CARING DEMOCRACY

Caring Democracy

Markets, Equality, and Justice

Joan C. Tronto

NEW YORK UNIVERSITY PRESS
New York and London

NEW YORK UNIVERSITY PRESS
New York and London
www.nyupress.org

Library of Congress Cataloging-in-Publication Data
Tronto, Joan C., 1952–
Caring democracy : markets, equality, and justice / Joan C. Tronto.
p.   cm.
Includes bibliographical references and index.
ISBN 978-0-8147-8277-4 (cl : alk. paper) — ISBN 978-0-8147-8278-1
(pb : alk. paper) — ISBN 978-0-8147-7045-0 (e-book) —
ISBN 978-0-8147-7034-4 (e-book)
1. Caring. 2. Democracy. 3. Equality. 4. Social justice.   I. Title.
BJ1475.T76 2013
306.2—dc23   2012043770

References to Internet websites (URLs) were accurate at the time of writing.
Neither the author nor New York University Press is responsible for URLs
that may have expired or changed since the manuscript was prepared.

New York University Press books are printed on acid-free paper,
and their binding materials are chosen for strength and durability.
We strive to use environmentally responsible suppliers and materials
to the greatest extent possible in publishing our books.

Manufactured in the United States of America

c   10 9 8 7 6 5 4 3 2 1
p   10 9 8 7 6 5 4 3 2 1

In memory of my parents

CONTENTS

In my previous book, *Moral Boundaries: A Political Argument for an Ethic of Care*, I made the claim that the world would look very different if we put care at the center of our political lives. In the intervening years, no mass movement to improve care has arisen, despite repeated attempts on the part of scholars and activists to make such a thing happen (Engster 2010; Stone 2000). Yet, despite the changes in the feminist frameworks within which the original argument was couched, despite the deepening insecurities wrought by terrorist attacks and continued globalization under the conditions of neoliberalism, I remain hopeful about the political possibilities raised by the visions of more caring and more just societies. In this book, I ask how we might differently understand democracy and caring in order to create such societies. I argue that, despite the voluminous discussions about the nature of democratic theory, politics, and life, nothing will get better until societies figure out how to put responsibilities for caring at the center of their democratic political agendas.

This argument will not seem at home in the context of much recent democratic political theory. Many political theorists have dedicated their recent work to demonstrating how *undemocratic* and brutal modern liberal democracies have become, and how often liberal democratic regimes end up reducing some people to "mere life." Other political theorists have become more concerned with ways to describe conflict in political life: Is democracy agonistic? Is deliberative disagreement a more promising way to think about politics? Others search for a form of democratic judgment that will set our thinking about politics aright again. While these issues are important and worthy of pursuit, they miss the fact that democratic political life has to be about *something*. In this book, I propose that thinking about caring in its broadest and most public form, as a way in which a society allocates responsibilities, offers a substantive opportunity to reopen the closed, game-like political system to the genuine concerns of citizens.

This is a book about an idea. The idea grows out of a word that does a lot of work in the English language: *care*. Care has many meanings: when we say "cares and woes," "care" denotes a burden; when we say "I care for you," we express love. Care always expresses an action or a disposition, a reaching out to something. When we use it to refer to ourselves, as in "I take good care of myself," we are in that instant thinking of ourselves as both the doer and that toward which we are reaching out. Care expresses relationships. It is used to express our deepest convictions, as when we say, "I care about dolphins"; it is used by advertisers in banal ways to make us like a company and perhaps continue to buy its products, as when we hear advertisers say, "McDonald's cares."

To put the idea of this book as simply as possible: what it means to be a citizen in a democracy is to care for citizens and to care for democracy itself. I call this practice "caring with." Citizenship, like caring, is both an expression of support (as when the government provides support for those who need care) and a burden—the burden of helping to maintain and preserve the political institutions and the community. Actually to engage in such democratic caring requires citizens to think closely about their responsibilities to themselves and to others. And it requires that people think about politics not simply as an election contest, but as a collective activity in which they guide the nation forward in time. While John Maynard Keynes was right to say "in the long run, we are all dead" (1971 [1923], 65), people are also always shaping the future by how they act. Caring about democracy's future is no simple task. Furthermore, it is already obvious that the conception of democracy I am using is not one that views democracy simply as a system for aggregating interests and choosing political leaders. For reasons I will spell out later, though, I am not going to focus here on offering a full-blown alternative account of democratic life and practice. That, it seems to me, is the task of citizens in a democratic society.

For nearly thirty years I taught at Hunter College, whose Latin motto is "mihi cura futuri." At Hunter we would loosely translate this as "The future is in my hands," or, still less literally, "caring for the future." Until 2003 most people thought this phrase was an example of the kind of made-up Latin that was popular in the nineteenth century, "a concoction of some doddy 19th century pedant," as the view was expressed around the college. A student of classics, Jillian Murray, found out that the phrase was, actually, quite legitimately Latin: it appears in Ovid's *Metamorphoses* in Book XIII. As Ulysses and Ajax argue about who should get the slain Achilles' armor, Ulysses draws this unkind contrast with his opponent: "Your right hand is useful in war, it's a talent . . . ; you lead men without thought, the care of the future is mine [*mihi cura futuri*]" (Murray 2003). To "lead men without thought" may make one more successful in the short run, but if one needs to care for the future, then one must act differently. So argues Ulysses, asserting that he is the true successor to Achilles.

We are living in a time in which too many leaders "lead men without thought." But I want to focus on an often overlooked but critical aspect of this current thoughtlessness: What has happened to our concerns about *care*? Why has so much in human life and in politics turned into discussions about selfishness, greed, and profit? Why has the language of economics seemingly come to replace all other forms of political language?

Here is the place where the little word "care" takes up another burden. What has gone wrong, I shall argue in this book, is that we have lost sight of the other side of human existence besides the world of the "economy." In addition to our economic roles as workers and consumers, citizens live in two other realms as well: in the world of intimate caring in our households, families, and circles of friends, and in the political world. In this book, I argue that we have misunderstood politics as if it were part of the world of economics. Instead, I shall argue, politics has historically been, and rightfully should be, closer to something we think of as part of our households: a realm of caring. Despite the feminist critiques of "maternal thinking" (e.g., Dietz 1985)—and neither I nor advocates for "maternal thinking" argue that there is an exact match between political and household concerns—there is a good reason that political thinkers have often compared households to polities. Both are kinds of institutions that rely upon bonds other than those that arise when people pursue their self-interest. In a democracy, politics requires our care, and we should expect from the state a certain kind of support for all of our caring practices. Government is something we care about, and something that reciprocates by providing "care" for us as well.

The great challenge of democratic life is to provide for economic production—which produces inequality—and at the same time to recognize everyone as equal participants in their society. Since democratic arguments began to resurface at the end of the eighteenth century, this danger—that democratic citizens will not want to work hard enough to produce enough for everyone to exist well—has lurked in the back of our political minds. Coercion of workers, "wage slavery" to early anti-capitalists, produced the remarkable growth of capitalism. Capitalism is a system for producing extraordinary wealth, and, as Karl Marx argued, one of the key roles of the state has been to support the growth and expansion of capital. But as so much of public life has focused on economic production and growth, an equally important set of human concerns took the backseat, namely, that humans need not only to produce but also to live lives filled with meaning. The intriguing aspect of this development is that, as economic life left the household and subsistence behind, the tasks of caring and producing meaning were left behind in the household as well. In the middle of the eighteenth century, arguments proliferated about men's roles as productive citizens. Thinkers such as Adam Ferguson (1995 [1767]) protested the new focus on economic well-being: to be interested only in one's own economic well-being was, he said, "effeminate." As economic production left the household, these "separate spheres" of a caring household and a remote worksite were also gendered. And the end result is that "care" became secondary to a state focused on tending to the economy.

In this book I will not offer a history of how this imbalance came about. But I will describe how, in a democratic country, to put it aright. To put the point succinctly, it requires that citizens take seriously the responsibilities for "caring with" each other. "Caring with" is not the same as judging one's self-interest, though it is about our collective and self interests in the long run. To do so requires a change in the values of citizens. It requires that citizens care enough about caring—both in their own lives and in the lives of their fellow citizens—to accept that they bear the political burden of caring for the future. That future is not only about economic production but also about caring for the values of freedom, equality, and justice. That future is not only about oneself and one's family and friends, but also about those with whom one disagrees, as well as the natural world and one's place in it. That future requires that we think honestly about the past and accept some burdens and responsibilities that have been deflected or ignored, realizing that if all such responsibilities are reconsidered, democracy will function more justly.

To care about and for democracy is a task for all citizens, and it is not easy. But when all citizens engage in such "caring with" practices, even though they will disagree about and dispute the best ways to proceed, one outcome of their engagement will be greater trust for one another, and thus a greater capacity to care for this collective purpose, this "res publica," this public thing. This book is an argument for why we have to make this change in our values. Whether or not we succeed depends upon the thought and action that will follow it.

When Bill Clinton ran for president, he famously hung a sign in his campaign headquarters that read "It's the economy, stupid." But beyond the emaciated account of democracy as periodic elections in which parties compete primarily to attract the attention of potential voters, people's daily lives are not made up of problems like "the economy," but rather the absence of jobs, inadequate health insurance, time-binds, how to take care of children and aging parents, trying to balance care and work duties, and so forth. As elected officials increasingly press to achieve agendas that have no resonance with voters, voters become more and more disinterested in their games. These cynical games become a vicious circle that leads to an even less accountable form of gamesmanship as a substitute for genuine politics. Voters lose trust in the system, but since their role is marginal anyway, gaming their absence from politics becomes a way to achieve victory. If more potential voters can be kept out of the system, it remains more predictable and controllable by the techniques of electioneering that serve the interests of those who have been elected, who in turn serve those who are part of the existing high-cost campaigning system.

In writing this book, I carry the brief for changing the subject of political life from an abstract set of concerns about "the economy" to a way of coping with real people's lives that is much closer to the way that people actually live. But what I do not do is to spell out in much detail a series of prescriptions about how responsibilities for care should be allocated. Democratic theorists have often observed the irony of theorists trying to prescribe outcomes for the *demos*, the people, at the same time they argue for giving power to the people. It will become clear in what follows what kinds of policies I think are best. But one need not agree with the details of my descriptions or my prescriptions in order to accept the overall point that I am making: that political life is ultimately about the allocation of caring responsibilities, and that all of those relationships and the people engaged in them need to be part of the ongoing political discourse. To be a small "d" democrat requires that one put ultimate trust in the people, who, well-informed and committed to democratic values, will make decisions consistent with those values.

This is a tall order. Most of what political scientists know suggests that citizens are largely disinterested and not very knowledgeable about politics. Many democratic theorists recognize that, at present, there is much obfuscation about democratic values, which are too often reduced to soundbites or to single words, such as "choice," "rights," or "freedom." Right now, it would be difficult to trust democratic majorities with making sound judgments about democratic values. Yet if, as democratic theorists, we are able to describe and analyze politics at a level that can be made meaningful in people's lives, and if some of the corrupting influences that now afflict "politics" were removed, then it might become possible to develop some trust for citizens' collective judgments. Care helps in bringing such discussions to a level that engages with people's real lived experiences and differences.

In arguing that democratic politics are themselves increasingly about institutions and practices that entail caring, I make half the case for connecting care with democracy. But the other half of this argument is equally important: democracy itself, as a form of governing in which citizens participate, requires care. A democratic state in which citizens do not care about justice, about their role in controlling rulers, in the rule of law itself, will not long remain a democracy.

I hope that my argument is not misread. We are living in an age in which "politics" has come to have such a strained and empty meaning that it is possible to think that I am suggesting that "politics" would be better if it were more like a caring household, that a nation should be like one big happy family, that thinking about care eliminates or mitigates conflict. I am not making such claims at all. To think honestly about the nature of care for only a few minutes reveals its complexity. Care relations are often relationships of inequality, posing an immediate challenge to any commitment to democratic equality. People think in many different ways about what constitutes good care; any account of care that is not pluralistic will end up imposing bad care upon some, and thus impinging upon people's liberties. Although some have tried to paint attempts to raise collective concerns for care as a creeping "nanny state," beyond that derogatory label it is clear that, given the complexities of modern society, most needs for care exceed the capacity of individuals and their intimate family members to meet them. The question is not *whether* caring responsibilities will be more broadly allocated, but *how*. The question is not whether democratic societies have to think about meeting their caring responsibilities without relying solely upon the family, but rather how they currently do so and whether these are the best ways to foster democratic citizens. Rethinking care on such a broad scale requires not only that we reassess human interactions, but also that citizens think, as democrats, about their location in a global society and on an increasingly fragile planet.

This book thus describes a way to rethink the subject matter of democratic politics. Because I am an American and most familiar with the dilemmas of caring as they play out in my own society, I draw most of my examples from this case. But I mean for the general argument to be used in many different political contexts. Indeed, if I am correct about the depth of the problems for care created by the contemporary economy, only solutions that transcend individual nations will ultimately succeed.

I hope that this book will be interesting to scholars of democratic politics, to scholars who think about care, and to ordinary citizens who are baffled by how wrongly our current ways of thinking reflect what matters the most to us. Humans begin and end their lives depending upon others for care; in between those times we never cease being engaged in relationships of care with others, and we never cease needing and providing care for ourselves. As our interdependence in caring grows greater, we need to rethink how we parse out our time, energy, work, and resources to make certain that we, as well as those around us, are well cared for. We cannot rethink these questions in isolation, we can only do so collectively. And in so doing, we will change how we see ourselves in the world and what should guide our most fundamental political choices.

Perhaps it is not too late.

ACKNOWLEDGMENTS

I am honored to be able to acknowledge the assistance that I have received from others in writing this book. The questions considered here have so preoccupied my mind that there is hardly a talk I have given, a conversation I have had, in the past nearly twenty years in which I did not learn from speaking to my interlocutors. To those who have agreed with me and those who have not, let me express my gratitude for your questions and arguments, your expressions of support and of indignation. I have learned from them all.

A number of institutions have provided material support. I have received teaching and research opportunities that forwarded this project from the University for Humanist Studies in the Netherlands; Princeton University Center for Human Values; the City University of New York (CUNY); Yale University; Goethe University, Frankfurt am Main; the Fulbright Foundation; Göttingen University; CIRSFID at the University of Bologna; and the University of Minnesota.

Many colleagues have served as close interlocutors throughout this project. None of my work on care would have been possible without the initial cooperative work that I did with Berenice Fisher, and I am forever in her debt for our long and productive conversations. Even when I am disagreeing with Berenice, I am thinking about her ideas. Selma Sevenhuijsen not only remains an inspiring colleague, but she also taught me about creating a long-distance and yet deep intellectual community. Over the years, a varied group of care scholars has emerged, and even when I disagree with them, or they with me, I learn constantly from Virginia Held, Nel Noddings, Fiona Williams, Julie White, Nancy Folbre, Kari Waerness, Olena Hankivsky, Paul Kershaw, Daniel Engster, Guy Widdershoven, Marian Verkerk, Hank Maschot, Deborah Stone, Rafaella Sarti, and Jennifer Nedelsky. Many other scholars and students, including Margaret Urban Walker, Martha Ackelsburg, Molly Shanley, Nancy Hirschmann, Jane Bayes, Joan Callahan, Lorraine Code, Alison Jaggar, Liane Mozere, Vivienne Bozalek, Sonia Michels, Wendy Sarvasy, Carol Nackenoff, and

Fiona Robinson, have raised questions and discussed matters of feminist theory and care with me across several continents. My Italian colleague Gianfrancesco Zanetti has provoked me, with good humor and intelligence, to resituate my work as a challenge to received hierarchies. Thomas Casadei has been a strong supporter in Italy as well, and I owe much to my hostess at Bologna's CIRSFID Institute, Carla Faralli. Rafaella Lamberti, Georgio Bongiovanni, Enrica Morlicchio, Eugenio Lecaldano, Roberto Brigati, Isabel Trujillo, Manuela Nardini, and Raffaele Rauti provided me with teaching and lecturing opportunities throughout Italy, for which I am grateful. Sandra Languier and Patricia Papermann have continued to support my work in France. Tove Pettersen and Per Nordtvedt have brought me to Norway several times, and I am grateful for the opportunity to work with them. Elizabeth Conradi organized a summer semester of teaching for me in Göttingen and remains a true colleague. Graciela Di Marco gave me the chance to bring these ideas to an audience in Buenos Aires, in a country that now has much to teach the world about democracy. Shahra Razavi's invitation to a workshop organized by the United Nations Research in Social Development group allowed me to develop some of the ideas expressed here. At a workshop at the Western Political Science Association's Feminist Political Theory group, Sarah Pemberton suggested that I use the language of "caring with" to capture the main idea here, and I am grateful to her and to the other participants in the workshop for their wise counsel. I regret that I can no longer express my debt to my colleagues who have passed on: Susan Moller Okin, Iris Marion Young, and Sara Ruddick offered encouragement and hard questions that remain with me. My former Hunter College/City University of New York colleagues Rosalind Petchesky, John Wallach, Ruth O'Brien, Joe Rollins, Ken Sherrill, Ann Cohen, Pamela Mills, Corey Robin, Young-Sun Kim, and Dorothy Helly have discussed the ideas here for longer than they can (or probably wish to) remember. Mark Larrimore, Callie Kramer, and Herlinde Pauer-Studer are dear friends who have discussed these and other ideas over many meals in our kitchen in New York and elsewhere. Graduate students from CUNY, Minnesota, and around the world have provided useful comments. My colleagues in political science at the University of Minnesota have commented on several of these chapters, welcomed me into a vibrant intellectual community, and provided me with kind encouragement to pursue my scholarly work. I am sustained by Mary Dietz and blessed to have her as a friend whose scholarship and conduct of life are an inspiration.

My editors at NYU Press have been more patient than I can describe. Ilene Kalish has been thoughtful and helpful, and, even though it was not warranted, has continued to be cheerful and encouraging. Aiden Amos has also been remarkably helpful in bringing the manuscript to its end. The anonymous reviewers of the manuscript and Jorma Heier provided useful comments on nearly final drafts for which I am grateful.

Chapter 4 began its life as the essay "Vicious and Virtuous Circles of Care: When Decent Caring Privileges Social Irresponsibility," published in 2006 in *Socializing Care: Feminist Ethics and Public Issues*, edited by Maurice Hamington and Dorothy C. Miller. I am grateful to Rowman and Littlefield for granting permission to reprint it in revised form in this book.

My final thanks are prospective: I want to thank in advance the readers who will come to this book and take the arguments offered here seriously. I offer the book both to scholars of democratic theory and life as well as to ordinary citizens who are looking for a way to make sense of our political possibilities at the present. These have been hard times for those of us who believe in democracy. I have sustained my hope that we can yet change the subject of political life to what really matters, that is, to what we do, and should, really care about.

.

Introduction

When Care Is No Longer "at Home"

Let's face it: care no longer seems to be "at home," neither literally nor figuratively. It used to seem so simple. Politics was something that happened in public, care was something that happened in private. Many societies followed one or another form of this public/private divide. Aristotle famously distinguished *polis* and *oikos* (household) at the beginning of the *Politics*. The nineteenth-century American ideology of separate spheres gendered the public as masculine and the private as feminine. In this separation, nonpolitical concerns, including sentiment and love, became attached to the private. "Home is where the heart is," pronounce needlepoint embroideries. Home is a "haven in a heartless world," intoned the psychologist Christopher Lasch (1995).

But this view of home as a place of comfort and care, marked off from politics, is a myth. While some (most?) homes do provide their residents with adequate, good, and even excellent care, not all homes are comfortable and caring. When the poet Robert Frost (1969) defined home as "the place where, when you have to go there, they have to take you in," he was not speaking sentimentally and presuming such a home to be cozy. And "home" has come to have some meanings in recent years that are no longer attached to the meeting of caring needs.

The last one hundred years have witnessed a revolution in care. Care requires not only nurturing relationships, but also the physical and mental work of taking care of, cleaning up after, and maintaining bodies. Throughout the twentieth century, with the growth of more professional ways to understand human development, care has become more professionalized and left the household further behind. This professionalization of nurturant care (Duffy 2011) has led to the creation of many forms of institution outside of the home to perform caring duties that used to be met in the home: schools, hospitals, hospices, nursing homes, care facilities for disabled people, funeral homes, and so forth. At the same time, care also involves a fair amount of necessary "dirty work"—cleaning, preparing food, bodily care, removing waste—that, as it moves out of the home, creates a new class of people, mostly women and disproportionately people of color, who are increasingly left behind by economic growth in the bottom rungs of society (see also Glenn 2010). Parents now report that they spend more time with children than in the past, but they do not spend time doing the chores required for the daily work of maintaining bodies and things. That dirty work is left for others. "Care" is no longer the work of the realm of the household.

In the face of these changing meanings of care, much mischief has occurred in unmooring "home" from being a grounded and concrete way to start thinking about human life. Consider how home has shifted its meaning in two of the largest political changes facing the United States in recent years.

If we peel away the layers of greed at the heart of the world economic crisis, precipitated by the credit meltdown of 2008, we find something worth contemplating. The derivatives packaged and sold around the world, which turned out to be basically worthless, all rested upon a classic economic "bubble" in which prices—in this case, housing prices—had climbed beyond their possible real value. On the global market, what was being sold was a debt. On the local level, what was being sold to people was a promise that transforming their homes into greater debt was a good investment for them. These "subprime" deals rested upon the assumption that the houses people were buying (often with no income check or any realistic possibility that they could make the mortgage payments after a few years of reduced charges) would continue to increase in value at such an astonishing rate that they would never have to face the fact that they were taking out mortgages far beyond their means to pay. By the time the mortgage payments became due, their mortgage brokers had told them, they would have sold their house for still more money and paid off this mortgage with the proceeds, with enough left over for another down payment. Fueled by the promise of easy money, encouraged by shady mortgage dealers and reckless banks, watching television series such as *Flip This House*, millions of people were caught in the hope that their houses would become a way to break into another economic status. People began to think of where they lived not as their home, but as their most clever investment. Everyone, it seemed, understood that they would never get rich working for a living. But now, for those lucky enough to begin to expand their assets within the bubble, the roof over their heads became a resource to exploit. Until, of course, the roofs all came crashing down.

Humans have a nostalgic attachment to their homes, "where," as Frost put it, "when you have to go there, they have to take you in." What does it mean that people ceased to think of their homes this way and began to think of them as investments? What convinced people to stop thinking of their homes as a place of safety and comfort, but to view them with an eye toward a calculated profit? Traditionally, as social scientists have explored, home is associated with warmth, a sense of comfort, a sense of being in the place where one can be oneself, and where one can regenerate one's energies (Windsong 2010). Now, a house was no longer a home but an investment. To make this switch, people had to start to think differently about themselves. One study of British citizens explored this point directly: cut out of the financial bonanza, people began to realize, they would no longer be able to live a good life simply by working for a living, or making a commitment to an occupation and developing a skill (Bone and O'Reilly 2010). Now one also needed to be a savvy investor, to play the market just right, and to expect that someone else would come along thinking the same way as you, but with less money, who would also be willing to invest. As "every man his own investor" came to dominate the economic landscape, nostalgic ties evaporated as people began to think of their homes as places for speculation. For those excluded, or too timid, to take a chance on the open market and change homes, their homes became a source of a different kind of cash flow through low-interest "home improvement" loans, which banks freely offered and which individuals took and used to pay for everything from capital investments to groceries. Consumer debt outpaced consumer savings. One way or another,

American consumers fell under the spell of seeing their homes as sources for revenue, and telling themselves that it was reasonable to act this way since their homes were, after all, increasing in value. Added to this illusion are the realities that real wages are stagnant, that pensions have been cut and continue to disappear, that finding good long-term employment has become an iffy proposition. Home as revenue became attractive as the hope for some economic security. People wanted to have money to spend, and in face of dislocations caused by economic and political uncertainties, they hoped that they could quell their anxieties with that one more thing, one more experience, one more set of "memories" that their borrowed money seemed to promise. This restless desire to acquire transformed how people thought. We can imagine how, in the style of a 1940s Looney Tunes cartoon, as Americans stared at their homes, the house became a gigantic piggy bank, and the ersatz mortgage and loan papers a huge hammer to break it open and get at the money. But as so often happened in those cartoons, when the deception ended, the broken pieces lying around on the ground had shattered not an illusion but something real: the historical and traditional value of owning one's home, in what President George W. Bush called "an ownership society."[1]

The economic crisis that began in 2008 brought this frenetic activity to an abrupt end. Banks were bailed out, but not the individuals who lost their homes or who now found themselves under the burden of a mortgage or home equity loan greater than the adjusted value of their house. While some banks are "too big to fail," individuals who had exceeded their household income had to bear responsibility for their actions. Now, as individuals begin to desert these mortgaged homes, as states and local governments suffer from lack of revenue and have to cut services to balance their budgets, the rippling waves of irresponsible behavior affect everyone. The most obvious scapegoat, as has been the case in the United States since 1980, is "big government," and the anger unleashed by this chain of events finds expression in the anti-government "Tea Party" movement— "taxed enough already." But the reality would place the blame differently, not upon government, but upon millions of people hoping to get ahead, and upon a vast network of banks, mortgage brokers, investment houses, and other businesses, operating on a global scale to take advantage of people's anxiety about their prospects for economic improvement.

What drives this clamor for "evermore"? Juliet Schor (1998, 2000) has suggested that Americans work too much and spend too much so that they can provide "more" for their children. In the past fifty years, the structures and work patterns of American families have changed dramatically. Parents eager to raise their children well find themselves caught in a "time-bind" (Hochschild 1989, 1997), and they use money and things to try to make up for this lost time. Parents now report that they spend more time with their children, but that time is literally spent engaging in activities that are organized around the children's likes and dislikes. This is not the same as having the children engaged with their parents in adult activities such as cleaning and cooking. The end result is that children, except for scheduled times in which they share in activities with their parents, spend much of their time in the company of other children; for many teenagers, virtually all of their waking time is spent in constant electronic connection with other teens. But teens and their parents now find it hard believe that these young people will be better off than their parents. For the first time, the next generation of Americans will likely be less well-educated and less likely to succeed than their parents. Americans are caught in a vicious circle of working harder, which takes more of their time and energy, and spending less time caring for their families. Then, in order to assuage their guilty consciences because they are caring less, they work more so that they can earn and spend more "making memories." No wonder the promise of "get rich quick" through selling one's home seemed so attractive. But there is no solution to this vicious cycle from within. The only way to end the need for more money and more stuff to substitute for time and caring is to begin to reshape delusional values of home as investment, of economic striving and success as the only value worth pursuing.

The attacks on the United States on September 11, 2001, have also profoundly altered our sense of "home." Although attacks from abroad are not unprecedented in American history, nor are attacks from within, the scale of the September 11th attacks, and their occurrence at a time when Americans felt themselves to be the single hegemonic global superpower, was profoundly shocking. When President Bush reorganized the federal government to create the Department of Homeland Security, which is now the third largest federal agency in terms of workforce (Congressional Budget Office 2012), few objected to the use of the term "homeland," which in its most recent common usage had referred to regions of South Africa designated by the Apartheid system for indigenous peoples. The term itself seemed to capture the anxiety that what had been disturbed were not sovereign boundaries, "order," or "peace," but "home" itself.

There is something much more partial about defending a "home" as compared to defending a conception of sovereignty or "peace." Defending home, "where, when you have to go there, they have to take you in," does not admit a challenge on the basis of judgments of right and wrong. It is, simply, home. The assertion that *our* home (but no one else's) needs to be free of violence and fear has resonated strongly in American life. Yet as wars continue in Iraq and Afghanistan, as Americans face the reality that their government has used and justified torture, as trillions of dollars have been spent, "home" seems to be less a place of security and more a place of anxious, unknown threats. Americans view their safety somewhat precariously; in a Pew Center survey in October 2010, 30 percent of Americans thought the threat of a terrorist attack was greater since 2001; another 41 percent through the threat was the same; only 25 percent thought the threat had lessened. Economically insecure, vaguely threatened by terrorists, Americans seem to retreat from public life. Citizens thus sat out the elections of 2010; on average around 40 percent of eligible voters bothered to go to the polls in the midterm congressional elections (Roberts 2010).

These ways in which Americans are no longer feeling at home are disturbing in themselves, but they raise an even more serious concern: How can people claim to live in a democracy if their fears and insecurities begin to override their abilities to act for the common good? We are living in a time in which the unreal has a great deal of appeal. From imagining cowboys fighting off aliens, or Abraham Lincoln battling vampires, much in our contemporary commercial culture seems ungrounded. This is not so surprising. As care moves out of the household, "home" becomes ungrounded, disconnected from the realities of living our lives. When care becomes mainly invisible—mired down in a messy material world below the "meaningful" world of social media (where teenagers now spend most of their waking lives), people float away from what really goes on in a home. Home becomes a way, instead, to tug at heart strings, to make people overlook economic risks and imbibe political snake oil. It also invites people to retreat into their own families and implicitly suggests that there is no one else to help out, little "caring with" to be done. To understand what is happening to people now and how to move forward, it seems that the idea "starting at home," to quote the title of an important book by Nel Noddings (2002b) about care and social policy, may no longer be the right approach.

The Need for a Democratic Care Revolution

What happens when care is no longer at home? The revolution in care institutions and practices that is already underway requires no less than a companion revolution in political and social institutions and practices. For the most part, the scholars who have studied this question have been sociologists, economists, and public policy analysts. They have tried to answer this question by exploring how care is transformed when it begins to take up places in the market, in transformed families and other social arrangements, and in the state. As valuable as this work has been, it has not gone far enough. Using the metaphors and language of the market leaves an account of care incomplete. Only a holistic and politically grounded rethinking of care can adequately address the present situation.

Thus, one of the key arguments of this book is to call for a rethinking of the meaning of democratic politics. Democratic politics should center upon assigning responsibilities for care, and for ensuring that democratic citizens are as capable as possible of participating in this assignment of responsibilities. While in the past the assignment of caring responsibilities may have seemed to be beyond the proper reach and scope of politics, I argue here that, given the changing nature of caring, nothing short of this reconceptualization of politics can address the political problems for democratic life that arise from our present accounts of care.

Care and Politics? Care and Political Theory?

In making this argument, I am flying in the face of a number of assumptions that are usually made about care and about political life. Indeed, there are three standard kinds of arguments that deflect us from seeing the need for this democratic rethinking of care. In each of these cases, the argument rests upon an unwillingness to recognize how thoroughly we need to rethink where caring responsibilities should lie.

The first argument is that care is "only natural" and that society is better when only those who are "naturally" good at caring do the care work in society. Although this argument harkens back to Aristotle's description of "natural slaves" as tools to help others, recent ideological accounts of who in society is most caring make women bear the burden of care. Charles Tilly's (1998) work on durable inequality notes that once relatively small differences in status emerge within a social system, many other forms of social practice continue to reinforce these differences. Feminist and other critical scholars have long noted that naturalizing a phenomenon puts it beyond the possibilities for change. Calling "care" naturally feminine has had precisely this effect, and it has also served to mark as "feminine" groups of men who are seen as caring. Within economics, debate is ongoing about the proposition that care work does not need to be well paid, since caregivers receive non-monetary rewards because caring matters so much to them.

In order for this argument to be true, though, care must be something that some people naturally do rather than others. However, while some people may seem more caring, practices of caring can be cultivated.[2] It is also the case, as we will see in chapter 3, that sometimes care practices are labeled differently in order to maintain the gendered ideologies about "care" as something primarily for women. In short, the claim—that caring is "natural" and its own reward for some people—is more ideological than real.

The second argument is the opposite one to the view that care is natural and therefore immune to market forces. This argument says that care is like any other good or service, and its distribution is best left to the market. If people want care, they will seek it out, and they will pay what it is worth to them. Thus, by this account, care is not a public matter but a private one.

While much care work is distributed through market mechanisms, and this pattern will be discussed at length in chapter 5, it is also a mistake to think about care only from a market perspective. There are several reasons why this is true. The market presumes, after all, the existence of a rational and able consumer. For a variety of reasons—incapacity, age (think of the very young or the very old), the disparity in knowledge between expert providers and less-knowledgeable clients or consumers (which produces the rules for market operation that presume *caveat emptor*)—the market model cannot be applied to all forms of care. Another problem with using the market to price care is that many forms of care are extremely expensive and do not adjust well to the market. If a society "costs out" all of the informal care that its members provide, it will discover a huge economy that is not accounted for in economic life (Folbre 1994, 2001, 2009; Waring 1988). Nor does care behave like other commodities on the market, since many of the costs of caring cannot be reduced through new technologies. Much of the cost of care suffers as much from William Baumol's "cost disease" (2012) as does playing chamber music (his original example): one simply cannot care without humans to do the caring (despite recent efforts to substitute robots for humans in such activities as bathing frail elderly people [Davenport 2005]).

The third argument takes the view that we can continue to muddle through. Relying upon existing forms of public policy, using the globalized market in care labor (McGregor 2007; Weir 2005; Yeates 2004; Pa-rreñas 2001), the existing care crises can be solved by incrementally adjusting public provisions and private costs, and by relying upon glob-alization to provide new sources of caring labor. The problem with this argument, which goes somewhat beyond the scope of this book, is that it ignores the injustice, unfairness, inequality, and lack of freedom in both current and proposed future arrangements. This book is designed to show that this assumption is pernicious because it leaves distorted forms of car-ing responsibilities in place that ultimately undermine the requirements of a democratic society.

Many scholars will also resist the claim that care is a matter for politi-cal theory. Even if there is some set of concerns to address within public policy, why should care be a subject of political theory? Does not the ex-pansion of the category of "the political" weaken its meaning? Given the nature of how laws, states, and social scientists have divided up the realms of social and political life, it is not so surprising that the care revolution, and its impact on how people live, has not been systematically thought about by political theorists. After all, previous theoretical starting points, from Roman law to Talcott Parsons, presumed that care was best relegated to the private sphere. Politics concerned only what was public; the pri-vate sphere was a world of unequal relations that could never be political (Aristotle 1981). Or, private concerns about sexuality, marriage, and nur-turing children were pre-contractual (Pateman 1988). Or, the repetitive work of "animal laborans" preceded the realm of freedom (Arendt 1958). Even when democratic theorists began to think about the ways in which women had been excluded from politics, their solutions did not at first change the care-is-in-the-home formula—they simply asserted that one should extend notions of equality (Mill 1998 [1869]) or justice (Okin 1989) to the household.

But when "public" and "private" themselves become reconfigured vis-à-vis the needs for human care, as has happened with the care revolution of the past century, a more fundamental rethinking of these fundamen-tal political categories becomes necessary. Absent such a rethinking, the market and public policy, following their own logics, fill in. This is not to say that the market and public policy analyses of care that are offered are entirely inadequate. There is much to learn from these analyses, and they inform much of the following discussion. As institutions for care emerge in the market, it has made sense to use market and public policy analyses to think about them. But to follow the logic of the market, or of policy, rather than to start from the logic of care itself, means that the basic questions about the nature and purposes of care never arise. Most profoundly, it occludes a question that has never been adequately answered: How should care happen in an inclusive democracy?

After all, care really is a problem for democracy. Taking care of people and things is often unequal, particularistic, and pluralistic. There is no universally equal solution to the problem of care needs. Indeed, care often seems to be highly non-democratic, especially if one presumes that care professionals know more than care receivers about the best way to care. Or, if one presumes that care receivers are dependent on others, it seems difficult then to return to a framework that presumes that people are independent. As mentioned earlier, and discussed at length in chapter 2, throughout most of human history the assumption prevails that unequal care is not a worthy part of political life.

As the historical records shows, if one wishes to exclude some people from participating in democratic life, then the problems of care are easily solved. One assigns the responsibilities for caring to non-citizens: women, slaves, "working-class foreigners" (More 1965 [1516]), or others who are so marked. But once a democratic society makes a commitment to the equality of all of its members, then the ways in which the inequalities of care affect different citizens' capacities to be equal has to be a central part of the society's *political* tasks. And furthermore, making care into a political concern will improve not only the quality of care, but also the quality of democratic life.

It would be a profound mistake, though, to expect the argument here to somehow re-create the sentimental home or to find a substitute for it. Politics is, after all, about people's pursuits of their interests and about power—and power and interest permeate all collective human activities. Since care is a fundamental feature of collective human life, there is no way to remove power and interest from affecting how care practices are organized. My goal is not to carry the banner for care in the hopes of eliminating conflict. Instead, my goal is to insist that at present we spend a lot of time arguing about the wrong things. What really matters, and what can be best expressed in terms of our values, has to go beyond the current default of explaining all aspects of human life in economic terms. Instead, the key question should be: How, at every level, can we engage in caring with one another? Precisely what this means, how care can be a ballast against overly market-oriented thinking, will be discussed in the chapters to come.

Indeed, rather than being nostalgic for a (mythic) golden age of care, this work is optimistic about care's potential in transforming current democratic life. Given the past exclusion and current inadequacy of incorporating care into political life, people are not wrong to think that somehow, what matters in their lives is not the stuff of politics. Although the concerns of political care are highly contentious, nevertheless to reintroduce the questions of care into the political agenda may act as a catalyst for more democratic ways of life. By demanding democratic ways to resolve the questions of how a society can best meet its caring needs, I hope to refocus attention not only on the importance of care, but also on the promise of democracy as kind of political system.

How to Think about Care More Democratically; How to Think about Democracy in a More Caring Manner

How then, are we to think about care more democratically? The central concern, it becomes clear, is the need for a more nuanced account of responsibility. The book is divided into three parts. Part I lays out the theoretical framework for conceiving of caring democracy. The first chapter describes the ways in which the problems of the current "care deficit" and the current "democracy deficit" are related to one another. The chapter also explains the meaning and scope of "care" for this work, and explains that "caring with" is an essential phase of democratic forms of caring. This leads to the claim that democracy is about assigning caring responsibilities. In chapter 2, the question of responsibility is viewed in this light. Drawing upon the work of Margaret Urban Walker, it offers an alternative metaethic—an ethic of responsibility—which, I argue, properly understood, requires a commitment to democratic values and to caring with others in order to evaluate how citizens assign responsibilities to one another.

In her revision of John Rawls's principles of justice, Eva Kittay (1999) makes a compelling argument for including care for caregivers as one of the basic principles required for a liberal democratic order. Daniel Engster (2007) also derives an admirable set of recommendations from principles that he thinks follow necessarily from the nature of care. The approach that I shall take here leans more heavily on the democratic than on the liberal concerns of contemporary political life. While it is possible for a philosopher to make arguments about what and how the values of care should best be inscribed into a democratic way of life, my goal here is to create a way for such decisions to be made democratically, by the people themselves. This approach requires a different kind of political philosophy or theory—not one that is prescriptive in all of its details, but one that sets out the parameters for how citizens might do this work concretely. This approach is not new; it bears a resemblance to the kinds of invitations to public participation that pragmatists such as Jane Addams and John Dewey raised in the twentieth century (Esquith 2010; Fischer, Nackenoff, and Chmielewski 2009; Sarvasy 2003).

The next part of the book, consisting of chapters 3–5, describes "how we care now." I begin by distinguishing between men and women, who each take a turn in chapters 3 and 4, respectively. In so doing I do not want to reproduce the view that care is only about gender, because care is also about race, class, and other ways of separating citizens into more and less important groups. Nevertheless, gendered language, assumptions, and frameworks remain a critical way in which care work has been distinguished. Focusing on masculinity and femininity in relationship to care allows us to see different and crucial elements of the complexity of our current non-system of care. Chapter 3 considers how men do engage in caring activities, but these activities are never described as "caring" and thus reinforce a gendered separation that permits care to be feminized and devalued. Chapter 4 explores vicious circles of unequal care in which the standards of "intensive mothering" are shown to divide up by class. Only upper-middle-class and middle-class women seem to care well for their children. Chapter 5 returns to the neoliberal view of care as a marketable commodity. In these three chapters, though it is somewhat artificial to do so, I make three parallel arguments in basic concepts in democratic political theory that change their demeanor when we look at them from the perspective of caring with other citizens. In chapter 3, I describe the effect of men's exclusion from care on "freedom." In chapter 4, on women's place as mothers in a competitive market economy society, I describe the effect of these practices on our value of equality. In chapter 5, on the market, I consider an account of justice if society uses the market to organize care.

Chapters 6 and 7 offer how we might start to think differently about a caring democracy. Chapter 6 considers how practices and institutions of care can be democratically organized and informed, and indeed, how improving the democratic quality of caring stands as another way to think about the value of democracy itself. Chapter 7 describes how changing the value of care in democratic societies permits us to recast issues of inclusion, dependency, and creating more just democratic societies.

In short, then, this book makes three arguments. First, our social, economic, and political institutions no longer fit with our modes of caring and need to be revolutionized. Second, in a democratic society, the way to rethink institutions and practices (even those that previously have seemed "apolitical") is to rethink them democratically. Third, caring democratically requires a democratic process by which citizens are able to care with their fellow citizens. Yet as they learn to renegotiate caring responsibilities, citizens' care for democracy solidifies and reinforces the democratic nature of society.

In this book, I do not wish to offer detailed specific policy recommendations. In part, the role of a political theorist in a democracy should not be to substitute one's own ideas for political discussion in the society as a whole, but rather to propose the issues and ways in which ongoing discussions and political negotiations should proceed. My hope, then, is to clarify how citizens caring with one another can reshape our political life.

PART I

Envisioning a Caring Democracy

1

Redefining Democracy as Settling Disputes about
Care Responsibilities

A Tale of Two Deficits

Scholars have begun to talk about a "caring deficit" (Bennhold 2011; Llana
2006), using the same economic language that other scholars have borrowed to describe a "democratic deficit" (Borooah and Paldam 2007; Nye
2001; *New Statesman* 2000; Durant 1995). The care deficit refers to the incapacities in advanced countries to find enough care workers to meet the
needs of people, their children, elderly parents and relatives, and infirm
family members. The democratic deficit refers to the incapacities of gov-
ernmental institutions to reflect the real values and ideas of citizens.

What no one seems to have recognized, however, is that these deficits
are two sides of the same coin. This chapter aims to demonstrate how
they arise out of the construction of a public/private split that is an out-
dated inheritance from Western political thought that misses important
dimensions of both contemporary caring and democracy. The goal is not
to abolish any separation between public and private life, but to reconfigure in a dramatic way what counts as public and what counts as private.[1]
Only caring democracy, a democracy that emphasizes "caring with," can
address both of these problems.

Such a synthetic approach requires justification. Even if people agree that caring is an important value, and one that should be included in thinking about political life, why connect caring with democratic theory, life, and practice? Questions about care are widely discussed, but why would it be better to frame these questions in democratic terms? Questions about democracy are widely discussed, but how are these discussions enriched by framing them in terms of care?

A first answer to these questions turns them around and asks instead: Why does a connection between care and democracy seem strange? Throughout most of Western history, care seemed beyond the reach of political life because it was private, or necessarily about dependency, or non-political in some other way.[2] Both because democracy makes demands for the equality of all citizens and because the nature of care has changed, it is no longer possible to rely upon the myth of a public/private split as a way to assign responsibilities for care. This book makes the case for conceiving of care as a public value and as a set of public practices, at the same time recognizing that care is highly personal and in this regard, "private." This is so not only because without more public care equality is impossible, though this is true, nor because without more public care some are not well cared for, which is also true. The larger case I want to make here is that without a more public conception of care, it is impossible to maintain democratic society.

This chapter explores what is at stake in the current understandings of the relationship between care and democracy. Although public life has required some way to account for the provision of care, the presumed "natural" or necessary splits between public and private life have functioned to simplify these choices. After exploring the nature of caring and of democratic caring, it will become easier to see why the current "neoliberal" assumptions disguise the problematic relationship that already exists between care and democracy. After this explanation, it should be clear why the care deficit will only be solved when caring becomes more democratic, and the democracy deficit will only be solved when democracy becomes more caring.

The Meaning of Care and Caring

One of the larger problems for all theorists of care has been to define the term. "Care" is a complicated term, with many meanings and connotations in English. One can say "I care for you," meaning something like "I love you." On the other hand, "cares and woes" makes care synonymous with a burden that weighs upon one's soul. Care refers both to dispositions and to specific kinds of work. Care seems natural, and is often believed to be feminine. It bears a family resemblance to Emmanuel Levinas's ethical notion of alterity, it was a central category in Martin Heidegger's philosophy, and yet, in its most daily meanings, it is associated with aspects of life that Hannah Arendt linked with "animal laborans," the least distinctively human of human activities.

Arising out of a long discussion about the nature of care and its possible relationship to moral theory, a large international body of scholarship has now emerged about the ethics of care.[3] This literature concerns the moral implications of care from the most local—we might even say most minute—forms of care to the broader social and political institutional settings of care in the modern age, and from caring attitudes to caring behaviors and practices. The ethics-of-care framework has been adopted for use by sociologists, social workers, lawyers, psychologists, political scientists, political theorists, philosophers, geographers, anthropologists, and in such disciplines as business, communications, education, literary studies, bioethics, urban studies, postcolonial studies, social work, theology, and even engineering. What sort of concept can be so flexible and widely adapted and yet remain valuable?

In 1990, Berenice Fisher and I offered this broad definition of care: "On the most general level, we suggest that caring be viewed as *a species activity that includes everything that we do to maintain, continue, and repair our 'world' so that we can live in it as well as possible.* That world includes our bodies, our selves, and our environment, all of which we seek to interweave in a complex, life-sustaining web" (see also Tronto 1993, 103; Fisher and Tronto 1990, 40). This broad concept of care is still the best one from which to begin this investigation. Even though this definition is often criticized for being too broad (Held 2006; Groenhout 2004), it contains within itself a response to this criticism. In arguing that care is an activity, a kind of practice, we left open the possibility that there might be other forms of care that are not on this "most general level." Thus, it is possible to think about other ways to understand the meaning of care as more specific caring practices that are nested within this larger practice of care. By this account, some more narrow definitions of care are useful in more narrow contexts.

For example, many sociologists conceive of care as a "labor of love" in which private or intimate *activity* is performed in a particular *emotional* state. For example, Francesca Cancian (2000, 137) follows the pioneering

British sociologists Janet Finch and Dulcie Groves in offering this definition: "A combination of feelings of affection and responsibility, with actions that provide for an individual's personal needs or well-being in a face-to-face interaction." As a sociologist, Cancian is eager to situate caring as activity and feelings in a particular locus, and so presumes that care is always face-to-face. By Cancian's definition, then, a social worker employed by a hospital to find placements for aged patients who cannot be sent home does not qualify as engaged in caring. For an economist who is trying to measure the costs of health care for society, though, such a worker would count within the calculus of care.

Every distinct account of care brings with it a particular focus, and it is desirable to have many such accounts. Tamara Metz's (2010b) definition of "intimate caring," for example, consists of three elements: (a) intimate caring is not monitored by outside parties; (b) the parties have worked out deep, diverse, particular terms, ties, and motivations; and (c) intimate caring is not characterized by relations of exchange. Intimate caring characterizes the care that members of a household provide to one another —both the unequal relations among parents and children and the more equal relationships that exist among adults. Her point in offering this definition is to allow scholars to distinguish the household from other kinds of caring institutions without having to resort to "marriage" to describe what constitutes the household.

Philosophers of care often stress that care is relational. Virginia Held points to several characteristics of care in her book *The Ethics of Care: Personal, Political, and Global*, including that "the focus of the ethics of care is on the compelling moral salience of attending to and meeting the needs of the particular others for whom we take responsibility" (2006, 10). Held also argues that care involves emotion as well as reason, shows concern for particular others, and entails a different ontology in which people are understood relationally. Held's definition presumes that care duties are focused on particular others. This is useful for some purposes, but it leaves out a way to discuss self-care or public forms of care.

These more specific meanings of care achieve particular purposes and emphasize and highlight some of the attributes and problems in care. But they also miss some other dimensions of caring. Mignon Duffy (2011) distinguished "nurturant" and "nonnurturant" caring. Nurturant caring is directed at the relationship with a particular other person, whose well-being is improved through the caring. But, as Duffy observes, nonnurturant caring—that is, caring directed at the physical world, which is a prerequisite for nurturant caring—is also care. Hospitals could not run without a cleaning staff and laundry. Furthermore, Duffy points out, in the United States, nonnurturant care is often performed by people of lower class, racial/ethnic, and gender standing. If one excludes "the dirty work" (Glenn 2010; Roberts 1997), from care, then there is a different view of who is doing care work than if such work is included. And if one only defines care as Held does, then one is not so likely to think about the philosophical qualities of nonnurturant care.

So the broad definition of care offered by Fisher and Tronto suits a particular general account of the place and meaning of care in human life. Care needs to be further specified in particular contexts. The Fisher/Tronto definition requires that care not be left on this most general level, but that the context of care be explored. How do we specify such contexts? As in Duffy's example, one way to distinguish a particular type of care is by its *purpose*. And such purposes might be nested within one another; that is, laundering clothes in the hospital is part of the larger goal of helping patients to recover from illness. On the other hand, the contextual meaning of care might arise from the purpose of the individual engaged in any particular caring activity. Laundering clothes might have a different meaning when performed in a household—for example, if one's partner has a big interview tomorrow and so an extra load of laundry is done to prepare a particular item of clothing—than in a large commercial laundry that provides clean uniforms to a hospital, and where the worker actually hates the work and does it only because it is a job.

Caring practices can be *nested* in several ways. First, drawing upon the way in which Aristotle described ends, we can imagine caring practices as nested within one another, from more specific to broader purposes. Thus, maintaining one's medical equipment is a caring practice nested within the broader practice of using that equipment, which is nested within the broader practice of medicine, which is nested in the broader practice of pursuing health. Second, one can reverse this process in order to think about the ways in which different caring practices rely upon other caring practices in order to succeed: if one supplies a doctor but no medical equipment, then one has not adequately provided medical assistance. Thus, to understand the different directions in which caring practices "nest" is to see their complex interrelationships, and not to create the conditions to challenge hierarchies among caring ends.

Power constitutes another important dimension of the context of particular kinds of caring. For some, care is always a dyad between one more powerful caregiver and a weaker care receiver (Noddings 1984). But the power dynamics are more complex in many other circumstances of care. Kari Waerness (1984a, 1984b) actually identified three forms of care: spontaneous care, necessary care, and personal service. Spontaneous care is a kind of good Samaritan act in which no ongoing relationship of care is established, but in which a person provides necessary care to another not expecting any reciprocal relationship to develop. Necessary care is care that the recipient could not provide for him or herself. As an example, doctors provide necessary care to patients. Not all of the care we call necessary care is highly skilled; young children need their diapers changed, but the skill level required is not very exalted. "Personal service," Waerness's third category, is the care that one could provide to oneself but someone else provides instead. One could wash one's own car but one takes it to the carwash; one could do one's own manicure but prefers to go to the nail parlor. Waerness's example is that husbands who expect their wives to clean up the house receive personal service. Notice that the difference between care and service is *not* the act performed, nor the intimacy of the relationship of the work, nor the nature of the relationship established by the care work. Within the Fisher/Tronto definition, all of these forms of care count as care, but Waerness's distinction between care and service captures an important element of caring. What is different is that in "service," the actors who command the care work that is provided by care workers are the ones with greater power, whereas in "care," the more powerful, actors provide the care work for less powerful or more vulnerable recipients. The care workers in both cases might have expertise, or they might be performing care work that is more routine and doable by everyone. The difference is in who appears to be in command.

Caring, as conceived by Fisher and myself, is also a complex process. We identified four steps in the processes of care:

1. *Caring about.* At this first phase of care, someone or some group notices unmet caring needs.
2. *Caring for.* Once needs are identified, someone or some group has to take responsibility to make certain that these needs are met.
3. *Care-giving.* The third phase of caring requires that the actual caregiving work be done.
4. *Care-receiving.* Once care work is done, there will be a response from the person, thing, group, animal, plant, or environment that has been cared for. Observing that response and making judgments about it (for

example, was the care given sufficient? successful? complete?) is the fourth phase of care. Note that while the care receiver may be the one who responds, it need not be so. Sometimes the care receiver cannot respond. Others in any particular care setting will also be in a position, potentially, to assess the effectiveness of the caring act(s). And, in having met previous caring needs, new needs will undoubtedly arise.

In order to think about democratic care, which is not on this level of generalization but a more particular kind of care, it now seems to me that there is a fifth phase of care:

5. *Caring with*. This final phase of care requires that caring needs and the ways in which they are met need to be consistent with democratic commitments to justice, equality, and freedom for all.

From this standpoint, the Fisher/Tronto definition is meant to provide a way to analyze when and how caring is done, and to be able to make assessments about care. It is not meant to be romantic or perfectionist. Sadly, within human existence and the larger global environment there are more needs for care than can be met. But some caring needs do get taken seriously and do get met, while others are ignored or met only in desultory fashion.

Adopting the broad Fisher/Tronto definition for the broadest possible discussions does not preclude the use of a more particular way of thinking of care in a particular setting. For example, the practice of caring for someone else's children requires some different competences than caring for one's own children. If a nanny sees her own child's first steps, she will be delighted. But if she sees her charge's first steps, she may not reveal it to the parents, who would be saddened to have missed this event. Knowing how to negotiate such issues is part of the caring practice of being a good nanny, which is different from the practice of being a good mother. Cancian's definition of care, which emphasizes these intimate emotional matters, might be a more useful definition to use in this situation. Nevertheless, there is a danger in adopting a narrower account of care before looking to the purposes and power relationships in a particular set of care practices. To do so might leave out some of the more important dimensions of care.

A criticism that is sometimes made against the Fisher/Tronto concept of care is that it does not provide an account of what constitutes good care

(Schwarzenbach 1996). While this is valid, it presumes that concepts necessarily denote their normative frameworks. Looking back at the various
concepts we have already described, it is clear that Held's definition contains a normative dimension, but Cancian's does not. We might draw normative implications from Duffy's distinction between nurturant and nonnurturant care, or from Waerness's distinction between personal service
and necessary care, but neither concept is normative in itself. And indeed,
the Fisher/Tronto concept works as well to describe bad or dysfunctional
care as to describe good care.

It is important, though, not to follow the philosophers' lead and to define all care as good care. For to do so is to allow ourselves to be misled
by the ways in which care can function discursively to obscure injustices.
Consider, for example, Uma Narayan's (1995) account of British colonialism in India, which points to a darker side of care discourse. Colonialism, Narayan observed, did not attempt to justify itself to the imperialist
population by claiming to be a system of the exploitation of others' goods,
property, and labor. Instead, the narrative of self-explanation was a discourse of care. The natives would be Christianized, civilized, made better
by their encounter with British, Western, and Christian ideals. Women
also were brought into the discursive spread of good colonialism in this
way. Narayan's example does more than simply show that "care" can be
deployed discursively to bad as well as to good purpose. It also points to
the limits of relying upon a *concept*, like care, for making judgments about
the world.

Care from Concept to Political Theory

Concepts are intellectual tools. They are designed for and serve particular
purposes. Thus, to have a concept of care is not yet sufficient for discussing care's place in the world. For care, like any concept, can be situated in
a number of theories, and depending upon the theory within which it is
placed, it will have different meanings. The normative adequacy of care
does not arise from its conceptual clarity, but from the larger political and
social theory within which it is placed. Thus, it is possible to talk about
care in a feudal society, in which case hierarchies of care will be prominent, and good care will, among other things, preserve the hierarchical relationships of lords and serfs. Or, it is proper to talk about care in a Con-
fucian theory of the good, and there care will stress certain relationships
as basic to human flourishing (Herr 2003). Or, as Narayan argued, care is

a discourse that provided a critical support to colonialism. Thus, simply to have a concept of care is useful, but we do not yet know to what ends this conceptual tool will be put.

Every political theory, explicitly or implicitly, contains an account of care. Sometimes—for example, in modern utopias—there are very explicit accounts of how caring work should be done. From Thomas More through Saint-Simon and Charles Fourier to B. F. Skinner and Ursula Le Guin, utopian writers have concerned themselves with the details of how, in reorganizing society, they needed as well to reorganize caring duties. These included not only nurturant caring duties (as when Plato and Aristotle described the education of citizens), but also, in some cases, the nonnurturant "dirty work." Fourier, for example, left dealing with bodily waste to the toddlers who seem fascinated with it. More usually, modern political theorists have simply left working out the details of care work to households or to a general conception of police power (which is explored at great length in chapter 3). One of the ways in which Michel Foucault's concept of "biopower" is a challenge to liberal theories of the state is that it suggests some ways in which, through state and non-state actors alike, the details of living—sanitation, health, and so forth—become controlled in the post-Enlightenment era without explicit forms of political intervention or consent. Leaving such matters beneath public regard, though, as if they are part of what is "natural," is still a way to deal with them.

If care is a basic aspect of human life, and if all political theories have to pay attention to care, what has been the status of care in democratic theories? In the ancient world of democracy, care was theorized as belonging to the private sphere (Aristotle's *Politics*). In the modern reconstructions of democracy, this aspect of the public/private split has persisted. The way that the franchise was conceived was to exclude those who were dependent. Over time, the franchise was expanded first to propertied men, then to working-class men, and, finally, to women. It is not surprising that women were the last to gain the right to vote since their association with dependency and care made them ineligible for public life. But this exclusion was not only about women; slaves, servants, and others, both men and women, who were viewed by their menial employment as too dependent were considered a threat to public life. The development of democratic practice in the past three centuries has increasingly been an attempt to include those previously excluded into the political realm: first working-class men, then women. But the process of this inclusion has been to presume that the previously excluded are simply the same as those included, no longer dependent and no longer weighed down by the burden of dependency. The problem with this argument is that it constructs the citizens as somehow independent. In reality, all humans are interdependent, relying upon the care of others in differing degrees throughout the course of their lives. To pronounce those previously marked by dependence with a new independence distorts reality; it glosses over the need for care in a society and everyone's condition of interdependency.

Thus, when T. H. Marshall (1981) famously described citizenship in the mid-twentieth century to include social rights, it was clear that what it meant to be a citizen was no longer to be a soldier, but to be a *worker*. Even though Marshall argued for the importance of social rights, and the extension of equality through social rights to all citizens, he also had in mind the traditional division of labor into gendered realms, men working in public and women in the household, and he conceived of social citizenship as the concern of men. As a result, feminist-friendly strategies in both liberal and social democratic states have largely focused on inclusion in the paid workforce as a way to make women fully citizens. These efforts on behalf of women were, opportunely, coincident with a change in the political economy in many advanced postindustrial economies so that the support of a middle-class household required two incomes (Stacey 1990). So women's entry into the workforce seemed appropriate for both political and economic reasons.

Care and Democratic Political Theory

This move toward inclusion through paid work left unanswered one large question: Who does the care work? Contemporary democratic theory has virtually nothing to say, on the theoretical level, in answer to this question. Why should this lacuna be a concern for democratic theory? Because unless democratic theory deals substantively with the question of "who cares," it results in an account of politics that misconceives citizens and their lives, overvaluing their lives as workers, devaluing their lives as people engaged in relationships of care. No state can function without citizens who are produced and reproduced through care. If public discussions do not explicitly address this question, then the care dimensions of life remain hidden in the background.

Most democratic political theory has ignored this large change in living circumstances, of citizens, and as well as the changing place of dependency in their lives. Indeed, contemporary democratic political theory has become increasingly concerned with procedures for democratic life, and with such matters as whether political life is better described as agonistic, deliberative, or communal. Very little attention is paid to how citizens live their lives. On the one hand, such a lacuna seems reasonable because, as Tamara Metz (2010a) has argued, intimate caring should be relatively free from monitoring by outside authorities. On the other hand, to ignore the ways that women, once left to the private sphere to "take care," must now find themselves also in the public sphere of employment is to consign them to a "double shift" in which the old division of responsibilities no longer obtains but no one is willing to think systematically about how to reorder them.[4]

Bruce Ackerman, one of the most creative and concrete of contemporary political theorists, has proposed that one way to improve public life is through the creation of a "Deliberation Day." Each year, everyone would receive pay from the government to attend a day-long discussion of important political topics. The goal is to reinvigorate citizens' abilities and willingness to take political problems seriously by having them mix with neighbors and hear new perspectives.

Deliberation Day is a nostalgic idea in many ways. Not only does it evoke the lost experience of the Town Meeting, it also requires face-to-face engagement of citizens, thereby ignoring the many clamoring voices whose chant "Let them use the internet!" is now the rage in discussions about democratic participation. But it is also nostalgic in another way, relying upon some subtly exclusionary assumptions about the citizens. Despite the hope that everyone will participate is this reality, not everyone will be able to participate. How will the people get to their gathering spaces? If they drive, will the gas stations be open? Who will watch the kids while the adults deliberate? Who will make sure that the lights are turned on, that there are enough chairs, and that the microphones work? Who will make lunch? Who will haul away the trash? Irreducibly, behind all human activities are care workers doing the barely regarded but essential work of caring.

Once we recognize the extent of caring as a part of human life, it becomes impossible to think politically about freedom, equality, and justice for all unless we also make provisions for all of the types of caring—from the intimate care of our kin to clearing away our waste. To pursue democracy while at the same time taking seriously how central care is for all human life requires a fundamental rethinking of questions about how we organize our lives, individually and collectively. Democratic theory has not yet finished its work if everyone is expected both to work and to be citizens, but some are left with disproportionate caring duties.

Furthermore, if everyone (that is, all able-bodied and able-minded adults) now counts as a citizen, what becomes of those who are not so "able," that is, those for whom prejudice and structural barriers continue to bar their complete acceptance as citizens, and what becomes of those who spend a disproportionate amount of their time caring for those others (Kittay 1999)? The solution to this problem lies in how we define the elements of democratic life that make citizens equal.

Several recent accounts of democratic theory do address the question of equality in more substantive terms. Nancy Fraser's (1997, 2009) distinction between "redistribution" and "recognition" draws attention to substantive concerns about equality, and her addition of a third "r," representation, furthers the connection of substantive equality with democratic modes of thinking. Iris M. Young (2000) understood the substantive concerns of democratic equality, and even the phenomenology of unequal relations, in her work. Carol Gould (2004) has argued that, thinking both within the nation state and on the global level, democratic equality requires the provision of equal human rights. Indeed, Gould considers care as one of the areas of concern for governments, and as a source of inequality for women. For Gould, the concept of "solidarity" better captures the need for citizens to work together than does the term "care," but perhaps the term used broadly, as "caring with," comes close to her conception of solidarity. Joseph Schwartz (2009) also relies upon solidarity to try to overcome the substantive disparities between supporters of "equality" and "difference" and ties such solidarity with care; he writes that "unless societies make a universal commitment to the particular needs of 'care' for those dependent upon others, a democratic society will not be characterized by the equal respect of social solidarity" (42). The current analysis builds upon these insights.

Equally Needy Citizens

Every political theory contains an implicit or explicit account of caring. Since we live in a democratic society, it makes sense to try to determine the meaning of care in that type of society. There are two reasons why this is so. The first justification for thinking about democratic care is its theoretical necessity to make care intelligible within a democratic society. The second justification, one addressed in chapter 6, is that democratic caring improves the quality of life for people living in a democracy.

Democratic life rests upon the presumption that citizens are equal. What equality means, however, varies among accounts of democratic theory. Equality can mean equality of opportunity or equality of outcome. It can refer to a basic starting point of equal human rights, or to a conception of equal respect toward human autonomy. Political theorists frequently explore these competing meanings. What is distinctive about democratic caring, though, is that it presumes equality rests upon a very different ground. It presumes that we are equal as democratic citizens in being *care receivers*. In being "care receivers all," citizens' needs for care and their interdependent reliance on others to help them to meet their caring needs become the basis for equality. Of course, the assumption that all humans are equally receivers of care is not the same thing as saying that all humans have equal, the same, or even necessarily similar needs. But it is to say that meeting needs is a feature of the life of each and every human, and that each of us is thus engaged in caring from the standpoint of the recipient of care. These needs vary not only from individual to individual at one moment in time, but for each individual, and for groups within the society, over time. People may be more needy as infants, when they are infirm, or when the approach frailty as they age. Nevertheless, this quality of being *needy* is shared equally by all humans.

Even if all citizens are needy, they are not needy in the same ways. It would be absurd to try to equalize the neediness of citizens; after all, being needy varies from one to another and within one's own life from day to day. From the standpoint of democratic life, however, it does make sense to think of an equal capacity to voice needs. This point is pursued at greater length in chapter 4.

A Feminist Democratic Ethic of Care

This book thus defends a particular view of care, of democracy, and the relationship between them. It requires that caring practices be carried out in a democratic way and that caring become a central value for democracies. These political conclusions follow from an account of a feminist democratic ethic of care. What is a feminist democratic ethic of care? How does it differ from more familiar accounts of justice, such as those described by John Rawls, or even from other feminist and non-feminist accounts of an ethic of care, such as those offered, respectively, by Eva Kittay and Daniel Engster? Most importantly, rather than being a set of principles from which one deduces proper action, a feminist democratic ethic of care begins by envisioning series of caring practices, nested within one another. The broadest of these nested practices are those that pertain to society as a whole (I leave aside for another book questions of international practices). The goal of such practices is to ensure that all of the members of the society can live as well as possible by making the society as democratic as possible. This is the essence of "caring with." While living in a democratic manner is not the only goal of care, or of human life, in a democratic society it *is* the goal of democratic caring practices. Thus, *democratic politics should center upon assigning responsibilities for care, and for ensuring that democratic citizens are as capable as possible of participating in this assignment of responsibilities.* The task of a democratic politics is to affix responsibility, and as we come to recognize the centrality of care for living a decent human life, then the task of democratic politics needs to be much more fully focused upon care responsibilities: their nature, their allocation, and their fulfillment.[5] Since this kind of caring practice has largely been excluded from political discourse by deeply gendered assumptions about human nature and about how to arrive at political and ethical judgments, to include this set of caring practices requires the interrogation of the gendered, as well as racially and class-biased assumptions that have been taken for granted in limiting the scope of questions addressed by democratic politics. It is from the insights of feminist theories and practices that these biases—and the means to overcome them—become visible. Much of this book will be an account about these hidden biases in how care is organized in contemporary (primarily American) society. But at the outset, a few points are clear. To recognize the centrality of care in human life requires a conversation about human nature, about politics and ethics, and about how to make philosophical and political arguments about all of these matters. Let me describe each of these alternative views in some more detail.

In terms of human nature (or, as philosophers might prefer to put it, *ontologically*), as many scholars have argued (see, e.g., M. Robinson 2007; Groenhout 2004; F. Robinson 1999, 2008; Koggel 1998, 2006), a feminist ethic of care has a different starting point. First, from the standpoint of a feminist ethic of care, individuals are conceived of as being *in relationships*. While individuals, and their liberty, can still matter greatly, it makes little sense to think of individuals as if they were Robinson Crusoe, all alone, making decisions. Instead, all individuals constantly work in, through, or away from, relationships with others, who, in turn, are in differing states of providing or needing care from them. Second, all humans are vulnerable and fragile. While it is true that some are more vulnerable than others, all humans are extremely vulnerable at some points in their lives, especially when they are young, elderly, or ill. Human life is fragile; people are constantly vulnerable to changes in their bodily conditions that may require that they rely on others for care and support. Third, all humans are at once both recipients and givers of care. While the typical images of care are that those who are able-bodied and adult give care to children, the elderly, and the infirm, it is also the case that all able-bodied adults receive care from others, and from themselves, every day. With very few exceptions, humans engage in caring behavior toward those around them. Children as young as ten months old imitate the activity of feeding; they try to feed their caregivers, and they open their mouths as the spoon nears the other person's mouth (Bråten 2003). Children describe their activities as caring for parents (Mullin 2005). People are both givers and receivers of care all the time, though each person's capacities and needs shift throughout life. At any moment in a society, there are those who are the most needy and those who are the most capable of helping themselves and others. This shifting in needs and capacities for care is an important way to think about how our human lives change through time.

Given these qualities of human life, a feminist democratic ethic of care has to be able to explain how individuals can balance autonomy and dependency in their lives. Most democratic political theories simply *assume the existence of autonomous actors* as the starting point for democracy. From this assumption, such thinkers then see human dependency as a flawed condition or problem. But this assumption leaves unanswered the question of how infants go from being children to adults, from dependency to autonomy. Ignoring this question is not just a philosophical or psychological problem, though, because it reiterates well-worn patterns of discriminatory attitudes. Why, in white-dominated societies such as the United States, do people of color seem disproportionately unable to qualify as "autonomous" actors, or disproportionately beset by "pathologies" that make them dependent? The assumption of autonomy also leaves outside of its scope the human reality of varying degrees of autonomy and dependency throughout one's own life, and among the members of a political community. When all of these elements of human life are left "in the background," political theorists and moral philosophers end up producing a distorted starting point for their thinking about the nature of people. We will see how and why this assumption is harmful to living fully human lives in subsequent chapters. But a feminist democratic ethic of care can allow and account for these differences in a way that respects both the desires for autonomy and the realities of human dependency by thinking of this practical problem as part of the central concerns of a democratic society.

Careful readers will notice that I have referred to this alternative way of thinking about human nature as being *relational*, not as being altruistic. This is an important difference. One can make arguments for more robust public support for care by describing people as altruistic. Deborah Stone has brilliantly made such an argument in her book *The Samaritan's Dilemma* (2008). But in this account of care as caring with, I think it is important that we realize the limits of an account of altruism. Altruism has, as Stone argues, many fine characteristics, and she documents a wide variety of practices that she calls "everyday altruism," demonstrating that they are a fundamental part of people's lives. Among other things, she points out that altruism is deeply empowering: helping others makes one better able to accomplish many kinds of goals. Surely, in a participatory democracy this is an important thing to remember about the nature of caring, altruistic action.

The problem with altruism is that it is presumed to start from the non-selfish motives of a self, rather than to be, as I have described caring, a natural (if untrained) impulse among all humans to connect to one another by thinking about, and helping meet, the other's needs. From the standpoint of the various moral doctrines of selfishness, that some people act in an altruistic manner is their "choice" and should have no bearing on others. From the standpoint of the relational nature of humans, doctrines of selfishness are themselves inadequate accounts of what it means to be human; that some people "choose" to be selfish is not an acceptable account of how humans should act. In this way, altruism can be reduced to an "identity"—some have it and some do not. But this view is not in fact accurate. Instead, an elaborate set of social and political institutions are in place that support the selfishness of some and the altruism of others. Until those conditions are unpacked, focusing on altruism alone is not a sufficiently deep challenge to the inequitable and unfree ways in which care responsibilities are distributed.

Politically, the feminist democratic ethic of care seeks to expose how social and political institutions permit some to bear the burdens (and joys) of care and allow others to escape them. To simplify the argument, which will be elaborated in the next chapter, I will use this metaphor: some people have to take up their caring responsibilities, while others are given "passes" out of such responsibilities. They are given these passes because they are engaged in other activities that they (and, presumably, society) deem are simply more important than caring. I will, over the course of this book, elaborate on a number of these passes: the protection pass, the production pass, the taking-care-of-my-own pass, the bootstrap pass, and the charity pass. Conversely, those who are given a disproportionate amount of responsibility for care are presumed to have less interest and concern with such matters as protection, production, self-aggrandizement, or wealth. In a democratic society, all of these issues would be concern everyone.

The position of democratic care originated in several feminist concerns about power. First, the initial separations of life into public and private spheres, which will be a recurring theme in this book, have the effect of removing some political questions from public consideration. Especially since these relationships are often tainted with being somehow "natural," they seem pre-political. Once feminists raise the question about the public/private split, their position is then easily caricatured as wanting to abolish all aspects of private life. Feminists have offered many analyses about how to rethink the public and private spheres so that meaningful forms of "privacy" are preserved for all citizens[6] (Allen 2003; Yuval-Davis 1997). Second, since all relationships of care inevitably involve power, and often involve deep power differentials, all care relations are, in an important way, political. Insofar as a central requirement of democratic political life is some relative equality of power, this view seems to doom care relationships to be anti-democratic, and therefore excluded from public life. Even theorists who try to be inclusive, such as recent advocates for "active citizenship," still make assumptions about who needs what, so that they exclude as "active citizens" those who are aged, for example (Barnes 2007). Such asymmetrical care, however, can be mitigated against in a number of ways. A feminist democratic set of caring practices, as we shall explore throughout this book, is aimed in part at reducing both these power differentials and their effects on people.

Caring democracy thus requires a commitment to genuine equality of voice, and of reducing power differentials as much as possible, in order to create the conditions for a meaningful democratic discussion of the nature of responsibility in society. But often in contemporary discussions of democratic theory, such ends as equal voice are simply posited, without the theorist providing an account of how society can arrive at a place of greater equality. Political theorists often seek procedural rather than substantive ways to address such challenges. Indeed, one of the major ways in which contemporary democratic theory is framed—deliberation versus "agonism"—is mainly a difference about the nature of democratic dispute. Within each camp, there are further discussions of procedure, but little engagement occurs between these approaches, or within them, about the substance of democratic discussion. Other democratic theorists, such as Harry Boyte (2004; see also Miraftab 2004), pay more attention to actual practices of individuals that we might describe as democratic in that they aim at balancing power, at improving public goods, and at caring.

Ethically, a feminist democratic ethic of care begins from a sensitivity to the traditional boundary drawn between politics and ethics. While much of contemporary political theory presumes that we first create a set of moral principles from which we derive political practices, many contemporary feminist and non-feminist thinkers have challenged this order (Tronto 1993). Often following Aristotle, they point out that the political values embodied in a given political community will often determine how ethical or moral qualities are valued in that community. In a society that has systematically devalued care, then, the kinds of moral qualities and capacities associated with care often are not seen among the most important ethical values, either. Thus, thinkers concerned with a feminist ethic of care began to provide accounts of other values that should be seen as important moral qualities. These values grow out of the complex processes of care itself, as well as out of the needs for citizens in democratic societies to be able to express their needs. In *Moral Boundaries* (1993) I identified four moral qualities that align with the four phases of care that Berenice Fisher and I had identified, and which were discussed earlier in this chapter. These ethical qualities are:

1. *Attentiveness—caring about.* At this first phase of care, someone or some group notices unmet caring needs. It calls for the moral quality of *attentiveness*, of a suspension of one's self-interest, and a capacity genuinely to look from the perspective of the one in need. (In fact, we might also be attentive or inattentive to our own needs.)

2. *Responsibility—caring for.* Once needs are identified, someone or some group has to take on the burden of meeting those needs. This is responsibility, and that is the key moral quality of this second phase.

3. *Competence—care giving.* Assuming responsibility is not yet the same as doing the actual work of care; doing such work is the third phase of caring and requires the moral quality of *competence.* To be competent to care, given one's caring responsibilities, is not simply a technical issue, but a moral one.

4. *Responsiveness—care receiving.* Once care work is done, there will be a response from the person, group, animal, plant, environment, or thing that has been cared for. Observing that response, and making judgments about it (for example, whether the care given was sufficient, successful, or complete?) requires the moral quality of *responsiveness.* The person cared for need not be the one who completes the process of responding, but some response is necessary. And the response will often involve noting that new needs emerge as the past ones are met, thus the process continues.

Selma Sevenhuijsen (1998) identified an additional set of qualities necessary for caring in a democratic society. They include, first, making care a priority, so that one has a commitment to handle the moral complexities of "dependency, vulnerability and otherness" in order to make life livable and worth living. Furthermore, Sevenhuijsen argues, care also requires commitments to "plurality, communication, trust and respect." These qualities identified by Sevenhuijsen help to explain what the critical moral qualities are that will make it possible for people to take collective responsibility, to think of citizens as both receivers and givers of care, and to think seriously about the nature of caring needs in society.

Thus, as a parallel to the fifth phase of care, we might add:

5. *Plurality, communication, trust and respect; solidarity—caring with.*

It would surely be possible to recognize other moral qualities as imprtant to an ethic of care. For example, Margaret Walker (2006) writes about the importance of hope, and Sara Ruddick (1989) describes a key for "maternal thinking" as cheerfulness. We might add other values to this set, for example, gratitude. But no list of these moral qualities is meant here to be comprehensive. It is important to note, though, that while such standard virtues as self-control and courage remain relevant, they may be less central here, or may change their usual meanings in order to be more connected to the needs for care.

While moral qualities are an important part of an ethic of care, it is also possible to overemphasize this dimension of caring. Some philosophers argue that care ethics is a kind of "virtue ethics" (Slote 2008). Indeed, different virtue ethicists emphasize different qualities and points of intersection with care. Some emphasize care's capacity to explain moral motivation, while others focus on moral consequences (Sander-Staudt 2006). But the problem with all theories of care-as-virtue is that they are not relational. They do not begin from the premise that the important ethical issues concern relationships and meeting needs, not the perfection of the virtuous individual. Starting from an ethic of care-as-virtue returns the focus to the caregiver's performance; this preoccupation makes too remote the political concerns of unequal power among caregivers and care receivers. Hence, Maureen Sander-Staudt concludes:

> [F]or many individuals, especially those with social privilege, a flourishing life precludes caring responsibilities that are burdensome, dirty, or tedious, whereas care ethics is committed to the practice of care on all levels. The flourishing of some individuals, including many women, is purchased by the caring servitude or employment of others, most of whom are comparatively disadvantaged women, but all of whom may nonetheless be judged virtuous by some community standards. (2006, 35)

This point about the limits of understanding care as a virtue also allows us to make a more general observation. An theory of care that does not include all of these elements—care as an alternative relational account of human nature, as a way to conceive of politics, and as a way to conceive of ethics—is not complete or adequate. Yet there is one more dimension to the ways in which a feminist democratic ethic of care differs from standard ways of discussing values and ethics in contemporary politics. This is what philosophers call the metaethical dimension, which will be considered at length in the next chapter.

On a theoretical level, feminist democratic care ethics differ from many other accounts of politics and ethics. On the broadest theoretical level, feminist democratic care ethics is *relational*. By this view, the world consists not of individuals who are the starting point for intellectual reflection, but of humans who are always in relations with others. To make sense of human life requires a relational perspective. This point will be extended in chapter 2. What is important to keep in mind is that claims made about individuals that do not place them in a relational setting will be incomplete.

Democratic Caring and Neoliberalism

This chapter began with the assertion that the caring deficit and the democracy deficit were two sides of the same coin. Now that the basic concepts of care and democratic caring have been presented, it is possible to explain that claim. It rests upon noting something else: that neoliberalism has minted this coin of the realm. This section spells out the meaning of neoliberalism and how it affects the prospects for recognizing problems of caring and of democracy.

Personal Responsibility and Neoliberalism

Care needs a home in democratic political theory, and democratic political theory remains incomplete without a way to explain where and how care gets done in a democratic society. Nevertheless, these concerns may only be the concerns of political theorists or philosophers. A much more serious reason to rethink the relationship between democratic political theory and care is clear if one glances at the contemporary political world, where a clear and anti-democratic account of how to solve the care problem has become a cornerstone of neoliberal political ideology. By neoliberalism, I refer to the economic system in which government expenditures are limited, the market is viewed as the preferred method for allocating all social resources, the protection of private property is taken to be the first principle of government, and social programs are limited to being a "safety net."[7] This economic system is supported by a political form of limited liberal democracy and an ideology of limited government involvement.

As an ideological position, neoliberalism has several tenets. The first is the assumption that the market is the institution that is most able to resolve disputes, allocate resources, and permit individuals "choice." Second, freedom comes to be defined solely as the capacity to exercise choice. From these two premises follows a third, that societies work best when they allow rational actors to make choices in the market; anything that interferes with such choice reduces people's freedom and is harmful to them and to society. Thus, under the banner of "choice," neoliberals seek to restrict all forms of *government* activity that might interfere with the "free market." We live in an age in which capitalism has not only taken a new form, neoliberalism, but in which this form of economic existence has come to function as an all-encompassing ideology. Neoliberal capital believes itself to be definitive of all forms of human relationships and of all ways of properly understanding human life. Neoliberalism is not only a description of economic life, it is also an ethical system that posits that only personal responsibility matters.

Wendy Brown (2005, 41) makes the important point that the neoliberal "market" is not, despite the claims of some of its adherents, a "natural" institution. Markets need protection, too. For example, if workers can organize too effectively, they can, through work stoppages, disrupt economic production, thereby (from the standpoint of producers) distorting the market. If states decide to tax corporations to provide welfare benefits for citizens, then the capacity of those in "the market" to act as freely as possible is constrained. Thus, neoliberalism requires that the state be enlisted into its political-economic project of constructing and maintaining the "free market," often at deep costs to the people. Naomi Klein (2007) has explored in detail the costs of this "shock doctrine": that the return to the free market will require dislocations among people who have become used to some modicum of social support. Once the state is involved in organizing and promoting the market, of course, it is no longer separable from "politics" (cf. Wolin 2008). But the logic of neoliberalism also directs the appropriate concerns of politics to be only those that support economic activity.

From the standpoint of an ethic of care, neoliberalism is a disastrous worldview. The neoliberal's political desire is to support the economy, but the economy requires "improvement"—that is, increasing efficiency —over time. One of the difficulties of care is that it is labor-intensive; it is difficult to make care more profitable (Razavi 2007). Thus, the logic of neoliberalism is to reduce the state's care costs, but they are resistant to being lowered.

From the point of view of a market, individual humans appear primarily as buyers and sellers, and since what most people have to sell on the market is their labor, the neoliberal world view thus sees people primarily as workers and consumers, who already have autonomy and clear ideas about their "preferences." People should therefore calculate about their expenses in taking care of themselves; if they end up, for example, with children or elderly relatives who need support, they need to accept the consequences of their own decisions and these costs for themselves.

Of course, the view that as buyers and sellers we act autonomously is largely a myth. As consumers, the incapacity to discern "true" "information" in the marketplace of ideas is difficult, given the extraordinary efforts made to affect our perceptions of the world and of products through advertising and public relations (Ewen 1996). The logic of consumption is relentlessly individualistic; Juliet Schor (2004) reports how marketing and advertisers have always sought to peel off more and more members of families from traditional loyalties to create loyalties to their products and brands. In the 1920s, women were the targets of advertising to attract them to "unfeminine" activities such as smoking. In the present, researchers study the importance of children in making families' purchasing decisions. Children can identify brands at the age of two and influence parents' buying between two and three years of age. Schor argues that advertisers spend a great deal of time and money to attach young children to their brands in order to develop customer loyalty. Despite the discursive presumption that consuming is all a matter of individual "choice," advertisers seek to attach infants to their products. This reality seems to undermine the model of the individual consumer as making only "rational" or "autonomous" decisions. On the contrary, it suggests the ways in which even consumption is relational. For an economist, a preference to consume what one's toddler seems to prefer is a just another preference. But when we realize that many parents say that they work harder than they would like in order to provide things that their children would like (Schor 1998, 2000), it becomes clear that "the market" has exerted pressure on parents through their children. The image of the autonomous chooser is, in this regard also, a myth.

Neoliberalism has also had a profound effect in changing the shape of people's lives as workers. "The market" is taken to be neutral in its effects on people. The reality is that "the market" has a bias of its own, toward "its own." Support for the market is actually a bias in favor of those who are most skilled at manipulating the market to their own advantage, since when they are able to do that, the market "grows," and since the assumption is that "a rising tide lifts all boats," growth in the market is taken as a universal human good.

We should stop, however, and examine these effects more closely. Martha McCluskey (2003) argues that the market is not neutral. Examining arguments that welfare is redistributive and reduces efficiency, she also notes that forcing welfare recipients to work may make more workers who will accept very low wages available. Thus, there is some advantage to employers in cutting welfare benefits, but we never think of such a cut as a benefit to them. She asks:

> Whose ability to get more of what they want by shifting costs to others should count as a societal gain, and whose should count as a private gain at the expense of others? By making the market stand for the public gain, neoliberalism implicitly confers superior citizenship status on those centrally identified with the market-they are members of the public whose gains count. (816)

Thus, McCluskey argues, though twentieth-century theories of citizenship recognized the need for solidarity with the working class, recent neoliberal theory has undermined this sense of solidarity. As a result, a bias toward those who have already succeeded in the market continues. Neoliberal ideology in this way is not neutral, but supports some at the expense of others. Nonetheless, since it is viewed as constraining government and supporting an indifferent (and thus, fair) market, neoliberalism is able to win the support of many.

From the standpoint of a neoliberal society, then, human life is viewed as the sum of an individual's own "choices," for which he or she will be responsible. Care thus becomes entirely a personal and private matter; individuals make "choices" about care for themselves and for those around them.

The problems with this ideological view are many, but let us begin by noting that the view that choice represents one's real desires leads to tautological accounts of freedom, equality, and justice.

"Choice," as we shall elaborate in chapter 3, is not freedom. If one is oppressed, then the choices before one will often be only bad choices. Indeed, one compelling argument against oppression is that it so diminishes people in their capacity to choose to act rightly (Tessman 2005). An alternative account of freedom would argue that one is only free after one has accepted one's responsibilities.

"Choice," as we shall elaborate in chapter 4, is not equality. Equality as equal opportunity is a myth if there is no equality of care for children. An alternative account of equality, defended here, requires acceptance of difference and plurality and a willingness to provide what is necessary to make certain that all have voice.

"Choice," as we shall elaborate in chapter 5, is not justice. Justice requires that each receive what is due, it requires honest exploration of the social, economic, and political institutions that constrain people's lives, and it requires that none are more subject to the vicissitudes of fortune than others. Support of the market does not produce these outcomes.

We mistake "choice" for freedom, equality, and justice because we have become too well trained by being workers and consumers. For most, work is a realm of compulsion; consumption is a realm of choice. So we have come to think of those moments when we are not constrained by the demands of our work life as if they were possessed of real choice. And we have come to mistake this economic account of our meaning for its political meaning.

Neoliberalism and "Personal Responsibility"

The moral and political theories that accompany neoliberalism presume that there is a simple account of care. To quote Wendy Brown:

> Not only is the human being configured exhaustively as homo oeconomicus, but all dimensions of human life are cast in terms of a market rationality. . . . [It results in] the production of all human and institutional action as rational entrepreneurial action, conducted according to a calculus of utility, benefit, or satisfaction against a microeconomic grid of scarcity, supply and demand, and moral value-neutrality. Neoliberalism does not simply assume that all aspects of social, cultural, and political life can be reduced to such a calculus; rather, it develops institutional practices and rewards for enacting this vision. (2005, 40)

We can call the moral dimensions of such neoliberal practices "personal responsibility."

As George W. Bush put the point in his First Inaugural Address, "America, at its best, is a place where personal responsibility is valued and expected." Is there something wrong with personal responsibility? How can anyone think this idea is not a good one? A close look at Bush's speech reveals the problem:

> America, at its best, is a place where personal responsibility is valued and expected. . . . Encouraging responsibility is not a search for scapegoats, it is a call to conscience. And though it requires sacrifice, it

brings a deeper fulfillment. We find the fullness of life not only in options, but in commitments. And we find that children and community
are the commitments that set us free. (Bush 2001)

Bush's elision from responsibility to "children" and "community" makes
clear that for him, personal responsibility is the solution to the problem of
care in the modern state. If you cannot care for your own children, your
own community, then if there is a problem in your family or community,
the problem is your inadequate sacrifice. His statement that "encouraging
responsibility is not a call for scapegoats" makes it sound as if one actually would entertain the idea that it *is* the search for scapegoats. What can
that mean?

As the Bush administration's policies demonstrated many times, this
notion of personal responsibility means that if you cannot take care of
your own family and community, then you, as an individual, are to blame
for not having made enough sacrifices or taken on enough responsibilities. There is no context for "children" and "community" other than that
of personal responsibility. Toting up individuals' willingness to take on
personal responsibility provides an answer to the question of how well
"children" and "communities" will do.

Such a politics is problematic. On the one hand, there is much to rec-
ommend personal responsibility; I am surely not arguing that it would be
better if people ignored their personal responsibilities. The problem with
personal responsibility is when it seems to be the only form of responsibility that is important in democratic life. Because when it is the only
form of responsibility, personal responsibility can have a profoundly *anti-
democratic* effect. "Personal responsibility" functions ideologically when
the expectations for responsibilities have been fixed along lines that reflect inequality and historic forms of exclusion. Taking care of one's "community" has a different meaning in a well-endowed gated community
or suburb versus a down-on-its-luck urban neighborhood. Going away
to college from an upper-middle-class household and living in a dormi-
tory will bring different responsibilities than attending university when,
as an eighteen-year old, one is already contributing to the family's income
and commuting. From the standpoint of the professor in the front of the
classroom, the first student may seem more "responsible"; to a child or an
elderly relative who depends upon this person's care, responsibility looks
quite different. When we act as if all of the starting and ending points
for everyone are the same, we miss an important feature of what justice

might require. From this perspective, personal responsibility seems anti-democratic because it pays no heed to the likely effects that great levels of inequality will have on individuals and on public life. It is anti-democratic because it presumes that all social institutions have the same form as an ideal market, where there is no past, no limits, and no concerns. It also presumes that the market is itself neutral.

But the market is not neutral—it advantages certain kinds of people and certain kinds of activities. In ignoring any past injustice, it permits no redress. It advantages those who are already in good standing within it, and disadvantages those who are not. As a result, the more committed we become to the "pure market," the less likely we are to reverse inequalities of wealth. Does this problem matter? Shouldn't we all just be content to take our chances? When something that claims to be neutral is in fact entirely biased, it seems important that we call its bias for what it is.

Consider for a moment that if we transform all responsibility into personal responsibility, then we have no way to describe collective *or* market *ir*responsibility. Brown (2005, 40) decried the loss of a more robust kind of citizen under neoliberalism: "The model neoliberal citizen is one who strategizes for her- or himself among various social, political, and economic options, not one who strives with others to alter or organize these options. A fully realized neoliberal citizenry would be the opposite of public-minded; indeed, it would barely exist as a public."

At the same time, economic irresponsibility can have no meaning if everyone is only responsible individually.

In a society in which no one is willing to accept responsibility for anything but their own choices, it is difficult to think about care beyond the household. Yet even that account of neoliberalism fails, for the truth of the matter is that we do not usually choose to whom we owe responsibilities. As Ruth Groenhout (2004, 88), referring to Annette Baier, observed, "We do find ourselves in the midst of responsibilities that are not always chosen." Indeed, as Brown noted, neoliberal thinkers know that they are making a normative claim, that it is *better* to think of the world this way, but that other possibilities of ways to think of the world exist. Nevertheless, for the people who are caught within this ideological system, it is difficult not to experience it as simply the way the world is.

Edward Bellamy, more than a century ago, described such an unequal society and how citizens within it would perceive one another in his widely popular utopian novel *Looking Backward: 2000–1887*. He used the metaphor of seeing society as a gigantic carriage or coach, in which the rich ride in relative luxury while the poor pull the coach down the road:

> The other fact is yet more curious, consisting in a singular hallucination which those on the top of the coach generally shared, that they were not exactly like their brothers and sisters who pulled at the rope, but of finer clay, in some way belonging to a higher order of beings who might justly expect to be drawn. . . .
>
> The strangest thing about the hallucination was that those who had but just climbed up from the ground, before they had outgrown the marks of the rope upon their hands, began to fall under its influence. As for those whose parents and grand-parents before them had been so fortunate as to keep their seats on the top, the conviction they cherished of the essential difference between their sort of humanity and the common article was absolute. The effect of such a delusion in moderating fellow feeling for the sufferings of the mass of men into a distant and philosophical compassion is obvious. To it I refer as the only extenuation I can offer for the indifference which, at the period I write of, marked my own attitude toward the misery of my brothers. (Bellamy 1888, 16–17)

Unless democrats, as people committed to both equality and freedom, are willing to offer an alternative account of how we might care, then the view of neoliberals, that all of caring is a choice one makes about how to exercise one's personal responsibility, receives no systematic answer.

Conclusion

From the standpoint of an ethic of care, citizens should be able to expect more from the state and civil society in guaranteeing that their caring needs, and those of their loved ones, will be met. At the same time, citizens must become more committed to producing the kinds of values, practices, and institutions that will allow democratic society to more coherently provide for its democratic caring citizens. Breaking the current patterns of fear and discouragement does not end the frustrations of the give-and-take that politics always involves. But within democratic care, politics will be closer to the concerns of the people, and, in this way, more fundamentally democratic. How such a transition might occur depends upon a deeper understanding of the problem.

Politics is always about both competition and agreement; if there is no common ground, then there cannot even be agreement about the methods and nature of competition (Wolin 1960). Political theory, too, is not neutral; it can never claim that its perspective is equally useful and adaptable to the views of all. The argument that I make in this book—that care and democracy need to be thought about together—has obvious and large political implications. It places greater value on the activities of caregivers, on the time spent engaged in caring, on human vulnerability, and it challenges the wisdom of a political philosophy that so fundamentally misunderstands human nature as to claim that we are primarily creatures of the market. Humans are not only or mainly creatures of the market, they are creatures of care. Democratic societies need to reorient their values away from support for the "market" to support for the means for people to live human lives. The independent rational actor whose life in the market is sufficient to provide for the other needs and wants of life, and whose freedom consists only in pursuit of life in this manner, is a myth. Thinking about how people's interdependence can be best organized through caring institutions that take everyone's equal capacity both for care and for freedom requires widely diverse and thorough democratic processes of agreeing and disagreeing. Only then will democratic societies move closer to realizing the ideal of democracy—equality and freedom for all —in everyone's life.

2

Why Personal Responsibility Isn't Enough for Democracy

Categorizing is not the sin . . . the problem is in the failure to
assume responsibility for examining how and where we set our
boundaries.
— Patricia Williams (1991, 102)

If citizens are going to take democratic care as a central political value,
how will this shift affect politics? To envision a society as caring is to envision a society engaged in the daily and extraordinary activities of meeting
peoples' needs. To envision a society as democratic and caring is to envision a society whose account of justice balances how the burdens and joys
of caring are equalized so as to leave every citizen with as much freedom
as possible. Such a vision requires that citizens see clearly how they care
with others, that is, how they think about responsibilities for care.

This chapter argues that rethinking politics in order to make it more
democratic and more caring also requires a fundamental rethinking of responsibilities. Indeed, we might want to substitute for Harold Lasswell's
(1936) succinct definition of politics, as "who gets what, when and how,"
one that sees it a way to divide up responsibilities: who is responsible for
caring for what, when, where, and how. I shall argue, though, that this
division of responsibility is often so deeply embedded in our collective
habits, practices, institutions, and political life that the assumptions upon

which they rest seem beyond the reach of normal political discussion. And these implicit boundaries not only determine caring responsibilities, they also permit many forms of irresponsibility to flourish. In deciding whether certain types of care are best addressed by the market, the family, or the state (or some combination of these institutional locations), assignment of care responsibilities describes a different way to think about political life. It casts politics in terms of actions (who *does* what), rather than distribution (who *gets* what). It describes how public and private life should interact. For example, luxurious care services (the services of a sommelier, for example) might always belong in the market. Public education has traditionally been a state responsibility, but one in which parents also share. Raising infants has been a family responsibility, though recent efforts to improve early childhood outcomes have also engaged market- and state-based institutions. Making these decisions in a public and transparent way refocuses attention upon how different settings (and mixtures of settings) can balance the achievement of collective goals (such as preserving public health) and at the same time further other values such as freedom of choice and plurality of visions about the good life and good care.

In this chapter, then, I make the case for putting the political process by which a society organizes its caring responsibilities at the heart of a new vision of the substance of politics. Both responsibilities and "passes" out of responsibility need to be reexamined. I will end the chapter by considering the idea of "personal responsibility," an embodiment of neoliberal ideology, and show its limits from the standpoint of a caring democracy. In the next several chapters, I describe how we care now, and how current caring arrangements rely upon many unexamined assumptions that have the effect of exempting some people from some of their caring responsibilities based on their gender, class, race, or economic situation. In a just democratic society, such distributions of privilege require a public evaluation. Using care as the broad framework within which to explore these questions permits democratic societies to face up to how well their institutions embody their values.

Why Focus on Responsibility?

But why focus on responsibility? It is only one of the four phases of care identified in the Fisher/Tronto (1990) definition, and as the exploration of care in the last chapter indicated, it is only one of a number of dimensions relevant in thinking about caring democratic practices. And yet, I assert here that democratic politics should center upon assigning responsibilities for care, and for ensuring that democratic citizens are as capable as possible of participating in this assignment. Is there something special about politics and responsibility? The term "responsibility" is often used in moral philosophy as well, so why do I assert its primacy to give an account of caring democratic life?

Other political theorists have discussed the importance of care, or a caring attitude, without linking responsibility and politics as strongly as I do here. Many other thinkers view caring as an originary source of the proper attitudes to have toward the world. William Connolly (1999, 36), for example, has used the language of an "ethos of care for the plurovocity of being." Several scholars have described Hannah Arendt's "love of the world" as akin to an ethic of care (Myers 2012; Kyle 2011). Harry Frankfurt (1988) wrote about "the importance of what we care about." And Michael Slote (2008) views care as a fundamental human virtue. Engagement of the sort he called care (*Sorge*) was a fundamental starting point for Martin Heidegger (1996; see also Paley 2000), and Emmanuel Lévinas's absolutist ethics found in the face of the other is often compared to care (Diedrich, Burggraeve, and Gastmans 2006; Groenhout 2004; Simmons 1999; Lévinas 1996). What distinguishes these approaches from a feminist ethic of care is that in all of these cases (except Lévinas), care begins with, and often ends on, the dispositional level. Care is seen as a kind of motivation, an existential account to the self for its reason (or one reason) for being. In this regard, care remains an attitude and a kind of approach that is a feature of the caregiver (that is, one who cares). Care functions in such accounts as a motivation (e.g., to be virtuous, or fully human). While such an attitude can be used to prescribe how people should act politically, it is not yet political in the sense that I am using it here. It is not yet even the same value "care" that I have invoked so far in this book.

The problem with these accounts of caring as an attitude or disposition is that they still center on the caring subject, rather than seeing the caring subject and object (which can even be the same person) in relationship and in actual caring practices. It is too abstract, too much an intellectual (even if not only rational, as in Connolly's account) rather than a practical and collective concern. One might say that such a disposition is necessary but not sufficient for care. But even that way of putting it misses the point. For one can care—that is, engage in practices of care—without any special attitude for it, though perhaps not very well. And to set this idea of caring—having the proper attitude as originary—misses the ways in which caring attitudes themselves arise out of caring practices. It ignores the fact, to employ the language used here, that attentiveness to needs can and must itself be trained. Care-giving is not (only?) natural and innate, one can become attuned to it.

Caring about something, the first of the four phases in the Fisher/Tronto definition of care, is the capacity to perceive needs. But it does not yet say anything about addressing unmet needs. To make the move to meeting needs, one must go to the next level and assign responsibility for meeting those needs to concrete people, groups, and institutions, in concrete places, vis-à-vis the unmet needs. This is the point at which caring for—that is, recognizing actual relations among those who have needs and those who might meet them—becomes key. Politics originates in making judgments about the relations that exist, about how needs might be met. It is, in this sense, the kind of "betweenness" that Arendt (2005) describes. It is true that if humans had no needs that they could not automatically meet by themselves, there would be no politics. But that is not because politics is the same as meeting needs; it is because politics involves meeting needs in a way that permits the pursuit of other goals as well, and because it involves making decisions about who does what for whom.

The most basic decisions about the allocation of responsibility underpin our political and social life. In the next three chapters, we will see, among other things, that caring responsibilities have been allocated through ideas such as domesticity in the nineteenth century, professionalization and institutionalization in the twentieth century, and marketization in the late twentieth and twenty-first centuries. That these appear "natural" rather than political does not change the fact that they are ways to allocate responsibility. The question in a democratic society remains: Are these ways to allocate responsibilities committed to inclusion, that is, to liberty, equality, and justice for all? To answer this question, the nature of responsibility requires further explication.

One last point is worth mentioning about the centrality of responsibility for the project of a political theory of democratic caring. To focus on responsibility is not to make the other phases of care unimportant. Indeed, each of the four phases of care also contains other phases nested within it. (We noted in chapter 1 that caring practices often nest within one another, but it is also true that within each caring practice there is a nesting of the four phases of care with one another.) For example, in order to make good judgments about who should be responsible for care requires that one think about the nature of care-giving, and about how to be responsive to a set of actions for caring. To be responsive to others is to be attentive to the development of new unmet needs. Thus, the politics of democratic caring does not end once some initial judgments about how to divide up caring responsibilities have been met. Nevertheless, these judgments are likely to affect profoundly what comes later.

Finally, if we think of "caring with" as an additional phase of care, it is clear that it also needs to be reenacted "all the way down" within all caring practices in a democratic society. While this is difficult both to imagine and to achieve in practice, it is one of the ways in which pragmatic commitments to democratic institutions, to organizing and participating in them, have effects throughout society (Boyte 2011).

Responsibility as a Political Idea

Responsibility is a multifaceted idea. Sometimes it is used as a synonym for obligation or duty. Used in this way, a responsibility is sometimes seen as arising from a right, and hence the idea that rights and responsibilities are tied together.[1] Understood as an ethical concept, responsibility is often used in the sense of something that is accountable or attributable, and hence worthy of praise or blame (Eshleman 2009). Yet the term is also a political term. Its meaning derives from the notions of "response" and "responsible," made into a more abstract noun by adding the suffix "-ity." In making something that is relational into something more abstract, the etymological origin of responsibility already points to some of its key elements: it is by nature relational, existing in the relationships among people rather than in individuals themselves. Further, by being a response, responsibility is dynamic rather than fixed, an abstraction about something concrete. According to the *Oxford English Dictionary*, the first use of the term occurred in the middle of the seventeenth century. An exemplary use occurred in the Federalist Papers, in Paper No. 63, defending the longer terms of the Senate, probably written by Alexander Hamilton: "Responsibility in order to be reasonable must be limited to objects within the power of the responsible party" (Hamilton, Jay, and Madison 1787). Moral praise and blame have existed throughout Western moral and political thought, but the English term "responsibility" is relatively new.

It is worth pausing over this appearance of the term. From early on, it seems, responsibility carried with it the danger that it could exceed its limits and become too great for the powers of those to whom it was assigned. These resonances of limit echo in most uses of responsibility in several ways. First, the goal of assigning responsibility is not only to tie a "responsible party" to a particular set of actions, but also to free others from that same responsibility. In describing the relationship of responsibility for some "responsible party," there is also an implicit denial of a general sense of responsibility for all other possible responsible parties. Second, the goal of assigning responsibility requires that the assigned party has sufficient power to carry out the assignment. It is not reasonable, asserts Hamilton, to ask too much of a responsible party. Third, the assignment of responsibility is diffuse. Nothing in the notion of responsibility itself explains who determines who should have responsibility, and whether particular responsibilities have been well met, though some accounts of moral responsibility attempt to do so with regard to particular actions (Feinberg 1970). P. F. Strawson (1962) suggested that all accounts of responsibility are ultimately social, but it is important to note that they are also all political. Fourth, insofar as responsibility is social and political, there will inevitably be ambiguity in ascribing and assigning it. Unlike rights, which can be adjudicated on the basis of a claim for a right, responsibility is much less clear. This lack of clarity makes responsibility not only more political, but also much less secure and straightforward for individuals and groups who try to determine where their responsibilities begin and end. We shall return to this problem shortly.

For the most part, accounts of responsibility stress its ties to the freedom of a subject to act and to the consequences of such action.[2] That is, responsibility is a way of assigning blame for past judgments and actions. Usually, legal forms of assigning responsibility are "backward-looking" in this way.

In recent writings about responsibility, many feminist scholars have found such "backward-looking" qualities in accounts of responsibility to be inadequate. Instead, feminists have begun to develop a model that is forward-looking and accounts for how to make change rather than simply to assign blame (Card 1996).

Iris Marion Young's (2006) "social connection model" of responsibility argues that all agents who contribute by their actions to the structural processes that produce injustice have responsibilities to work to remedy these injustices. She distinguishes the social connection model from a "liability" model. She allows that in legal proceedings, the liability model still has an important role to play. Writing about the example of college students

boycotting the production of licensed college wear in sweatshops, however, lead Young to realize that the "liability" model was inadequate. One
can say that the sweatshop owner had committed a moral wrong, but the
response—"At least those workers, underpaid though they may be, have
some work"—is also somewhat persuasive. Young recognized, as had
Marion Smiley (1992) before her, that trying to parse out who is wrong
and deserves blame does not *solve* the problem of irresponsible action.
Drawing upon her career-long meditations on the complicated relationships of agency and social structure, Young recognized the more complex
nature of "structural injustice," in which, though we can see an ongoing
social injustice, the actions or particular others may not be traced through
complex social institutions to clear causal paths. As a result, Young argued, everyone involved bears some, albeit different, level of responsibility. She averred that different conditions of power, privilege, interest, and
capacities for collective action might make some more responsible than
others. Thus, while everyone who perceives a situation of structural injustice has a responsibility to address it, "by virtue of this structural posi-
tioning, different agents have different opportunities and capacities, can
draw on different kinds and amounts of resources, or face different levels
of constraint with respect to processes that can contribute to structural
change" (126). From here, Young needed only to add the obvious point
that such complexities cross national borders to provide an answer to the
question of how our responsibilities might cross national borders.

   But which relationships are significant enough to create conditions of
responsibility? Again, scholars have provided a range of answers to this
question. Soran Reader (2007) argues that relations are a particular kind
of interaction (not only among humans, but also with other living and
inanimate things in the world). By her account, what makes a relation is
that its engagement of the moral actor is constitutive of the relationship
with the "relata." So, while a person might be a member of the group "recipients of heart transplants," that status, condition, substantive property,
does not become a relation until one heart transplant recipient seeks out
another, becomes engaged with her about how their lives have been affected by their common experience, their initial conversations blossom
into a friendship, and so forth (374). Such relations, and not merely sharing properties, argues Reader, make agents responsible. "The mark of
obligation-constituting features of real relationships is that they are not
merely properties that the relata happen to share. Rather, they are properties that literally connect, constituting the relationship. Such features

both connect and obligate agents" (370). Thus, Reader's agents have vol-
untaristic qualities to some extent that make them responsible, but not all
responsibilities arise voluntarily. This is so since they may have been the
relata, that is, the object of a relation created by someone else—just as,
say, an infant does not choose her caregiver.

Reader specifies that relations that can lead to responsibility can arise
in a number of ways, including presence, biology, history, practice, environment, shared projects, institutions, play, trade, conversation, and other
"less structured interactions." The resulting responsibilities will vary, but
not because there is a moral principle that describes some as more valuable than others. Rather, they vary with the depth of the relationship that
exists; "obligations are also stronger if the relationship is fuller" (377).

Reader's account of relations thus recognizes that responsibilities are
necessarily partial, yet depending upon the agents' deeds and activities,
they can be far-reaching and myriad. In this regard, she claims, partialists
are correct to see that relationships matter, but wrong "in the kinds of relational properties they have hitherto singled out." The relationships that
matter, she claims, are intrinsic to the nature of the relationship itself. She
notes that her account "is unlike other partialist accounts, in seeing moral
obligation as a part of not just some but all relationships, and in accounting for the way moral obligations diminish, and thereby accommodating
the impartialist intuition that strangers may obligate us morally" (379).
But strangers do not obligate us simply by sharing with us the substantive
property of being human. Some form of relation—presence; biological,
historical, or institutional ties; or some other form of "interaction"—occurred to create a responsibility.[3]

Most important for the purposes of this book is Margaret Urban
Walker's (2007) concept of responsibility. Walker's concern with responsibility grows out of a metaethical critique: her notion of moral understandings, she observes, are "mainly about moral epistemology, that
is, about the nature, source, and justification of moral knowledge" (4).
Walker distinguishes two kinds of metaethics: the theoretical-juridical
model and the expressive-collaborative model. The former is concerned
with elucidating clear moral principles following standard rules of philosophical practice; the latter denies that any moral actor's position, including the philosopher's, is superior to others. Instead, only through moral
practices—the expression, agreement, and collaboration about the meaning of morality in any community—does moral life take form. Walker
calls the practice of the expressive-collaborative metaethic an "ethics of

responsibility": "An 'ethics of responsibility' as a normative view would try to put people and responsibilities in the right places with respect to each other" (2007, 84). As a result, morality becomes "a social negotiation in real time, where members of a community of roughly or largely shared moral beliefs try to refine understanding, extend consensus, and eliminate conflict among themselves" (71).

Walker (2007) distinguished these two kinds of approaches to metaethics. To her, the theoretical-juridical model is flawed because it makes an unjustifiable assumption about the superiority for moral life of the kind of knowledge produced through standard practices in philosophy. It allows philosophers to engage in discussions at a level of abstraction that grow out of a failure to recognize the distinctive location of philosophical discussion. She adds: "It also shields from view the historical, cultural, and social location of the moral philosopher, and that of moral philosophy itself as a practice of intellectual and social authority" (41). The usual basis for such claims is that moral philosophers have grounded their arguments in carefully honed philosophical standards of logic and reason. But, asks Walker, why do these standards bear special status in making moral argument? Why are moral philosophers exempt from the biases that they might attribute to all others? Walker suggests that a more appropriate way to understand ethics is as an outcome of an expressive-collaborative process in which various moral actors come to agreement about an acceptable set of moral standards. Expressive-collaborative morality thus makes no claim to being beyond time or place. Instead, it "looks at moral life as a continuing negotiation *among* people" (67). As Lorraine Code elaborates,

> Beginning and ending in practices of responsibility, both epistemic and moral, this model shifts attention to questions about how moral agents, singly and cooperatively, *express* their sense of self, situation, community, and agency in the responsibilities they discover and/or claim as theirs. Expressing and claiming are no impersonal processes but the actions of specifically identified, located deliberators, trying to work out how to live well in the circumstances in which they find themselves; starting not from an unstructured, uncontaminated "original position" but from the possibilities and constraints consequent upon the hand they have been dealt. (2002, 160)

This approach "displaces formulaic deduction from theoretical principles with negotiated understandings; and displaces legislation from first principles or categorical imperatives with cooperative engagement in producing habitable communities, environments, and ways of life" (160).

Thus, as Walker argues, the only way to avoid such biases is to engage everyone in the process of expressing and collaborating to produce an account of moral life with which everyone can live. As noted above, Walker insists that "an ethics of responsibility as a normative moral view would try to put people and responsibilities in the right places with respect to each other" (2007, 84).

It is important to note that the kinds of discussions that Walker and Code envision informing an expressive-collaborative morality, the kind of "judging with care" that Sevenhuijsen endorses, can only occur in a society in which real, everyday people have an opportunity to express themselves and to be heard by others. Only a democratic political order can do so. In any other political order, even one that is "liberal" but not democratic, there is a claim of authority made on the part of some to trump the exchange of views in which all are able to participate.[4] Everyone needs to engage in the kinds of affixing of responsibility that Walker sees as fulfilling the metaethical need of collaboration.[5]

Although Walker does not use this language, it is clear that her account of responsibility makes it a political process. On some level, then, the process of allocating responsibility is at the heart of the political practices of care. Political "care work" also requires that those responsible for the allocation of care responsibilities throughout society are attentive to whether or not those processes of care function. This can be done through a variety of means, but the best ways will require the participation of actual care workers and receivers in providing responses about how well caring needs are being met.

What distinguishes a feminist democratic ethic of care from Walker's more general "ethics of responsibility" should now also be clear: a care ethic provides a substantive basis for applying the ethics of responsibility. It directs our attention to certain aspects of life in order to determine responsibilities. Some forms of responsibility can appear to be contractual, but for an ethic of care, one needs always to go beyond simple agreements to look more closely at the power allocation in exchanges about responsibility. One needs to focus also upon relationships among people, and not simply upon isolated individuals, in making decisions about care.

While this assimilation of responsibility and responsibility to care may have begun to sound like a problem of distributive justice, and to some extent it is, we need to recall that politics is about power not only in this distributive sense, but also in the sense of the creation or assumption of collective capacity to act.

It is never, then, simply a matter of distribution. Furthermore, if "ought implies can," as Thomas Haskell (1998) observes, then what follows is a very complicated understanding of what is necessary and what is transformable in human life, and hence, what constitute the limits of responsibility. How should we think about the converse: to what extent does "can imply ought"? Haskell glosses Bernard Williams's (1994) discussion of slavery in the ancient world and observes that since ancient writers simply assumed that slavery was necessary, they did not imagine it could be immoral. Haskell then asks, "How do 'necessary evils' such as slavery come to seem remediable, thus shrinking the domain of necessity and expanding the realm within which the imperatives of responsibility can operate?" (297).[6] From this standpoint—of what is beyond the scope of responsibility and what is within our power to change—Nancy Fraser's (1989) concern about the "politics of needs interpretation" assumes a new salience. For if we are unwilling to question the necessity behind a set of practices, then we will not see ourselves as responsible for them.

In a democratic society, we might presume to answer that everyone in the society should be around the table making decisions about the allocation of responsibilities. But with limited time and resources, not everyone will be involved in every decision about allocating responsibility. One way to think about a society's political values, in the broadest possible terms, is to ask the question, What are the primary decisions that have been made about the allocation of responsibility? For example, if a society leaves questions about how much and what kind of education children should receive to their parents, then one allocation of a basic responsibility has been made about who sits at the table and makes judgments about the child's education. Whether this is a wise decision never reoccurs on the political agenda because the prior allocation to a very narrow circle of responsibility has already occurred. On the other end of this spectrum, allocations of responsibility also operate on a global level. If democracy should be a global value, the artificial limit of national sovereignty seems an unsatisfying answer to the question of whom to seat within the circles of responsibility that concern the safety and flourishing of people. Nevertheless, in real terms, responsibility is allocated, either through some past decision that now looks fixed, or through some new process for allocating responsibility.

Questions about allocation of care responsibilities do not follow the traditional division of "left" and "right" in predictable ways (cf. Seven-huijsen 2000). Walker, for example, has turned to the problem of moral repair, which requires that we see a relationship between ourselves and our past actions, the actions of others who were in our position, or those to whose actions we remain connected. The question of whether slavery's legacy has been overcome in the United States, for example, remains a vital concern for those who see themselves having a historical connection to slavery. Whether all citizens will also find this relationship compelling requires that we think more about the place of time and history in the construction of ongoing relationships. Or, to use another example: most Americans live in racially segregated communities. The creation of racially segregated housing is a long-term effect of formal institutions and laws, as well as of informal practices. If physical proximity is one of the factors that determines our degrees of responsibility, then such practices and institutions affect our current ways of thinking about responsibility.

Such a reallocation requires, however, that we rethink public and private duties and separations, whether needs can be defined collectively or individually, and whether people can be treated individually and equally at the same time. Turning more directly to some of the political complexities of allocating responsibility helps to explain the current allocation of care benefits and burdens, and to imagine a more democratic alternative.

Responsibility and Power

What does a democratic politics of care, understood as fixing responsibility, require? Drawing upon the account of responsibility so far developed here, the democratic element of such a politics is substantive as well as procedural. The concern is not the choice offered by current democratic theorists among aggregative, deliberative, or agonistic forms of democracy, but about whether democratic methods are focusing upon the right questions. I have suggested here that the right questions concern the nature of responsibilities for caring. There are several dimensions to making certain that such processes really confront the important questions about caring.

First, such a democratic politics of care as responsibility requires that we specify who will participate in the decision-making process. As political scientists have long noticed, who "sits at the table" to make decisions can have as large an effect on the outcome as what the people who sit at the table do. The question of who gets to decide is a critical one.

To clarify this point, let us continue to elaborate this metaphor. Imagine a whole series of tables set up in a large room. At each table are the people who will make judgments about how to put people and responsibilities in relationship to each other. Let's call these the responsibility-setting games,[7] or circles of responsibility. Obviously, people will be able to affect the outcome of a responsibility-setting if they are able to *exclude* others from that process. Imagine a game about racial injustice in which one race is excluded from the process of setting responsibility.[8] Exclusion is one effective way to control the outcomes of a political process. Democratic theorists have long realized how important it is that everyone is included in processes like responsibility-setting games in order to create genuinely democratic outcomes. And usually the more powerful are able to exclude the less powerful; this is one of the things that it means to be more powerful.

But exclusion is not the only way to rig the outcome of a circle of responsibility. Another way is to *absent* oneself or one's group from the "people" whose roles are under discussion in the responsibility-setting game. If individuals or groups in society are granted a "pass" out of being assigned responsibility, then they also effectively exercise power over the outcome by virtue of being able to absolve themselves of responsibility. I have previously labeled this kind of behavior "privileged irresponsibility" (Tronto 1993, 121). Thus, when it comes to dividing up the responsibilities for managing a household, the traditional breadwinner model allows the head of the household (usually the husband in this traditional model) a "pass" from most daily domestic duties because he has already brought home the money that organizes the household (Bridges 1979). But it is important to see this mechanism both from a moral perspective (as a way of shirking responsibility by claiming that one's own responsibilities lie in some other circle of responsibility) and from a political perspective (as a kind of power by which one is able to force others to accept responsibilities —perhaps even too many responsibilities—without having to make the case for one's own exclusion from the discussion or the responsibilities).

Much of the frustration of recent American politics, I suggest, arises out of our inability to have honest political discussions, and to make convincing judgments, about who is responsible. To some extent, such irresponsibility rests upon "epistemological ignorance." Charles Mills described such ignorance as arising out of an unwillingness to know anything about the lives of those who are dominated through structures such as racism (Pateman and Mills 2007; Mills 1997). By controlling the "we," some are able to affect the apportioning of responsibility without really owning up to the responsibility of setting these conditions. Such exclusions and absences are thus vitally important in shaping how political discussions go forward.

A second key issue is what people will decide when they come together to allocate responsibility. This matter is greatly complicated, of course, by the fact that "the table" at which they will sit always has a context. There is a history among these people, and past decisions and judgments shape what can be decided now.

One of the challenges in negotiating responsibility and authority is that most matters pertaining to them seem to have been settled in the past. As a result, there will be some places and some conditions under which these settlements come into dispute, when settled social questions seem no longer adequately resolved. We can well see, then, why new technologies and capacities would raise issues of authority and responsibility. With new forms of power, new forms of responsibility will be necessary. Following Bernard Williams (1985), Walker observes that existing settlements will often seem questionable when they are brought forth into the light of day: "In the case of moral life, transparency consists of seeing how we live, both through and in spite of our moral understandings and practices of responsibility. In seeking transparency, people are looking at what they think they value and care about, at the mutual understandings they believe organize their practices of responsibility around these things, and at their places in the order that results" (1998, 216).

Issues of responsibility will be made more difficult by cases of power differential. Walker continues, "All significant differentials in power are critical hot spots in social-moral orders, marked out as sites for transparency testing" (218). This is not to say, Walker adds, that all relationships of authority and responsibility should or could be equal. But it does show that power is one of the locations likely to produce moral conflict. In a democratic society, in which one begins from assumptions of equality, it is a key question how power differentials are deserved. Why should some be exempt, for example, from cleaning up after themselves while others are overly responsible for such cleaning up?

The Irresponsibility Machine?

At this point, the discussion of responsibility seems somewhat overwhelming. There are few limits to the kinds and varieties of responsibilities to which humans can be assigned, and the more aware people become

of their interconnectedness with others, the more responsible they become as well. In such circumstances, it is no surprise that, in addition to
controlling who participates in responsibility-setting, people have devised
other ways to avoid responsibilities.

A first way to avoid responsibility is through ignorance. Not knowing
about a problem seemingly absolves one from trying to solve it.

A second way to avoid responsibility is to create an institutional structure that deliberately diffuses and obscures lines of authority. Philip Petit
described one such mechanism in his essay "Responsibility, Inc." (2007),
where he described how the Exxon corporation managed to evade responsibility for the oil spill caused by the *Exxon Valdez*.

Another source of such irresponsibilities is the kinds of political, social,
economic, and cultural decisions that operate in the background. I previously called such conditions *privileged irresponsibility*. By backgrounding
(Plumwood 1993) the ways in which the public/private split was created
and making it appear natural, those who take on "public" duties are able
to leave behind "private" duties. In making a distinction between the more
"spiritual" and more "menial" (Roberts 1997) or "dirty-work" (Glenn 1992)
aspects of maintaining a household, white women were able to racialize
an already gendered set of responsibilities (Duffy 2011). Similar separations will be traced in the next few chapters in this book; how responsibility and irresponsibility coexist is a matter that is open for reexamination.

A very important effect of high levels of responsibility bears noting. As
people grow up, probably all of them have greater responsibilities, widely
understood, than anyone can ever meet. Parsing responsibility makes it
easier to live. As lines of responsibility become more ambiguous, one result
is an increase in the amount of uncertainty and anxiety in people's lives.

The present moment is one of great anxiety. On the one hand, this
greater anxiety arises from the greater capacities of humans. If "ought
implies can," then the more sophisticated human capacities become, the
more lives that can be saved through medical intervention, the more food
that can be grown, the more easily military intervention might stop geno-
cide, then the more it appears that somebody should take responsibility to
address such circumstances. As burdens of responsibility increase, though,
and the old solid lines become more blurred, levels of anxiety about which
responsibilities people should meet also grow. This increase in anxious
fear, I suggest, occurs in large part because the lines of responsibility—and
people's sensibilities about whether they do, in fact, have the power to meet
their responsibilities—are now much more varied and unpredictable. One

way to try to reduce this anxiety is to try to offer a simple and simplistic way to resolve all such questions of expanding responsibility. The ideological construction that evades these new problems of responsibility is very strong, and democratic caring is meant to be an antidote to it.

It should now be clear that the neoliberal economic world view, which posits individual responsibility as the only meaningful level upon which to understand responsibility, functions as one of these irresponsibility machines. It cranks out a standard answer to the question about responsibilities for care: "They're your own. You're on your own. If you did not make a provision for yourself, then it is your tough luck." In the next three chapters, some of the structural reasons why individuals may encounter responsibilities that they cannot meet, through no fault of their own, will become apparent. It is important to keep in mind that if there is no public process for thinking about responsibility, the irresponsibility machine will provide the constant answer: "It's your own fault." As Edward Bellamy said over one hundred years ago, it is surprising how easily one accepted this harsh view of others.

Rethinking Responsibility from a Caring Democratic Standpoint

At its most basic level, care is particular: different people think that specific forms of care are good care, while others think differently. In a pluralistic society, some decisions about the proper way to care are best left to individuals, families, and other institutions. On the one hand, for example, it would violate people's liberty to intrude upon families' abilities to make their own decisions about the appropriate kinds of activities for children. On the other hand, rules about whether and how to license care professionals seem appropriately within the public domain.

On some matters, citizens owe an accounting to one another about the nature of caring; on others, they do not. At what level does such general concern end? Ian Shapiro (2001) tried to sort out this arrangement by distinguishing between children's "basic needs" and other needs that they possess. By his account, society has a role to play in insuring that basic needs are met, but not other needs. To an extent, Shapiro's analysis accords with some ways in which society now approaches intervening in family care arrangements. If children appear to be neglected, then the state intervenes. But how does one draw this fine line, and where does it end?

The analysis offered in the previous chapter can begin to suggest a flexible but perhaps more clear way to answer this question: What is it that public discussions of care should concern? If we return to care as a set of practices, each of which goes through four phases in its process, then it becomes clear that the public part of caring concerns allocating caring responsibilities.

In this chapter, we have come closer to a general answer to the question: Under what conditions do people see and understand their responsibilities to care about, and care for, others? I have argued that it is not just or fair that some citizens, based on such qualities as who they are, what they do, or what they own, receive "passes" out of helping to apportion responsibility for care. On the contrary, I argue that if a democratic society has any commitments at all, it must have a commitment to making care —both receiving and giving care—equally and widely available to all. This means especially that we accept our responsibilities to care for the young, the elderly, and the infirm or differently capable among us. It also requires that democratic citizens recognize that freedom depends upon our capacities to exercise our freedoms, and such capacities are not the same thing as exercising a "choice." This understanding of freedom as a capacity to engage in deep and superficial relationships of care requires that we go further and think about what it requires for us to exercise such capacities. While our rights can be defined negatively in terms of "freedom from" government intervention, in a complex modern society we also need broader assistance in organizing the world around us so that we can care for ourselves and for others around us. Our political responsibility to other citizens, which is how we might define justice, is that we must ensure that, in our democracy, no one goes without care. Justice thus comes from the public decisions about caring responsibilities that we make collectively. This is the proper role of government in a contemporary state. Although in the past several years we have heard many complaints about a "nanny state," in truth, we have not yet considered seriously what are the caring needs of contemporary life.

A Responsibility for Democracy

A potential problem with Walker's account of an expressive-collaborative morality is that it presumes that those who are relevant to the moral problem will be engaged in the expression and collaboration. But what happens when the boundaries around responsibility are drawn too narrowly? In her recent writings, Walker stresses the importance of "the story" as a way into moral reflection. Surely, a story is a richer starting point for philosophical accounts of responsibility than, say, the usual perspicuous examples that are the tropes of ordinary-language moral philosophy (for example, Philippa Foot's famous "trolley problem"; see, e.g., Thomson and Parent 1986, chap. 7). Yet there still remains, especially when the storyteller is primarily focused upon her "identity," the very real danger of what Charles Mills (1997) calls "an epistemology of ignorance." Mills points out that whites are largely ignorant of the history of racial exploitation of which they are beneficiaries. Yet when any dominant group is able to "background" the "other," there is a danger that they will never tell stories that de-center their own experiences and accounts of the world.

When we incorporate our concern about responsibility, we now see the main problems inherent in care—paternalism and parochialism (Tronto 1993)—in a new light. Both can now be understood as distortions of the kinds of responsibilities that people should appropriately assume. For paternalists, the problem is that they claim too much authority in the allocation of responsibility to themselves. Parochialism is a problem in which we set the boundaries of our responsibility too narrowly. In both of these cases, we will better understand the moral problems we face if we think in concrete terms about who is involved in making decisions, how they are involved, who they have excluded, and who is exercising various forms of privileged irresponsibility.

Here we arrive at another way to rethink the roles of caring democratic citizens. One of the challenges of an expressive-collaborative morality is to include the views of everyone in setting the agreements of what moral principles should hold. *Whose responsibility is it to see that the scope of the discussion is wide enough?* In a way, this might be the ultimate form of all democratic citizens' responsibilities: to ensure that all are engaged in caring with others. They must keep a commitment to the very forms of democratic discussion and to the process itself. If, by a responsibility, we mean a response that grows out of an existing relationship, then this form of responsibility requires of citizens that they take inclusion seriously.

To review, a feminist democratic ethic of care requires that we reconceive democratic politics as the allocation of social and individual responsibilities, that we ensure the adequacy of the democratic process by making certain that people neither absent themselves nor exclude others from these processes. The democratic process itself is no guarantee that members of a political community will arrive at the correct decision, but including all in allocating responsibilities might make it less likely that some potential changes are hidden behind the claim of necessity, or that paternalistic or parochial ideas will prevail without challenge.

There is one final point that we should make about responsibility, which brings us back to the point that we made at the beginning of this chapter. While it is possible to speak about "responsibility" in abstract terms, the goal of connecting care to responsibility is to bring responsibility back to the real and actual practices in any given society. We noted the limitations of "personal responsibility." We noted the ways that some groups may be able to give themselves "passes" out of certain forms of responsibility. We usually do not describe these passes this way, but I propose that we consider them as forms of *privileged irresponsibility*. That is, by focusing on irresponsibility we will be better able to see how some people end up with less, and other people with far more, of the responsibility that might be better allocated in society.

Thus, the level of discussion about the nature of justice and care shifts to the question of how relationships matter, and of which kinds of relationships are strong and which are weak. Here is another way in which the relationship-dissolving effects of neoliberal ideology remove forms of responsibility: if our only relationships exist among "us," then we have no larger responsibilities to "them." In a democratic society, such a premise must be challenged.

In this way, then, what actually happens when we try to fill in the lineaments of caring responsibilities is that we revisit questions of "justice" that go beyond the narrow conceptions of justice as concerned with current breach of rights. Nothing I have said should imply that justice, understood as the capacity of individuals to gain redress when their rights are violated, is not important. What I have suggested, though, is that such an account of justice is too narrow because it leaves issues of responsibility unasked and unresolved. To ask "Who is responsible?" is now to ask the basic democratic political question. In allowing citizens to see how *irresponsible* they are, especially in the construction and acceptance of caring responsibilities, this perspective allows a rethinking of what it means to be caring democratic citizens.

The next section of this book turns to a discussion of a variety of current passes out of taking more responsibilities seriously. Such passes implicate many of the deep structures of our society: gender, class, and race, as well as institutions like the state, the market, and the family. After this exploration, the final section of the book considers what a caring democratic society might require.

PART II

How We Care Now

3

Tough Guys Don't Care . . . Do They?

Gender, Freedom, and Care

Engendered Responsibilities

Ludovic, the young boy who is the protagonist in Alain Berliner's 1997 film *Ma Vie en Rose* [My Life in Pink], presumed that he would someday fulfill his dream and turn into a girl. It is lucky for Ludovic that he is not a middle- or high-school boy in the United States today. Here, boys and young men intensely police the boundaries of being a boy, searching to weed out "gays" and "fags" or boys who they think are otherwise different either sexually, sartorially, or in terms of academic ambition (Pascoe 2007; Ferguson 2001). Some of the victims of this harassment take their own lives (Warner 2009). As Judith Warner notes, it is ironic that as what it means to be a "man" becomes more vague in the culture as a whole, boys take deeper offense at threats to their particular notions of masculinity. These developments are a sign of a time of anxiety, but it is also a crisis of caring and, ultimately, of democratic possibility. As long as masculinity continues to be constructed around the idea that "tough guys don't care," so long as to "man-up" limits how to care, there is no hope that our society can rethink caring responsibilities to become more caring or more democratic.

The first and most obvious point to note as we turn to how caring is actually practiced in contemporary society is that caring is *gendered*. Caring is also deeply marked by all other cultural and social values and formations, including *race/ethnicity* and *class*. As recent scholars have noted, to use any one of these lenses without recognizing their intersectionality is likely to distort social reality.[1] While such intersectional analyses are a central part of any full picture of care, it is also remarkable how persistently, across time and place, care is viewed through a gendered lens: in our usual sense of the term, "care" is seen as women's work. It is important not to lose sight of what this gender claim means. To say that care is women's work is not to make an essentialist claim that "women give birth, and therefore they are naturally better caregivers." It is not to say that all women do, or should, care well. And to say that care is women's work is not to deny that men care. It is, however, to say that the current constructions of masculinity and femininity permit men to avoid having to take, or to think much about, the responsibilities for the caring tasks assigned to women. Indeed, conceptions of masculinity and femininity change as caring tasks and their distribution change. Still, what it means to be masculine is to be given a "pass" out of thinking about "girl things," including the caring responsibilities assigned to women. It is at this level that the ideologically gendered division of care affects our prospects for envisioning a more inclusive democratic alternative.[2]

Do men care? Of course they do. Men *care about* providing for their families. Men *care for* themselves, their property, and others. Men even *give care*, increasingly, to their own children, spouses, friends, and elder parents. And men *receive care*, too; when they are boys, elderly, or infirm, and when they manage, by themselves or with others, to receive the care that they need every day to keep themselves alive. Yet the *image* persists that what it means to be a man is not to care, or, at least, not to care well. Lori Campbell and Michael Carroll (2007) conducted in-depth interviews with men who were serving as the primary caregiver to an elderly parent. They discovered that, despite the caring work they did, even these men still thought that men were not very good at caring and that women were naturally better caregivers. Throughout society, women are more closely associated with care; indeed, the idea that women are good at caring and men are not is one of the characteristics of the current form of what R. W. Connell (2005) calls "hegemonic masculinity."

How do we explain this discrepancy between what men *do* and what people *believe* about men and care? Indeed, how do we explain the persistence of an ideology of "tough guys don't care" even when the facts belie this understanding? This is a complex task that requires digging down into some questions about the nature of masculinity, or better, competing views of masculinities in society. Looking closely at masculinities will in turn reveal many dimensions of how care's place is obscured in contemporary American life. Exploring these points clarifies how dominant ideologies about economic life, masculine superiority, the fear of dependence, and the split between public and private life distort our capacity to make sense of our current political predicament, and thus prevent us from becoming more fully democratic. But these beliefs or ideas are not simply a "misreading" of society; they also rest upon institutions and practices to which such ideas gave rise and which reinforce those ideas now. Transforming the ideas about men's caring will require a large political commitment. We need to change values, institutions, and practices about the relationships of masculinity (and, by extension, femininity) and care. This is so great a change that it can probably be called the next phase of democratic revolution.

In this chapter, I focus on an account of "hegemonic masculinity," rather than on multiple forms of masculinity.[3] As Connell and many other scholars of masculinity have made clear, there is no single form of "masculinity"; what it means to be a "real man" varies across time and place. Masculine men care more in some cultures than in others. Furthermore, as Connell observes, some men retain a position of social superiority by constructing their form of masculinity as better; others are made subordinate by adhering to a view of men that is part of marginalized or subservient masculinities. In the United States, the interrelationships of these different types of masculinity closely follow lines of class, race, ethnic, religious, and sexual privilege. It is not that these other forms of masculinity are not important, or not worth exploring. Yet because "hegemonic masculinity" plays the central role in defining masculinity for the culture as a whole, I will focus on it.[4]

The work on describing multiple and overlapping conceptions of masculinity has just begun to receive scholarly attention. I invite others to explore my findings and these broad questions within other configurations of masculinity as well. But I also do not wish to make a definitive pronouncement about what masculinity and care might mean. In the end, democratic life and public policy do not rely upon the judgments of one scholar, or even many scholars. In the end, the task of scholars is to point out what directions might better fit with the goals of a democratic society. But the task of working out *how* to accomplish such changes rests with a democratic community's sense of how to go forward.

My plan in this chapter, then, is to explore why "care" is gendered as feminine and why masculinity, as a gendered ideal, means something other than care. This pursuit requires an exploration of several central aspects of modern life, most importantly, the construction of "protection" and economic participation as the central aspect of an adult, mature, life. To frame this problem in the language that was used in the previous chapter, masculine aversion to some forms of caring is an outcome of some responsibility games. Men don't care because, to make this ideological framework more concrete, they are given a "pass" out of what we normally regard as caring responsibilities because of two other forms of contributions they make to society.[5] For the sake of argument, I call these passes "protection" and "production."

In a way, both protection and production are kinds of care. But they repair, maintain, and preserve daily life at one remove, rather than in the direct and intimate ways usually associated with care. Both protection and production are essential for living well, and for living well in a democratic society. But they are not all that is required for living well. Bringing these two aspects of life back into balance with other elements of care, then, will make visions of more democratic societies possible. Indeed, at the end of the chapter I will propose that the imbalances created by the gendered scripts of caring responsibilities also distort how we think about freedom itself.

This exploration begins by examining (the typical, majority-culture versions of) these scripts, to see why tough guys don't care—or, perhaps, why tough guys do not call their caring work "care."

Why Is Caring for Girls? Why Don't Tough Guys Care?

Why is care identified so strongly with the feminine? This chapter will provide a number of complementary answers to this question. The oldest arguments, which persist to this day (see Campbell and Carroll 2007), make a biological claim that since women become pregnant, give birth to babies, and provide milk from their bodies to infants, they care "naturally." The more traditional the ideology, the more likely it is to include a strongly biological basis for distinctions in caring roles. Of course, the problem with these biological arguments is that they do not admit how humans have frequently altered "natural" processes. While artificial wombs (ectogenesis) do not yet exist (Simonstein 2006), women now sometimes bear children as surrogates for other women, a practice that increasingly occurs across national boundaries (Hochschild 2012). The practice of feeding infants foods other than breast milk has been a feature of Western culture in the past century, and before that, wet-nursing was widespread. So there is no reason why the "natural" mother "naturally" cares; mothers also sometimes kill their infants (Oberman 2004–5; cf. Ruddick 1989). Yet the idea that women's reproductive roles determine their political and social roles has been widely accepted in Western culture, from Aristotle to Rousseau to contemporary thinkers.

Psychological explanations also can be offered about why women are more closely associated with care-giving than are men. Some psychologists, drawing on object-relations theories, argue that men's separation from their mothers diminishes their capacities to develop deep relationships. Some scholars, such as Nancy Chodorow (1978a, 1978b, 2004), base these claims on contemporary psychoanalytic theories; others, such as Carol Gilligan (1996, 2002, 2004), have explored this theme as deeply embedded in cultural practices as well. For Gilligan and David Richards (2009), the hierarchical ordering of patriarchal societies requires a split within each human's psyche, which, deeply damaged by this split, then tries to banish and control pleasure, love, and connection. Patriarchal order describes a sharp binary of traditional gendered roles and organizes these roles hierarchically (Richards 2010). Gilligan and Richards argue that trauma thus inflicts everyone in a patriarchal society. The psychological damage of this order requires that everyone abandon attachment to their caring mothers, though for boys and girls the separation occurs at different ages. At this point, patriarchal societies inscribe men's control over women's daily activities, but not the need to engage in those activities, as both a responsibility and privilege of their superior gendered location.

Philosophers describe this dualizing process somewhat differently, in terms of knowledge. For Val Plumwood (1993), dualisms such as culture/nature, reason/emotion, and autonomous/heteronomous express two sides of the same coin, in which the second quality is repressed or backgrounded. The result of such dualisms, according to Plumwood, is always to denigrate the second term. Sociologically and anthropologically, differences created through such separations take on a life of their own. As Charles Tilly argued in *Durable Inequality*, one of the effects of any system of domination is that it takes on a life of its own. With the appearance of any form of oppression, the lesser parties begin to engage in what he calls "opportunity hoarding," that is, they begin to accept their inferior status overall but try to find ways to put themselves, individually, in the good graces of those who are oppressing them, and thus, to make themselves exceptions to their own class and to gain some resources through such cooperation (Tilly 1998, 2003).

Women do disproportionate amounts of housework and child-care around the globe. The end result of these presumptions about women's greater caring nature is a highly sex-segregated workforce around the globe. An International Labor Organization study observed "how closely the characteristics of 'female' occupations correspond to typical stereotypes of women and their supposed abilities"; the first such stereotype was women's "caring nature" (Anker 1998, 22–23).

So, sharply distinguished gendered activities are reinforced by social conditioning, by ideas of their naturalness, by patterns of gendered activities and practices. These broad social patterns are both result from and are the cause of social attitudes about the different capacities of men and women to care. Unquestioned attitudes and social patterns reinforce one another. No matter where in society we look, girls and women are marked as "more caring." A stroll through a toy store, with the contrast between metallic-colored toys for boys and the ubiquity of pink and pastel toys for girls, makes clear that rigid gendered stereotyping continues (Blakemore and Centers 2005). Within medicine in the United States, women are still concentrated in less prestigious subspecialties and excluded from higher-ranking positions. (Kilminster et al. 2007) Indeed, this pattern of gender is so deep that it appears as if it is universal and timeless. But if we make that assumption, we ignore some keys to understanding how responsibilities have been allocated, and also what we need to do to bring these responsibilities more in line with how a democratic society might equally divide them in order to create freedom and equality for all.

Men's Caring I: The Protection Pass

Protection of the body politic from its enemies, external and internal, has always been an important part of the responsibilities of citizenship. Using the broad definition of caring as "to maintain, continue, and repair" the world, protection is an element of care insofar as it prevents, and tries to mitigate against, harm. One place where protection emerges in the modern period as an important form of non-caring care is the "police" and "police powers." In the American legal system, the "police powers" extend broadly to include provisions for public health, safety, and education. In reality, the historical notion of police is even broader and deeper.

In the eighteenth century, William Blackstone codified the English common law in his *Commentaries of the Laws of England*. There, he included this account of police:

> By the public police and oeconomy I mean the due regulation and do-
> mestic order of the kingdom: whereby the individuals of the state, like
> members of a well-governed family, are bound to conform their general
> behavior to the rules of property, good neighbourhood, and good man-
> ners: and to be decent, industrious, and inoffensive in their respective
> stations (Dubber 2005, xii)

Note the connection between police and economic life, and the analogy between the state and a family. When the state acts as the head of a household, it is exercising its police duties. In a recent study, Marko Dubber (2005) emphasized the breadth of these powers and their patriarchal tinge. As a result, Dubber says, we really should understand that law and police are two different systems of government regulation:

> While the state may govern its constituents through law, it also man-
> ages them through police. In contrast to law, police is defined by heter-
> onomy, or other-government, of the people of the state. . . . These two
> modes of governance, law and police, reflect two ways of conceptual-
> izing the state. From the perspective of law, the state is the institutional
> manifestation of a political community of free and equal persons. The
> function of the law state is to manifest and protect the autonomy of its
> constituents in all of its aspects, private and public. From the perspec-
> tive of police, the state is the institutional manifestation of a household.
> The police state, as paterfamilias, seeks to maximize the welfare of his
> —or rather its—household. (3).

This expansive understanding of police, which is related to the processes that Michel Foucault (2007) called "governmentality" and which incorporated both economic and other forms of life, was widely discussed in the eighteenth century. For Dubber, it draws upon ancient and medieval roots. For Pasquale Pasquino (1991), the writings about "police" in the eighteenth century are the beginnings of discussions about the origins of capitalism. In any case, these public activities were carried out *by* men, to control all people, including women and children. Notice that "police" thus encompassed both the regulation of public space and economic life. For men, to care for the public realm was to participate in public life in a way that helped to organize and produce "happiness" (literally, one understanding of the role of eighteenth-century "police powers") through economic organization, controlling the disposition of people, and so on. The implicit strength of these police powers has been spelled out in U.S. jurisprudence for over two centuries. But it is important to note, as does Dubber, that this was a *gendered* power, essentially expanding the notion of the father as head of the household to the state as the responsible party for insuring "good order" in society as if it were one big family.

The breadth of the term "police" narrowed considerably; indeed, Mark Neocleous (1998) reminds us of the fact that Adam Smith himself uses the term in this expansive sense in his *Lectures on Jurisprudence*, but in the narrow sense of providing order against criminality in the *Wealth of Nations*. In nineteenth-century England, a more contemporary understanding of police work emerged, conceiving it in the militarized sense of a war on crime, rather than a broader power for the protection and maintenance of order. This change also later happened in the United States as a response to urbanization (Monkkonen 1981). Modern policing has become militarized and masculinized and receives unquestioned public support, but "police" was originally a kind of care work, which included economic life.

While in American popular culture the police are now viewed as heroes, they also remain, less visibly, servants. "Protect and serve" is the motto of the Los Angeles police department, emblazoned on police cars viewed throughout the world in Hollywood television and film productions. Although the military has occupied a different place in public imagination, its clear function (once wars of aggression became less acceptable politically) is protection. In a way, protecting the territory of the state is a kind of care work, and the Army Corps of Engineers, a main engine of early American economic development (Klyza 2002), still embodies the older meaning of "police" and seems to be engaged in care work. Although there are ways in which military service is care, however, it is not conceived this way. Furthermore, as the actual military forces become more integrated by race and gender, it becomes increasingly necessary to refine the meaning of the military to make its mission more masculine.

Once the exclusive realm of male citizens, military service has been converted in recent decades in the United States to an avenue of upward mobility for those who are less well off in the society, and given the difficulties of recruiting an all-volunteer force, increasingly the military includes poorer people, people of color, and women. Within the military itself, those feminized care tasks that were once performed by conscripts (cooking, cleaning, maintenance) are now performed by outsourced men and women, often from third world countries (Stillman 2011), reemphasizing the hierarchical and gendered conception that what men do in the military is fight. Increasingly in the United States, the term "warrior" is being used to re-masculinize the duties of soldiers and to separate essential military functions from the care work (provisioning supplies, providing for the soldiers' lives and comfort) that is also essential for the military.

If protection is a form of care, then a set of questions about protection arise from the standpoint of a democratic caring society. If care concerns needs, who determines the needs for protection? And protection is "protection from whom"? Iris Marion Young (2003) argued that there is a great danger if citizens simply accept the story about their need for protection and do not question it.

Protection, as a form of public care, is care provided by citizens and for citizens, with both providers and recipients of care marked by masculinity. As Dubber might suggest, an important question is, Who participates in law and who is at the mercy of "police"? Recipients of "masculine" care are perceived, by their nature, to be citizens who, for one reason or another, find themselves *in extremis*. Houses catch fire, firefighters respond. A citizen is robbed, the police respond.[6] Recipients of "feminine" care, on the other hand, are people who are found in the private sphere and who are usually marked as dependent: children, the disabled, the ill and infirm, the elderly.[7]

This is a critical distinction. Men and women remain citizens even when they need the care of the police. No one questions their status as citizen because they have been robbed. One reason, then, that protection does not appear to be a form of care is that its recipients have a different status in society. When people are dependent and need care, they become *feminized*. In becoming feminized, people are no longer seen as capable of making autonomous judgments. This last point requires us to pursue a bit more philosophically the ways in which care, and masculine versus feminine care, match up to an historical separation between public and private life. This investigation is important, too, because it allows us to see the dimensions of public and private care in a new light. When only private care counts as "care," then care follows deeply gendered separations of public and private life.

Violence: The Dark Side of Protection as Care

One of the puzzling features of protection as a form of care still needs to be considered. What happens when (men's) protective care (for women) is not so protecting, but becomes instead a "protection racket" (Young 2003; Stiehm 1982a, 1982b)? As Judith Stiehm has long noted, protectors sometimes cannot protect, they sometimes use the need for protection as a justification for other forms of bad treatment, and they sometimes turn on the ones they are supposed to protect. Violence seems to pose special problems for an argument of democratic care.

Perhaps we should begin by explaining why, from the standpoint of a democratic ethic of care, anyone should be concerned about violence. There are two reasons. First, violence, at least in many of its manifestations, seems to be the antithesis of care. Inflicting harm on others seems to be at the other end of the spectrum from caring for others. Yet if care is so central to human life, how can it account for the nature of, and existence of, violence? Second, as we know, there is actually a great deal of violence inflicted in intimate settings; in the places where we expect to find care, we often find violence, and often violence and care are intertwined. How, especially if I am right that they are at opposite ends of a spectrum of how humans should treat one another, can violence and care cohabit intimate space?

Let me begin by reviewing some claims made about care and violence. An ethic of care has long been associated with *nonviolence*. Sara Ruddick's important early book in the care discussion, *Maternal Thinking* (1989), is subtitled *Toward a Politics of Peace*. There, while Ruddick acknowledged that mothers are often among the most vehement supporters of war, nevertheless she believed that a commitment to preservation, growth, and becoming a member of society, the values that she attributes to an ethic of mothering, if kept in balance, necessarily lead to a politics of peace. In making this claim, Ruddick follows the political practice of an earlier generation of feminists, like Jane Addams, who were staunch pacifists, even in the face of World War I. Addams's (1907) argument rested upon an assumption that as human societies evolved, people would realize the folly of using war to solve their problems. She also believed that as the world grew smaller, it would become more difficult for nations to pull people apart, and thus to generate sufficient hatred for them to make war.

Whatever insight care theories provide to an understanding of violence in general, another kind of violence is especially important to care ethics: intimate household violence. Feminists have long despaired that a "marriage license is a hitting license" (Straus, Gelles, and Steinmetz 1980). Domestic violence poses a challenge to the claims about care and its centrality in human life. If care is so much a part of the human condition, then why is there also so much violence? Why is there so much violence among people who are intimates? Why do high levels of domestic violence persist in the United States and around the world? If domestic violence is intrinsic to the institution of the family itself, then is it wrong to presume that a "protection pass" excuses men from care work in the household? Is domestic violence akin to, or different from, forms of violence outside the household?

In her book *In a Different Voice*, Gilligan (1982) described one of the more solid and disturbing gender differences that she found in her work: men were much more likely in viewing the Thematic Apperception Test to create stories that were about intimate situations in which there was violence. Something about intimate settings made them presume violence in the situation. In her later work, Gilligan (1996) described how boys are less likely to provide a cognitive account of their fears of intimacy because they suffered the trauma of the loss of their mothers at an age that was, in many ways, precognitive. As a result, they remain fearful and unsettled by intimacy.

Another psychoanalytic theorist whose views might provide insight into intimate violence is Jessica Benjamin (1988), who argues that sadism and masochism—putting oneself over and over again into a situation where one either does or suffers harm—is likely a longing to repair broken and inadequate kinds of relationships.

The relationship of emotions to violence is also confusing. On the one hand, some psychologists think of violence as a result of dissociative thinking, an incapacity to be fully human at that moment (Moskowitz 2004), a kind of absence of emotion. On the other hand, many view violence as an outcome of damaged emotions or provoked emotions; the *Chicago Sun Times* (2008) quoted a teacher who was coping with the epidemic of murders there as saying "kids are killing because they are hurting." Thinkers such as Robert Jay Lifton see the violence produced under military duress as resulting from an "atrocity producing situation," which can affect anyone and triggers deep emotions of rage and anger (Peltz 2008). Regardless of which of these views of emotions in relation to violence is correct, however, it is clear that violence can and does arise in families. As Elaine Leeder writes, "The family is a paradox; it is the most loving institution in our society, and yet it is also one of the most dangerous" (2004, 239).

What do these competing accounts of the relationship of care and violence signify? On the one hand, one might denounce violent care and point out that it is harmful to those cared-for. On the other hand, one will hear arguments that in some communities and cultures, violence, especially intimate violence, is simply a part of the way that people live, and that we have no capacity to judge their notions of caring, which include some uses of corporal punishment. Is there any way to sort through these complications?

Generally, scholars think of violence as serving one of two broad purposes. On the one hand, violence is sometimes understood as instrumental, as attempting to achieve some other end (cf. Arendt 1970). On the other hand, in the Marxist tradition, violence is understood as serving the purpose of domination and oppression (Young 1990). Either way of thinking of violence fits with an explanation of intimate violence. Nevertheless, framing the question of violence in relationship to care provides new insight. In a recent Canadian study, Paul Kershaw, Jane Pulkingham, and Sylvia Fuller (2008) found that many recipients of public assistance had become "dependent" as they escaped from settings of domestic violence. The welfare problem, then, is in no small part a problem of those who have lost their agency through being victims of violence. The authors conclude: "We expand the idea of 'caring more' to include not just performing more child rearing or personal care for other dependents, but also the adoption of a more caring disposition which defies masculine norms that continue to sanction violence" (187).

Vittorio Bufacchi (2007) argues that the best way to think of violence is as a harm to the integrity of a person. While there may be limits to Bufacchi's way of thinking (for example, he is unwilling to include economic or structural violence), it is nonetheless the case that his notion captures some important elements of the nature of violence. Violence is a means, Hannah Arendt argued, but we must realize that its ability to destroy the capacity of its victims to act is among its great harms. Arendt wishes to argue that violence and power are opposites, but we cannot also forget ways in which violence destroys the power of one's opponents, and thus makes the victorious violent party able to exert power over others with brutal efficiency. George Orwell described the future in *1984* using this violent image: a boot, stomping a face, forever. This is an age of such disproportionately spectacular forms of violence (from nuclear weapons to the imaginary Martian invasion, zombies, toys that turn into weapons, films where everything is blowing up, the dream of the "Mission Accomplished" destruction in Iraq). Yet it remains important to remember these more local and still horrific forms of brutality.

What does it mean to live in a culture where violence is a commonplace, everyday event for many in their own homes (Leeder 2004)? How do these patterns of abuse and acceptance affect everyday life? While most violent people are men, most men are not violent (Connell 2005). So, how do we explain that some men seem more prone to violence, and they are, in fact, recruited to be violent (Huggins, Haritos-Fatouros, and Zimardo 2002)?

Indeed, the movement for "moral repair" against acts of horrific violence have also recently been applied to less horrific acts in such programs as "RSVP: Resolve to Stop the Violence Project." This program, operated first in association with the Sheriff's Office in San Francisco, aims to address the problems of violence by calling for victim restoration, community restoration, and perpetrator restoration. One surprising point is that the violent men who eventually have to listen to victims speak of the effect of violence on their lives had no idea of these effects of their actions on others (cf. Baron-Cohen 2011). Another example of an anti-violence project that has yielded positive results is the Atlanta-based Men Stopping Violence, which tries to help violent men see their actions as part of a larger community's problems (Douglas, Bathrick, and Perry 2008). And bell hooks (2002) believes that the violence against women and children is often rooted in men's violence against other men, which is not acknowledged or dealt with in a serious way. By her account, until men's violence is more generally addressed, there is little hope of ending widespread violence.

This section has suggested that protection is a kind of care and needs to be understood in this way. Why is protection not now discussed as a part of care? The answer is that hiding the caring dimension of protection allows those who are in control of protective work to earn themselves the "protection pass" out of responsibility for other, more feminized forms of care work. Keeping these boundaries between care and protection in place helps to maintain the gendered hierarchy of men above women. We will return to another way in which protection figures into the construction of masculinity and femininity shortly. First, though, let us follow how economic life becomes gendered after it has been historically severed from household and "police."

Men's Caring 2: The Production Pass

Production also emerges as an important form of care-at-one-remove in the modern era; perhaps it is the most important form of such care. The separation of the household from the space of production in the early modern period changed the gendered nature of production and care. Ideologically (if not in reality),[8] men cared by providing a paycheck, and women cared through "the other side of the paycheck" (Bridges 1979) by maintaining domesticity and performing the necessary reproductive labor to allow men to continue their work.

"Domesticity" is the name that the legal scholar Joan Williams (2000) gives to this deeply entrenched pattern of the separation of the household from public life. In domesticity, men go out to a workplace, and women attend to home and children. It is a pattern that became prevalent throughout the world, beginning in the eighteenth century when the site of work moved outside of the household and men followed this work. Prior to the eighteenth century, and in some classes until now, women were not excluded from "production," nor, for that matter, were children, whose "care" looked very different in a pre-industrial age. It would be hard to exaggerate the importance of this view for the differential status of men and women in our time. For some, this separation of "production" and "reproduction" (to use the language of socialist feminists) describes the main reason that men are more powerful than women in society. But before we leave the initial separation of household and place of production, we should notice that there is no reason why this separation is "natural." Although it is no longer a reality for most households in the United States, the traditional view of the household as consisting of a "breadwinner" and a "caregiver" persist in cultural thinking and in many of our public policies.

In the historical tradition in Western societies, what it meant to be a citizen was to present oneself to the political order (the polis, the king, the state) as ready to serve, and that ability to serve qualified one as a citizen. Thus, for some ancient Greek city-states, a citizen was one who could equip himself with the requisite tools for military combat; in post–World

War II Western societies, a citizen is one who can present himself as ready to work, unencumbered by household responsibilities.[9] Throughout much of the history of Western societies, women have been barred from those activities that qualified men as citizens: excluded from military service, political participation, some parts of the workforce, and so forth. Thus, women have only been included as citizens in a different way. Citizens have to be born, after all, and women are involved in the creation of citizens. Women's citizenship has usually been mediated by their connection to the political order through men: husbands, fathers, sons.[10] What women have done for male citizens is to take care of them.

Models of citizenship define the boundaries between public and private life and determine which activities, attitudes, possessions, and so on are to be considered worthy in any given state.[11] Citizenship shapes deeply held values about justice and fairness in determining what good citizens do. Models of citizenship also include an implicit account of what citizens are like before they come to the public arena. States exclude from active citizenship children and others who have not been thought to have achieved "majority." In previous historical eras, property or arms were conditions of citizenship. Through inclusion and exclusion of some people, citizenship reflects winners and losers in the political game with the highest stakes—a political game in which the deck is stacked, since one can only win by achieving the favor of previous winners, who dilute their victory by allowing anyone else to join them as winners.

Societies conceive of citizens in terms of the contributions that they make to the society. Historically, citizens have been conceived as warriors, as burgher-merchants, as farmers, as artisans (Isin 1997). The chief discourse on citizenship in welfare states has followed the lead of T. H. Marshall in identifying citizens primarily as workers (see, e.g., Marshall and Bottomore 1992 [1950]). It is instructive, perhaps, to recall here the Aristotelian model of the citizen as one who participates in public life, but whose actual conditions of life presuppose a separate realm for both economic activity and care work (see, e.g., Yak 1993; Stiehm 1984). Thus, the Aristotelian citizen floats his (sic) citizenship on previously accomplished work that is beneath the observance of political institutions, but nonetheless essential for his life.

Whereas property was once conceived as a necessary prerequisite for independence, and thus for citizenship, that model of the citizen has by now faded (Isin 1997). As many astute observers have noted, the conception of the welfare state that informed postwar life presumed a particular

model of citizens (see, e.g., Knijn and Kremer 1997; Lister 1997; Bussemaker and van Kersbergen 1994; Pateman 1988). This model presumes a
citizen worker and a "support staff," traditionally conceived as the wife in
a nuclear family, whose task it was to perform the "reproductive labor" of
"the other side of the paycheck" (Schwarzenbach 1996; Bridges 1979).

This model of the household no longer accurately describes the way
most people live, but the notion remains that citizenship attaches to those
who leave the household to go out to work. By providing for the material
needs of their families, then, men earn a "production pass" out of doing
the caring that has been located in the household. If anything, recent
welfare reform in the United States has reinforced the view that citizenship depends upon paid labor. Indeed, the second wave of feminism has,
as one of its profoundest consequences, increased the participation of
women in the paid labor force. Yet as many more women now work, they
are caught in a bind, the "second shift" (Hochschild 1989), in which they
must do both their previously assigned caring work and the paid work
outside of the household. Although men have made minor increases in
their contributions to work within the household, and though this idealized description does not match the realities of caring families within
particular households (Hochschild 1997), nevertheless it provides a pass
out of household-based care responsibilities.

The Work Ethic and the Care Ethic

When feminist scholars began to use the language of "care ethic," they
were thinking of a philosophical contrast between an "ethic of rights" and
an "ethic of care" (Gilligan 1982). Interestingly enough, the language of a
"care ethic" can take on a different cast, also highly illuminating, when we
contrast it with that of a "work ethic."

The phrase "work ethic" is attributed to the German sociologist Max
Weber, who in *The Protestant Ethic and the Spirit of Capitalism* (2003
[1905]) argued that because of their anxiety to demonstrate their spiritual fitness before others in their community, early Protestants became
committed to a form of "worldly asceticism," which provided the basis for
the remarkable accumulation of capital in early modern Europe. While
Weber's causal argument is widely challenged, his characterization of
Protestants as committed to godliness through their hard work, "the work
ethic," persists as an account of a certain frame of mind that seems to fit

well with how Americans value hard work. For Weber, an unintended consequence of the religious views of these godly Puritans is that they created a society that rewarded hard work, savings, and looking toward the future, and that recognized individual economic effort.

The work ethic suggests that what people deserve is what they have worked to obtain. From work flows desert. While humans may have irreducible needs, the work ethic presumes that people will work to meet those needs if they are real needs. Two corollary views follow: if one does not work hard, one will not get what one needs; those who are needy have not worked hard enough to get what they need. In the United States, there is a widespread endorsement of the work ethic. Studies have shown that men and women do not diverge in their support of the work ethic (Meriac, Poling, and Woehr 2009), and even studies that purport to show that there are racial differences among African Americans and white Americans in their support for the work ethic nonetheless demonstrate high levels of commitment (Cokley et al. 2007).

The relationship of the individual to society has a different meaning from the perspective of the work ethic than from the perspective of the care ethic. From the standpoint of the work ethic, the citizen is an individual who is capable of, and ready to, work. Government's role should be to protect property and preserve order so that those who are industrious can enjoy the fruits of their labor. What individuals owe to each other is a responsibility to do their own best, and not to become a drag on others. The basic point of the work ethic is that humans must work to meet their needs. Those who work hardest will have the most with which to meet their needs. Those who refuse to work hard will suffer from their lack of effort.

The work ethic resonates with a number of strands in American intellectual history. The work ethic harkens back to, and coheres with, values that stress rugged individualism. We can also think of the work ethic as a way to operationalize Social Darwinism; it explains in practical terms what "survival of the fittest" meant: those who will survive and flourish are those who are able to work hardest and to use their talents most directly. The work ethic also resonates with some accounts of equality and definitions of "what's fair" that have been popular in American thought: provide people with equality of opportunity, and their success or failure will depend upon their own willingness to work (Hochschild 1981). The work ethic reinforces the remarkably persistent strand of individualism in American life. It also justifies an expansive reading of liberty, especially economic liberty: people are entitled to their own views and possessions, since they derived those ideas or earned those things themselves.

Surely it is a good idea for people to be responsible and to work hard to earn what they need, and people who do work hard should be rewarded for their hard work. But there are other dimensions of the work ethic that make it less attractive as an account of the proper way for individuals and society to interact.

First, the work ethic is deeply gendered. It is inscribed into a masculine world of work, which is separate from a feminine world at home. To make this point, we need to realize that to say something is gendered is not the same thing as saying that it reflects a difference between men and women. If we think of "gender" as if it only means the differences between men and women, then we might well conclude that the work ethic is not gendered (Meriac, Poling, and Woehr 2009), since both men and women endorse it. But the term "gendered" expresses more than differences in the attitudes of individual men and women. It is no surprise, really, that women as well as men articulate the beliefs that are mainstream and strongest in their society. The "gendered" dimension only becomes clear when we look more deeply at "work" and the location of "work" in our culture. Here the story becomes more complex; work is markedly more masculine than feminine. The heroic actors described by Weber in *The Protestant Ethic* were men; women appear in the text only as an example of workers who are inured to arguments for efficiency and profit (Weber 2003 [1905], 62). Weber himself used categories that are deeply gendered (Hearn and Collinson 1994; Bologh 1990), but we cannot understand the ways in which the work ethic is fully gendered unless we take one more step.

The idea that the only socially valuable work is that which produces monetary income reflects a bias in our thinking about public and private life, and further, about the place of men and women in these two spheres. The separation of public and private spheres has been a characteristic of Western thought since ancient times. In recent years, feminists began to explore how deeply the public/private split generally reflects the separation of men's worlds from women's worlds and the denigration of the feminine as part of private life.[12] Indeed, the English word "idiot" derives from the ancient Greek term for "private." Where this difference plays out in contemporary life is still central. Women are more likely to put their family lives before their work lives; men are much less likely to allow their family roles to interfere with their work lives. While various scholars have disputed the degree to which such claims are true, a study by D. J. Maume (2006) looked at married heterosexual couples who thought of themselves as committed to gender equality in their relationships. Despite their professed egalitarianism, these men and women still had made fairly gender-stereotypical decisions about their own resolution of the work-life balance. Men rarely took their status as parent into account in making work decisions, whereas mothers frequently did so.

Now it may not be a necessary or logical element of the "work ethic" that it requires separate spheres for men and women and the assignment of production to one sphere and consumption, reproduction, and "care" to another. It is possible to imagine a "work ethic" in an integrated economic system in which work and play, physical exertion and leisure, production and care, teaching and learning, were somehow part of an organic whole, and that as people balanced out these activities they managed to produce enough to allow for extra accumulation. What was key for Weber, though, was the one-sidedness of this work ethic. It provided the basis for the accumulation of capital because, and only because, people were motivated to break their old habits and work harder in order to demonstrate their godliness, which for Weber also turned out to be the way to make profits.

That this work ethic fits so well with the separate spheres of economic and personal life, or, as current parlance describes it, "the work/life balance," is no doubt due in part to its alignment (Weber might have said its "elective affinity") with dichotomous accounts about the nature of gender. Such a separation has never existed among all economic strata in society: lower-class girls and boys went out to work; working-class women often continue to work; and within systems of slavery both men and women were put to hard labor. Nevertheless, as an ideological view, the work ethic matched nicely with the gendered predispositions of the late nineteenth and early twentieth centuries. Social theorists from Weber to Ferdinand Tönnies (2001) and Sigmund Freud (1958) assumed that their particular assortment of dichotomous gendered qualities were ahistorical and universal. Gender dualism fit well with an ideology in which men worked as hard as possible and left the work of care behind them in a realm of women.

Thus, when historians such as Nancy Cott (1977) and, following her, Joan Williams (2000), make the claim that "domesticity" stood as an "implicit critique" of capitalism, they make a grave mistake. Seeing the existence of the other side of a two-sided coin is not a critique of that coin's existence. Arguing that women's work in the household was essential does not undermine the existence of a capitalist economy in which men's work occurs outside of the household. On the contrary, ideologies of domesticity support the existence of separate spheres.[13] Insofar as the "work ethic" endorses the view of worthwhile human activity that separates out and privileges work in the paid political economy, then, it operates in a manner that reinforces gendered roles and makes the existence of this separate economic sphere appear to be "natural."

The work ethic is not only or primarily a description of the economy of separate spheres. Crucially, the work ethic also makes a moral claim, that is, that desert should be measured by one's work. This view fits well with the neoliberal worldview and account of responsibility that I began to explicate in chapters 1 and 2. If one starts from the idea that all of one's economic fortunes and misfortunes are a result of one's own hard work, then there is no place from which to argue that factors beyond one's control may also influence the outcome of one's economic life. The idea that the individual worker remains somehow autonomous, and that the only basis for deciding whether one earns more or less is how hard one works, does not make sense in a globalized capitalist economy. Decisions made far away from the shop floor, for example, by the new owners of a company, determine whether the factory moves or stays, not the willingness of the workers to work hard.

The work ethic suggests a standard of judgment that excludes emotion, context, and relations of power. The work ethic lays out a clear standard for evaluating equality: equality of opportunity. It defines liberty in terms of the ability to work as hard as one would wish. It posits, finally, a standard by which people can judge others as morally deserving, that is, whether they are willing to work hard. It thus offers a simple way to judge others. If they fail, it must be because they did not work hard, or because they were not like us. Hence, those who fail are not to be understood and met with attentiveness; they are to be demonized for their moral failing of not working hard enough. And "we" know that they do not work hard enough because they have failed (cf. Gilens 1999).

Such thinking also marginalizes those who are dependent. The logic of the position that hard work is the way to meet all of one's needs, attached to the self-assessment that one works hard, leads to the tautological view that citizens are not receiving care from anyone else so long as they are earning an income. As long as most American citizens are able to delude themselves into thinking that they do not receive care, then they are able to exclude both the "needy" and their own caregivers from full citizenship (see Kittay 1999).

Neoliberalism requires citizens as "ideal workers." Such citizens are unencumbered by whatever decisions they have made about their lives in the private sphere. These citizens work as hard as they can. (Or, they succeed as much as is possible in the new political economy; note that hard work is not necessarily what pays off, though the ideological commitment has not caught up to reality here.) And they receive what is due to them on the basis of this hard work. In this way, the work ethic reinforces the view that the most important contribution that a citizen can make is to work. But what happens when, as in the neoliberal economy, there are not enough jobs?

Neoliberalism, Competition, and Freedom

There is a second way in which a focus on men's caring as production affects men's ability to care. Men are assumed to be in competition with all other men. As a result, they do not care for others but are in a state of competition against them, as Karl Marx argued. The economic crisis that has gripped the world since 2008 demonstrates that workers are more abundant than jobs. And the competition among workers intensifies. Men cannot waste their time and energy "caring," by this account; they need to be heavily invested in their economic activity. Thus, many American men work more than forty hours a week; they set their priority on earning.

Here, perhaps the deepest difference between the approaches of a care ethic and a work ethic become visible. The work ethic model is highly individualistic. As an ideology, it describes the social world as relatively flat: if an individual is willing to work hard, that is all that is necessary to enjoy the benefits of hard work and to live a good life. The worldview of the work ethic is thus compatible with the worldview of neoliberalism: everything important to know about collective life is a reflection of different individuals' capacities to operate within the free market.

On the other hand, a relational care ethic views individual effort from a different standpoint. Given the complexity of care, caring well requires that any worker be attuned not only to his or her own welfare but also to the ways in which others also have needs—intimates in one's household, friends and neighbors, and more distant others. The care ethic, with an emphasis on care for the self, also permits an understanding of the social structures that shape the conditions of workers' lives. Effort, by itself, cannot suffice to make one's actions proper when one understands the complex contexts of care. As a result, a care ethic view of work requires a broader understanding of the place and nature of working for income.

A global neoliberal economy does not need workers, it needs capital. While Marx argued that only the exploitation of labor produces surplus value, increasingly the sources of profit derive from finance (Madrick 2011). Hard work itself, as David Harvey (2005) has explained, is no longer what pays. What pays is the capacity to be ready to take advantage of the fluctuations in capital. We will consider what this different capacity means for workers in the next chapter. But before we leave men demanding a "production pass" out of caring, let us consider the conditions under which this demand is made, and the assumptions it brings with it as an account of human freedom.

Freedom

To argue that hard work alone is worthy as a measure of one's public contribution to society is to adopt a view of society in which individuals, left to their own devices, will find ways to improve themselves. From such a perspective, freedom is easily described as the kind of "negative freedom" that Isaiah Berlin (1969) described—freedom from government interference. Yet freedom, defined as freedom from government interference in economic activity, ignores the ways in which, in a globalized and capitalist political economy, many activities of government are oriented toward creating a hospitable environment for capital.

The idea of freedom as lack of attachment is deeply embedded in American culture; it did not begin when Janis Joplin sang of freedom as "nothing left to lose." Commentators on American conceptions of masculinity frequently note that, in the end, what it takes to be manly is to exercise the freedom to escape from the complications and ties of a home with its embedded and obliging relationships (Leonard and Tronto 2007; Faludi 1999; Kimbrell 1995). Men on the road, freed of binding ties, are a symbol of American manliness and freedom. But what have such men given up in order to be "free"? Is this the best way to understand freedom?

Feminist scholars, thinking about ways to break out of many of the dilemmas of public/private splits and of the institutionalized gender patterns in society, have adopted a more complex view that equates freedom with the capacity to make a "choice" (Hirschmann 1996, 2002). From the standpoint of a relational ontology, free choice means more than simply an individual exercise of will; it requires a complicated interaction with the structural conditions of life.

Feminist theorists who have written about "relational autonomy" emphasize that sometimes decisions that appear to be the result of a choice may nonetheless violate one's autonomy. As Carolyn McLeod and Susan Sherwin explain this perspective:

> Whereas traditional accounts concern themselves only with judging the ability of the individual to act autonomously in the situation at hand, relational autonomy asks us to take into account the impact of social and political structures, especially sexism and other forms of oppression, on the lives and opportunities of individuals. . . . In particular, a relational view of autonomy encourages us to understand that the best way of responding to oppression's restrictive influence on an individual's ability to act autonomously is to change the oppressive conditions of her life, not to try to make her better adapt to (or simply to manage to "overcome") those conditions privately. (260).

Because women have been located ideologically in the private sphere, and because their view of citizenship therefore has included calculations about leaving or changing these conditions, scholars investigating their condition have noted the importance of dependence in women's place in society. As noted earlier, if one needs the care of protective care workers such as police officers or fire fighters, needing such care does not make one into a dependent. To need the kinds of care that have historically been privatized and confined to women's care, however, is to be seen as a dependent (Fraser and Gordon 1994). As Fraser and Gordon argue, the term "dependency" is applied disproportionately to those who find themselves within the private sphere. Scholars such as Theda Skocpol (1992) and Barbara J. Nelson (1986) have noted the gendered ways in which some kinds of needs are treated as transparently the needs of citizens (e.g., those requiring veterans' pensions or workers' compensation) while others are considered as beneath the level of citizens' needs and their recipients cast as dependents (e.g., welfare assistance, needs for children and the elderly). Nancy Fraser (1989) called this the "politics of needs interpretation," since in every society a political fight produces the assumptions made about which needs are worthy and how they should be constructed and controlled.

Thus, a different account of freedom is necessary in order to go beyond the model of individuals competing in a market as the vision of social life. Whatever else autonomy might mean, it has to include the kind of freedom that Philip Pettit (2002) describes as the freedom from domination. In a discussion in which he tries to describe the nature of the loss of freedom, Pettit distinguishes between the harms of non-interference and those of domination. Interference with one's wishes, for example, by a city ordinance that prevents one from making too much noise late at night, is not as significant a form of violation of liberty, Pettit argues, as one that produces domination. Domination is worse because it makes us into a different kind of person, one who is dependent upon others. Such dependence distorts who we can be as humans. So, Pettit, following Quentin Skinner, argues:

> The person who is dominated will tend to second-guess the wishes of the dominator, wanting to keep him or her on side and to restrict their own options accordingly. In the traditional language, they will tend to toady and fawn, bow and scrape, placate and ingratiate—in a word, abase themselves; furthermore, they will censor everything they say and do, tailoring it to an assuaging effect. (348)

Nancy Hirschmann (2002) takes Pettit's idea further. For Pettit, she notes, the "dominator" has to be identifiable, but other social formations, such as sexism or racism, can also create domination even if the dominator cannot be identified. As she explained,

> Social norms do not come into being by themselves, and they cannot persist without people's actively calling on and deploying them. So the domination that might result from such norms cannot persist without individuals' activating within larger frameworks of cultural meaning to interfere with other individuals' self-conceptions, desires, and choices. But at the same time, the power of norms, practices, and meaning far exceeds the grasp and control of any individual, so that this power can be used and called into play without the explicit awareness of anyone, either dominus or dominated. (28)

Given the reality of social construction, many freedoms are constrained in ways that individual actors may not understand. How can one make sense out of such a situation, then? When does one know that freedom has actually been constrained? Hirschmann takes the next logical step, and uses inequality as a likely indicator that a form of dominating social construction has constrained people's liberty.

Specifically, equality can help determine whether a particular context constrains any group of people less or more than it does any other. For instance, if a society repeatedly, systematically constrains women more than men, blacks more than whites, lesbians more than heterosexuals, then there is a theoretical presumption in favor of the conclusion that the society—or the rules, norms, institutions, practices, and values in question in a particular context where freedom is at issue—presents a barrier to the more constrained group (Hirschmann 2002, 231).

Thus, Hirschmann shows that, given how social constructions become constraints on people's freedom, the absence of equality becomes a useful tool for evaluating the absence of freedom. The analysis of freedom does not end with the establishment that there are choices available—it requires that these choices somehow be free and equal.

Freedom to make choices is the freedom described for an autonomous actor operating in a world that is well described by the market. Since all else is equal, one simply makes choices. But in a world in which there are forms of domination, making choices is not an adequate definition of freedom because it ignores the context and social structures that shape those choices. The world inhabited by men and women in the neoliberal market is not a world free from domination. Although right-wing ideologies portray the state as the great force for domination (and it is potentially such a force, to be sure), they ignore the ways in which capitalists under neoliberalism force individuals to act and manipulate the institutions of the state so that capitalists are the main beneficiaries. As a result, individuals are left with "choices" that no one can really describe as "free." Should an upper-middle-class woman "opt out" of work and raise her children? The question cannot be answered if it is posed in this way, as we will see in the next chapter.

But before we turn to the dilemmas of mothers in thinking about how we care now, let us summarize the traditional bargain that men have struck to get them out of caring. Men provide two forms of broader social care: they protect the society and they engage in productive economic activity. Thus, the argument goes, they are due a "pass" from engaging in the daily activities of care. They are historically "on the ready" to become involved in the defense of women and children, and must therefore think of themselves as invulnerable and project that sense of their own capacities.

They are, through their engagement in protection, granted a pass from caring. Furthermore, men "care" for their families by providing them with the economic means to survive. Men do so through earning a living. In so doing, they take care of the people in their households, and, in exchange, they expect the women and children in the household to concern themselves with "the other side of the paycheck" (Bridges 1979).

What is interesting about this account of men's care is that it leads to a conception in which freedom means not having to care. It does not recognize *real embedded human* choice—that perhaps one would want to return to caring for the others with whom one is in relationship, or for the public realm—as freedom. Instead, it presumes that if one were only somehow wealthy enough, and protected enough, one could secede.

If this definition of freedom ever made sense, it no longer does. Men need to renegotiate their protection and production passes and rethink how masculinity has been constructed as an alternative to caring. From such a standpoint, care might again become a part of public and collective life.

Changing the Gender of Citizenship

One argument against the approach that I have taken here in this chapter is to suggest that it is impossible to change the gendered nature of citizenship because it is *natural*, or so otherwise deeply rooted in human society, that men care by protection and production and that women's caring is constrained to the private sphere. Yet it cannot be that gendered roles are entirely natural; it is possible to explore historical moments in which gender underwent a transformation. One such change in the "gender of citizenship" accompanied the shift away from republican and toward more liberal political values at the end of the eighteenth and beginning of the nineteenth centuries in the Anglo-American world.[14]

The gender script of the republican arguments in the eighteenth century did not expect that men's primary duty as citizens was to create their own private wealth. Indeed, to be concerned with one's private life, one's own level of economic comfort, one's appearance, and so forth, was condemned by eighteenth-century writers such as Adam Ferguson (1995 [1767], VI.3) as "effeminate." By the beginning of the nineteenth century in America, though, as Michael Kimmel (1996) argues, what it meant to be a "self-made man" began to take on the terms of economic success.

As the economy has changed, so has the possibility for men to live out ideals of masculinity. As Susan Faludi (1999, 38) noted, "It's often been observed that the economic transition from industry to service, or from production to consumption, is symbolically a move from the traditional masculine to the traditional feminine. But in gender terms, the transition is far more than a simple sex change and, so, more traumatic for men than we realize." Indeed, Faludi argues, this change made it impossible to uphold older masculine virtues of self-containment, hard work, sacrifice for one's family. Instead, we are now living in an era that "elevated winning to the very apex of manhood while at the same time disconnecting it from meaningful social purpose" (598). Faludi now sees men as "surrounded by a culture that encourages people to play almost no functional public roles, only decorative or consumer ones" (34).

If conceptions of gender have shifted in the past, then it is also possible that they can shift again. Men do care, and the changing meanings of care in men's lives currently produce a remarkable amount of anxiety in American life. There is a need, then, for a thorough rethinking of how care responsibilities do and do not align with gender roles.

That this question is currently one of the large issues lurking beneath the surface of American politics is not difficult to see. How else might one explain the elections of 2010, in which candidates won support for expressing rage rather than making policy proposals, and in which candidates were admired for threatening to take a baseball bat to the existing political order? Even the women who find themselves in this political position try to express themselves as "momma grizzlies," a version of a caring that is closer to the masculinist account of care as protection than to traditional versions of maternalism. The old categories of right and left cannot guide voters or citizens through these waters. Americans will be able to escape from their anxiety and rage only when they are able to face these realities: the current economic, social, and political order cannot adequately express the scope of caring concerns. And they cannot express these concerns because they speak only in the languages of economics, interests, and rights. People in democratic societies need as well to speak politically of needs, cares, and people's fears about their inabilities to care well.

Conclusion

This chapter began by examining the "passes" that describe men's caring responsibilities not in the traditional language of care, but in the language of protection and production. Protection and production *are* critically important forms of caring. Nevertheless, insofar as they have been deeply gendered, their allocation has not been part of any discussion of the proper allocation of caring responsibilities. In gendering protection and production, men's care has been presumed to be individualistic. This results in incapacity to understand the place of violence and the individualistic competitive "work ethic" that underpins much social thinking. It also underscores a broken connection between "freedom" and freedom from dependency. I argued that while it may seem that what one gains from avoiding dependency is freedom, in fact it just substitutes other forms of dependency.

"Choice" is not the same thing as freedom from dependency, and economic dependence on conditions that are beyond the reach of ordinary people is a fact of our lives. Yet even if we could be free from all forms of dependence, that would not be a free life, it would be a life devoid of meaning. Dependence marks the human condition from birth until death. What makes us free, actually, is our capacity to care and to make commitments to what we care about. This is a kind of choice, but it is not choice understood simplistically. It requires action rather than consumption. It requires engagement with others. It is often not presented to us, or does not seem to come to us, as a choice. When people make commitments, aware of and yet regardless of the constraints around them, and hold to those commitments, then we can define them as making a free choice. But I do not know a better way to think about freedom.

4

Vicious Circles of Privatized Caring

Care, Equality, and Democracy

Few if any governments in the world today can rest content with
the job they are doing of protecting the basic interests of children for whom they are responsible.
—Shapiro 2001, 101

Nancy Hirschmann's (2010) essay and the subsequent discussion in the
Boston Review about "mothers who care too much" explored the problem of how much caring from mothers is "enough." Should mothers work,
or should they devote themselves to their children? Of course, to put the
question this way is already to limit the "mothers" about whom one is
speaking. Upper-middle-class women may be able to exercise the "opt-
out" option, but most cannot. Many commentators note the injustice of
starting any discussion about mothers' proper roles if one is discussing
only *some* mothers. Hirschmann recognizes this problem, but lays blame
for it at the feet of a gendered division of labor. It is telling how rarely discussions about mothering get beyond this class division, as if there were
no other interesting questions to consider.

In the previous chapter, I largely followed this class-based script, too,
leaving issues of race and class more distant than they actually are. What
we discovered there is that the failure of men to take up some of their caring responsibilities is a result of their sense of privilege because they have

two other "passes" that let them off the hook for household caring duties: the protection pass and the production pass. At the end of the chapter, I argued that part of the reason that these passes seem salient to us is because of the presumed connection between "freedom" and freedom from dependency. I argued that while it may seem that what one gains from avoiding dependency is freedom, in fact it just substitutes other forms of dependency. "Choice" is not the same thing as freedom from dependency, and economic dependence on the conditions of the economy that are beyond the reach of ordinary people is a fact of people's lives.

In this chapter, I will take up another piece of how we care now, that is, how we care for children. I will use this focal point to explore two important themes about care now. First, since caring for children remains intensely feminized, I will explore the gendered dimensions of caring for children. Second, I will use this chapter as an opportunity to think about the concept of equality. I shall argue that the current construction of the political economy, which heavily rewards "winner-take-all" victors, requires caregivers to try to subvert equality in order to care for their wards. Thus, a vicious circle of unequal care promises only to reinforce and entrench itself more deeply.

As women want to become full citizens, their way to demonstrate their appropriateness as citizens is also to "attach" to the paid labor force. The resulting chaos in caring work cannot be well understood within the scope of this worldview. The fact that work makes them unable to provide care means that they receive a "production pass" out of caring. Coupled with the high demands placed upon them to care for their children, then, parents (especially mothers) demand a pass to care-for-my-own; they should only be obliged to provide direct care for those who are within their immediate scope of care.

Bernard de Mandeville in *The Fable of the Bees* (1714) described how the pursuit of private vices could produce the public good of greater social wealth. This argument bears a close family resemblance to the contemporary neoliberal ideology. Neoliberals believe that encouraging the private pursuit of wealth, and limiting the public intrusion in this process, is the surest way to achieve collective happiness. Mandeville's fable tells the familiar story that our responsibilities do not extend beyond ourselves or our families. In this chapter, I shall argue a converse position: out of admirable personal conduct can arise a public harm. When unequal citizens only care privately, they deepen the vast inequalities and the exclusion of some from the real prospects of being full citizens. Unless caring responsibilities are rethought with the concerns of genuine equality in mind, then there can be little progress toward a more democratic society.

This chapter also tells a cautionary tale. Many powerful individuals and organizations in the world tout the organization of social and political life in the United States as a model of how a modern society can provide a fine way of life for its citizens. American military, political, and economic power also spreads this neoliberal ideological message around the globe. Indeed, Americans live surrounded by material wealth and express satisfaction with their lives. At the same time, however, a widening gap between rich and poor makes it doubtful whether the equal standing of all citizens, a starting point for democracy, will describe the United States in the not-too-distant future. Of course, citizens are never equally situated, but we assume that equality of rights and equality of opportunity are sufficient to create political equality.

In reality, we should be quite worried about the prospects for equality in our society. As Eva Kittay (1999) established in her account of care workers' unequal access to the resources that make political life possible, as long as care continues to shape differently the capacities of citizens to be citizens, there can be no genuine equality among citizens in their capacity to exercise political rights. As seriously, as I shall show here, as long as neoliberals continue to insist that the separation of public and private life accurately describes the limits of government's power, they provide an ideological justification for the deepening circles of unequal care. Without some basic equality of care for children, there can be no such thing as "equal opportunity" (Harrington 1999). In this chapter I shall argue, however, that if unequal opportunity poses a threat to democratic society, then democratic citizens have to take seriously care responsibilities that extend beyond their own households.

Unlike the last chapter, when some unusual locations for care were identified, this chapter deals with what is commonly taken to be paradigmatically "care," that is, direct care provided by parents to children. This is care in the classical "private sphere" of the home, family, or household. Many feminist scholars have pointed to the kinds of vulnerabilities that are created by this arrangement in thinking about women's status vis-à-vis men's. For example, Martha Fineman (1995) has argued that rather than think of a family as a married couple with children, it makes sense to define the household unit as a woman and her children, since the dangers of vulnerability almost all accrue to women. It is important to continue to observe that women are harmed by the idea that they as a group are the primary caregivers. Other scholars have considered ways to redefine or think differently about family or household as if this, alone, would solve the problems of unequal care (Metz 2010b). Yet Nancy Folbre (2001, xiv) pointed out that just because women have "challenged the double standard of care work," this does not answer the question, How much care we should provide, and to whom? Nor does a challenge to the public/private split help to explain why some mothers' children are so much better taken care of than others'. Assessing these differences and problems, this chapter argues that nothing short of redefining and renegotiating care responsibilities, their institutional and personal loci, and their public nature can move this debate forward. Instead, discussions of care will remain caught in a vicious circle in which care reinforces social and economic inequality.

Some Care Imbalances

At present, most of the intimate direct caring for young children occurs in the default institution of the household or family. Given the widely disparate capacities of such households to provide care for their members, large imbalances result in the kind and quality of care that children receive. There are measurable, material imbalances in the amount of care that various people receive and in the amount of resources that people have to accomplish their caring work. These imbalances closely mirror the configurations of social class and status (primarily racial/ethnic status) in the United States.

A consensus has emerged that the most important years for a child's development are the first three (Shonkoff and Phillips 2000). The care one receives or not at the beginning of life greatly influences one's future. Jody Heymann (2000, 2006) has exhaustively demonstrated that working-class parents are less likely to have such resources as "personal days" at their disposal, and working-class children's poorer school attendance correlates with such lack of resources.

Children whose early care is inadequate never make up the care deficit that they have suffered, and so we should not be surprised to learn that those who have been poorly educated and received inadequate health care become adults with fewer resources to draw upon and are less successful in the world. Globally, "poverty and ill-health are intertwined" (Wagstaff 2002), and this is so in the United States as well (Shi et al. 2005). Martha Wadsworth and her colleagues (2008) conclude that "growing up and living with persistent poverty is detrimental to one's psychological, physical, and educational health." The literature finds "a pervasive tendency for children born in socially disadvantaged families to have poorer health, education, and general welfare" (Fergusson, Horwood, and Boden 2008).

In every category of caring for oneself and one's family that we might mention, the more affluent have greater resources for caring and better take advantage of these resources than those who are less well off. Nursing-home care provided for the more affluent is more pleasant than that provided for public assistance recipients. The more affluent are more likely to have access to better food and eat more nutritiously, are more likely to engage in exercise as a form of leisure activity, are more likely to seek help from doctors and mental health practitioners. The more affluent are more likely to have access to resources that provide the "infrastructure" of care as well—for example, better access to transportation and more, better, and safer housing. There is no doubt that people who are more affluent have the opportunity to receive better care.

Those who receive better care, however, are also somewhat less burdened by the demands to care for others. In the formal economy, care work is among the lowest-paid work in our society. While some caring positions are professional, those are disproportionately held by white women. Those who do less skilled, "nonnurturant" caring work, both within and beyond the household, are disproportionately women, people of color, immigrants, and working-class people (Duffy 2011). Furthermore, much care work occurs in informal and unpaid sectors of the economy, so that care workers are likely to be the least well protected and organized and to receive the fewest benefits (Heymann 2000) in order to care for their own families.

Structurally, several aspects of care practices contribute to such inequities. First, in terms of the allocation of resources, care work is both undervalued and ascribed to women and people of lower class and status. They are the result of long-standing discrimination in the workforce, and of structural differences in the ways that we think about paying for care work (Nelson 1999). Second, in terms of the allocation of power, since needs for care are overwhelmingly ascribed to "vulnerable" people, such as children, the elderly, the infirm, the disabled, and others who are dependent, *control* for meeting these needs is placed in the hands of those who are deemed competent and independent. Thus, it is difficult to generate a public discourse in which the voice and views of the vulnerable can even be heard.

As we observed earlier, Charles Tilly (1998) has argued that small initial advantages of one group over another embed themselves into large-scale patterns of oppression by using ascriptive differences to structure social institutions and practices. The ways in which care is provided, and for whom, seem to illustrate this point. The wealthier you are in the United States, the better you are cared for and the less likely that you are to be employed doing care work for others. This is the initial pattern, then, that is reinforced in a vicious circle of uncaring for others.

The Social Psychology of Unequal Care

We might expect that such inequalities of care and access to care resources would generate some concern in American society and among political leaders. After all, among children, the quality of care someone receives is an important indicator of the child's capacity to develop into a productive citizen. If Americans are serious about equality of opportunity, then they should be quite serious about the adequate provision of care at an early age (cf. Heymann 2000; Harrington 1999). President George W. Bush's labeling of his educational reform as "No Child Left Behind" might have been merely rhetorical, but it captured a commitment to equality of opportunity. And for the elderly, viewed as senior citizens, there is a greater level of support for making their lives easier than for other social groups. Similarly, the infirm receive public benefits through the Social Security system, and their care seems to be partly a public concern. The problem is, however, that these commitments do not translate into any real commitment to equality of care. Indeed, for a variety of reasons, I shall argue, the opposite happens.

First, since Americans generally conceptualize care as a private concern, the language and framework of market choices guides how to describe and think about care options. The effect of this framework is to make care primarily outside of public concern. One way to understand care inequalities is to see them as the outcomes of "choices" that competing actors make in the marketplace. Through monetary and temporal resources, both in the market and outside, one way to understand care imbalances is to see them as the result of long chains of individual choices. For example, if parents choose to spend their time, money, and so on in ways that do not benefit their children, while that choice may be deplorable, it is their own individual choice and not a social responsibility. The language of the market and of choice here diminishes abilities to see the ways in which economic inequalities contribute to social incapacities.

Because care seems to be about intimate life, it makes sense to think of the "unit of analysis" or "level of analysis" at which to think about care as the individual actor or family. Each family or person wishes to care for its/her/his/their charges as well as possible. The consequences of assuming that all actors are intimate care–giving actors is to see all care activities as the result of actions by particular individuals, a kind of methodological individualism. In thinking about how others act, the market becomes a leading way to describe all such behavior, and thus the market serves as a powerful way to describe how care distributions operate in capitalist societies (Slater and Tonkiss 2001).

This worldview obscures how people make judgments about others' choices, and for that matter, how individuals make choices for themselves. A variety of social-psychological mechanisms seem to be at work in justifying inequality of the amount of care available to different individuals. Consider the following three.

1. Competitive Caring

This argument for equality of care presumes that care can be distributed within liberal frameworks of justice. Yet there are limits to starting from liberal principles of justice and expecting care simply to fit within that framework. Jody Heymann (2000) argued that equality of opportunity demands that family time for caring should be equalized. Heymann argues that if time were organized more rationally around care, then more children would have chances to succeed in school, more elderly relatives would receive adequate care, work and productivity would improve, and society would be better.[1]

There is a basic flaw in this argument: as long as caring remains a subordinate activity and value within the framework of a competitive, "winner-take-all" society, caring well within one's family will make one not a friend but an enemy of equal opportunity. When people care, almost by definition they think not of society, but of intimate others and their concrete and particular needs. In a competitive society, what it means to care well for one's own children is to make sure that they have a competitive edge against other children. On the most concrete level, while parents may endorse a principle of equality of opportunity in the abstract, their daily activities are most visibly "caring" when they gain special privileges and advantages for their children. Arguments about the value of public education, for example, lose their force when they affect the possibility of *one's own* children's future. This example demonstrates that when care is embedded in another framework of values, it does not necessarily lead in a progressive direction.

Idealized middle-class family care in the United States thus requires, structures, and perpetuates some of the very inequities of care that Heymann describes. A "career person" (Walker 1999) only wants what is best for his or her family. This leads to the assumption that such people care for themselves, and that "care" is only a concern for the dependent and infirm— the young, the unhealthy, and the old. In fact, the model of the self-caring person is a deception: while working adults may not require the *necessary care* of others (that is, the expertise of professional caregivers), they may use a great deal of other people's *care services* (that is, routine caring work; cf. Waerness 1990) to keep their busy lives on keel. In American society, the more elite one becomes, the more dependent one becomes upon others meeting one's basic caring needs: providing edible food, clean clothing, attractive shelter. Thus, the parents who have flexible work schedules, whose children succeed at school, are probably using a vast array of care services. Such labor is among the poorest paid and least well-organized in our society. Heymann's widening gap is thus also a caring gap, though the ideology of "caring" covers up its roots and makes it more intractable.

2. Unsympathetic Disregard

A second social-psychological mechanism that might explain why people are not willing to assume the responsibilities to care for others in a public manner arises when people make judgments about whether other citizens deserve their support—that is, unsympathetic disregard.[2]

In his recent writings on why inequality persists in the United States, Ian Shapiro (2002) described an "empathy gap": individuals tend to identify with those who are better off than they are, but not with those who are less well off than they are.[3] Further, geographical segregation between rich and poor in the United States makes empathy more difficult.

Another important element that Shapiro could have mentioned, but did not, is the way in which, as long as care is individualized and privatized, it is possible to praise oneself for one's caring and decry the ways in which others care. Such praise and blame will likely follow lines of race, class, ethnicity, region, and religion, and will likely make it more difficult to see inequalities as a result of lack of choice. Instead, they may be viewed as the product of others' deliberate bad actions, decisions, or ways of life. As a result, people are likely not to be very sympathetic to such lapses on the part of others.

One reason this element is especially important is that when we ask people to make public judgments, they are often wise enough not simply to generalize from their own experience. What they are likely to do, however, is use available generalizations about "others" to make judgments. An illustration of this tendency is found in Martin Gilens's (1999) account of why Americans hate welfare. Since, Gilens discovers, most Americans presume that the majority of welfare recipients are African American, and since Americans are only willing to support welfare if they believe recipients work hard, and since Americans believe most African Americans are lazy, then they are unwilling to support welfare. People here are not evaluating their own beliefs and actions, but those of others that come up short. Note, though, how this psychological mechanism of making judgments based on second-order generalizations means that people do not have to claim responsibility for attitudes such as racism. They do not think that they are making a racist judgment; after all, their starting premise is that all hard-working people deserve help. They just take "as a fact" the premise that blacks are lazy. Although this is a subject for empirical research, it would be interesting to discover to what extent such thinking influences how people think about care. Everyone believes that they do the best that they can for their charges. But when other people fail to act in the same way, regardless of the reason, they can be dismissed, "they simply don't care."

If we recall the ways in which absence of resources prevents less well-off individuals from caring for their own families, we can see how care becomes a vicious ideological circle. Parents who see that the other parents do not show up for school plays, for example, might conclude that those parents "don't care," not that they work in jobs where they cannot get time off from work to attend. Thus, in addition to the lack of material resources that unequal care presents, it also may create the conditions for diminished sympathy.

3. Privileged Irresponsibility

"Privileged irresponsibility" refers to the ways in which the division of labor and existing social values allow some individuals to excuse themselves from basic caring responsibilities because they have other and more important work to perform (Tronto 1993). To use the conceptual distinction of Kari Waerness (1984a, 1984b), privileged irresponsibility is a special kind of personal service in which the recipient of others' caring work simply presumes an entitlement to such care. Furthermore, the existence of such an entitlement permits it to "run in the background," that is, not to be noticed, discussed, or much remarked upon. Consider, as an example, the ideological version of the traditional division of household labor. A breadwinning husband "took care" of his family by earning a living; in return, he expected his wife to convert these earnings into comfortable shelter, edible food, clean clothing, a social life, management of the household, and so forth. Nor did the breadwinner husband think it was a part of his responsibility to know very much about the complexities of food preparation, household management, and so on. Such a man rarely learned how to "take care of himself." Care work, invisibly and efficiently performed, was a privilege of his role. As to the caring needs he had met by the labor of those around him on "the other side of the paycheck" (Bridges 1979), he felt no sense of responsibility. Hence, privileged irresponsibility.

Peggy McIntosh (1988) and others (A. Johnson 2001; Hobgood 2000) who write extensively about "privilege" assume that when people learn that they are privileged by ascription, they will go through a process of "consciousness raising" and surrender their privilege, since it is unjust. Privileged irresponsibility operates under a somewhat different logic. Like the more usual form of "privilege," privileged irresponsibility is rarely visible. One of the great benefits or privileges that comes from being in a position of superiority in a hierarchical system is that one need not exert conscious and daily effort, or consider one's role or responsibility, in maintaining that system. Thus, such systems come to rely upon the peculiar ignorance of their beneficiaries. Such privileged irresponsibility usually takes the form of complete ignorance of a problem, but it may also involve misinterpretation or unclear perception of a problem (Mills 1997).

Nevertheless, when privileged irresponsibility does become visible, privileged people need to do more than alter their consciousness. They need to reassess and take up their responsibilities. Unless basic questions about the nature of social responsibility are rethought, there is no reason to expect that noting this privilege will cause any discomfort. It may be the case that (to use the same example) the husband recognizes that he is getting a good deal, but he is likely to think that his wife is also getting a good deal. Especially in a culture that emphasizes how much each of us is only responsible for our own lives, and ignores the caring that supports such lives, such privilege is very difficult to unseat.

To carry this analysis one step deeper, different types of care reflect the terms of power relationships differently. As we observed in chapter 1, Kari Waerness (1990) distinguished between necessary care (which someone else must provide) and personal service (which is care that one could provide for oneself but relies upon another to provide). In necessary care, the caregiver is relatively powerful because he or she is essential to the well-being of the care-receiver. In personal service, the caregiver is not essential to the well-being of the care receiver, and the latter could thus dispense with the caregiver's role. The result is that care receivers have more power in personal service than they do in necessary care.

Because caring is complex, and because we might only think that we are caring when we engage in necessary care activities, people may come to believe that they fulfill their necessary caring obligations at the same time that they demand very high levels of personal service from others. What they fail to recognize in doing so is that they are taking advantage of those from whom they are demanding personal service. Privileged irresponsibility concerns personal service, not necessary care. Yet this distinction is not usually made or present in our thinking. The situation becomes more complex still. Usually, the privileged also expect that others will provide the personal service that they require on terms that are agreeable to them. The idea that this situation reflects a proper division of labor in society, however, prevents any reconsideration of responsibility. Thus, by using personal service to fulfill their own necessary care roles, those who can afford to hire others to do their personal service work for them think of themselves as accomplished in caring while they are able to ignore the ways in which their own caring activities continue to perpetuate inequality (see, e.g., Tronto 2002).

The privatization of reproductive care that has accompanied the growing public nature of productive work reflects as well the relative social power of different groups to make their contributions more highly prized and recognized. Relatively more powerful people in society have a lot at stake in seeing that their caring needs are met under conditions that are beneficial to them, even if this means that the caring needs of those who provide them with services go unmet. More powerful people can fob the work of care onto others: men to women, upper to lower class, free men to slaves, those who are considered racially superior to those whom they consider racially inferior groups. Care work itself is often demanding and inflexible. People who do such work recognize its intrinsic value, but it does not fit well in a society that values innovation and accumulation of wealth.

Regardless of what assumptions we make about humans—whether they are greedy or benevolent—once there is inequality in care, thinking about how others take care of themselves and their charges is likely to make people feel less inclined to take their care problems seriously. Ideologically as well as materially, then, inequality in care creates a vicious circle.

Gender, Class, and the Ecology of Care

These social-psychological factors that obscure people's abilities to understand the "caring choices" that others make are not the only problems with thinking about class difference and the absence of caring solidarity. It is also the case that what constitutes "good care" varies along some ascriptive characteristics as well. For example, Annette Lareau (2003) has explored the differences between middle- and working-class parents' attitudes about the kind of care that their children need. For middle-class parents, children's talents and opportunities require constant cultivation. Such cultivation often requires the intervention of professional service providers (piano teachers, tennis coaches, etc.) and that the parent negotiate the interactions of children with others (for example, in learning how not to be too deferential to doctors but to ask questions). For working-class parents, on the other hand, children will develop naturally and according to their different natures if left to their own devices. Once children are adequately protected from danger, letting nature take its course will result in their growth in the ways that are naturally intended (Lareau 2003). Note that the cultivating, intensive form of child care that characterizes middle-class upbringing requires more extensive reliance upon the professional and skilled services of others. It requires, obviously, resources of time and money to pay for such services. The ideology of what Sharon Hays (1996) has called "intensive mothering" is primarily a middle-class phenomenon. Although Anita Garey (1999) found a way to classify mothers' activities across class lines, it is clear that the categories that she uses to define what is important for mothers will vary by class. For example, "being there" will have a different meaning to a middle-class parent who can get leave from work to attend a child's school than to a working-class parent who cannot. Francesca Cancian and Stacey Oliker (2002) have also explored the differences among working- and middle-class families in their accounts of "good caring."

Although this discussion has focused on class, we could make a similar argument about ethnic and racial differences in attitudes toward child-rearing (Omolade 1994). These differences apply not only to children, but also to elders and disabled or infirm members of the family and community.

Gender differences also dictate that girls and women are presumed to be the "default" givers of care when a situation arises. On a global level, scholars have demonstrated the serious mortal consequences of such assumptions for girls and women, who are expected to eat last, be less educated, receive less health care attention, and so forth (Sen 1992). Women may demand care appropriate for their station, but they still remain the caregivers in their own homes, either by directly providing care or by being responsible for organizing such services.

To point to these differences is not simply to make an argument that some people care one way and others another way, though this point is also true. The differences are not simply about preferences, but about a structure of inequality that is deeply embedded in other structures in society.

Rethinking the Meaning of Equality

Political theorists and feminist scholars have devoted much thought in the past generation to debating the many possible meanings of equality. Philosophers have debated what it is about humans that should be equal: their capabilities, an intrinsic standard of human dignity applied to them all, their capacity to suffer pain, their vulnerability, their equal possession of a unique bundle of interests, and so forth. I will discuss only those dimensions of this set of concerns that are relevant to our purposes.

For some, equality implies sameness, and when so understood, virtually no one is willing to endorse it as a political value. Often, though, equality as sameness is presumed to mean the same thing as "equality of result" as opposed to "equality of opportunity." In a vague sense, such a notion of equal opportunity is different from its more specific legal meanings in the past fifty years, which are tied to the elimination of the effects of racial discrimination. In the widely accepted sense, "equality of opportunity" is more closely connected to arguments about the "level playing field." Since everyone starts off in the same position, people through their own actions are responsible for where they end up. Indeed, if we had to

pick a standard meaning for equality in the United States, it would probably be such a notion of equal opportunity.

A number of critics have objected to this understanding of equality.
Here, I draw upon the view of Elizabeth Anderson (1999), whose conception of equality fits better with an account that recognizes that some of the
ways that our responsibilities come to us are already allocated, historically
and politically. Recall Margaret Walker's (1998) point:

> Sometimes it is a privilege or a mercy to be exempted from respon-
> sibilities: sometimes it shows you are nobody, or less of a somebody
> than somebody else. Assignments of responsibility are a form of
> moral address, but some are addressed as peers, others as superiors
> or subordinates.

In an expressive-collaborative moral setting, then, the goal is for all to
be addressed in assigning responsibilities as equals. The only way this can
happen is if everyone has equal moral standing to participate in these assignments. Thus, we arrive at Anderson's view that the "proper positive
aim is not to ensure that everyone gets what they morally deserve but to
create a community in which *people stand in relations of equality to others*" (1999, 288–89, emphasis added). Other political theorists have also
stressed that, in the context of a commitment to democracy, having the
power to voice one's concerns and to be heard is a crucial way to understand equality (Young 2000).

Understood in this way, equality is not about equal opportunity, but
involves some kind of equality of standing, that is, all are equally eligible to be heard, about their status and concerns, in making assignments
of responsibility.

What is important to note about this account of equality is what it excludes: it will not be enough to say that if person X had a choice and person Y had a choice, then the two are equal. If they had no equal standing
at the beginning, then they do not have equal standing through the offer
of "choice." All too often, this is what current conceptions of equality do.

To achieve this kind of equality will require more than simply pass-
ing laws against discrimination. Since equality looks different across the
life cycle, at least three different steps are required. First, when people
are young and in a state of dependency, they need equal access to adequate care in order to grow into fully capable adults. Second, when people are adults, they need to be able to exercise their voices equally and

independently, and provisions need to be made to guarantee that their voices are not silenced or drowned out by others. Third, when people are ill, elderly, or disabled, institutional arrangements need to be made to ensure that their voices are also heard.

Although I have described some ways in which inequalities manifest themselves in current household organization, it is always possible that new patterns of domination will occur. As has happened in the past, the shape of oppressive assignments of care-giving roles change (Duffy 2007). One way in which these patterns are now changing concerns the employment of migrants as private servants.

Care Inequalities and Servanthood

One last problem emerges out of the current capacity of relatively wealthy families to provide ever larger amounts of care and service to their members: servanthood. After its long decline throughout the late nineteenth and early twentieth centuries, domestic service is once again on the rise. Early in the twentieth century, "the servant problem" was not only the concern of bourgeois women who discussed it frequently (Sarti 2005, 2006), but of socialists who took a different approach. For socialists, the disappearance of domestic servants would result both from the egalitarian commitment to wider education, and from the capacity of new technologies and collective forms of organization to make domestic work less arduous. Regardless of whether the argument was that domestic work was a burden for the workers or for the employers, it seemed to have fallen out of favor.

It is surprising, then, to note that domestic service is once again on the rise. In the exhaustive analyses of the Servant Project, Rafaella Sarti (2005) and her collaborators identified some important shifts in the nature of servants from the eighteenth and nineteenth centuries to the present. Most importantly, while servants in the eighteenth century were marked primarily by *age* (they were young people who worked as servants before they created their own families), and in the nineteenth and early twentieth centuries by *age, class*, and, increasingly, *gender*, by the contemporary period, what distinguishes servants are their *class, gender*, and *nationality* (Sarti 2005, 7). Women primarily, but men as well, are now crossing international borders to become servants.

Whereas service "opened" households in the past (Sarti 2005, 12), and where service was a temporary employment during one part of the life cycle rather than a permanent status (in Europe), this is no longer the case. An important feature that distinguishes contemporary forms of servitude from past forms is that it is increasingly marked by race, class, gender, nationality, ethnicity, and language. The result is that some of the fluidity that might have characterized earlier forms of servanthood have now solidified.

As Sarti observed, in the past, the benefits of domestic service on the servant were not one-sided. In the eighteenth century and nineteenth centuries, being a servant was often a route for improving one's social or economic situation. So too current servants negotiate positive and negative features of their situation. We might begin by noting that some good effect does come to the women and men who place themselves in situations of transnational domestic service.[4] In some ways and in some cases, service abroad allows men and women to make better provision for the children they left at home. Many who retain ties to or have left families in their home countries are able to return home to display an enviable kind of life. While it is a great hardship for women to leave their children, remittances make up a large percentage of the balance of payments of sending countries, and many nations have policies that favor training care workers to go abroad. There is evidence that the money sent back by *women* who have sojourned abroad improves the quality of the education that their children receive; the United Nations Population Report discovered that "56% of female remittances were used for daily needs, healthcare or education" (Workpermit.com 2006; see also Morrison and Schiff 2007).

What does it mean to think of these individuals' choices from the standpoint of autonomy and dependency? On the one hand, subjecting oneself to such humiliating treatment is a kind of submission. On the other hand, though, leaving one's home to travel abroad appears to some degree to be an autonomous act. (We leave aside the question of those who have been coerced or tricked into such service, whose autonomy and freedom have been compromised.)Yet to what extent does it make sense to use such language as "choice" when an individual confronts a global "necessity" such as the need for money, and is schooled in a society (such as the Philippines) that encourages such "service"? The question of "choice" is thus more complex perhaps than simply describing a situation of poverty versus wealth, or the absence of coercion in making a decision to migrate.

Domestic workers are often treated poorly and discriminated against. Increasingly, because they are so exploitable (Romero 2002), transnational migrants who are not citizens are sought out as the preferred domestic servants because they so relatively powerless. As the feminist geographer Linda McDowell (2007) has indicated, often the person brought into the home to care for children brings values, ideals, practices, and languages from a different class (to say nothing of a different culture). In this circumstance, the employer wants to be able manage the ways in which the children are raised as much as possible.

Domestic workers, especially those who are most vulnerable, receive low wages. Although they are expected to be "one of the family," they realize that they are not, and they suffer indignities and hardships to live in this manner. Mary Romero (1992, 2002) wrote extensively about the complications of being a *Maid in the USA*, and in her subsequent work, she has found that the situation for domestic workers has not improved. Romero concludes, "While intimate relationships between employees and employers have been material for novels, films, and myths, studies indicate that such relationships are much more exploitative than personally or financially rewarding to workers. . . . Rather than treatment as 'one of the family,' the occupation is characterized by everyday rituals of verbal and spatial deference" (Romero 2001, 1660).

Bridget Anderson (2000, 19–20) observes how domestic workers contribute to inequality of standing:

> The employment of a paid domestic worker . . . facilitates status reproduction, not only by maintaining status objects, enabling the silver to be polished or the clothes to be ironed, but also by serving as a foil to the lady of the house. The hired productive worker is reproducing social beings and relationships that are not merely not her own but also deeply antagonistic to her own interests. Her presence emphasizes and reinforces her employer's identity—as a competent household manager, as middle-class, as white—and her own as its opposite.

Yet, from the standpoint of the role of the family in creating a democratic society, the more serious effect remains to be explored. The service relationship not only creates a servant, it also creates a master, or a set of masters.

Domestic service is undemocratic because when such care workers become marked, as the anthropologists put it, with the stigma of care work, they are viewed as part of a feminized, multicultural workforce. They are distinctive because they are marked by a brutalized or privatized form of work,[5] and the work they do becomes marked because it is done by those who are brutalized or privatized.

From the standpoint of justice in a democratic society, we should also be careful of such markings of people as the appropriate ones to do banausic work. Such marking of people as different, even by dress, persists wherever a class of servants exist. They are different people in different regions and historical eras, but they are clearly designated as appropriate to do servile work and are marked by race, color, religion, creed, accent, national origin, and so forth. Audre Lorde recounted in *Sister Outsider* (1984, 126): "I wheel my two-year-old daughter in a shopping cart through a supermarket in Eastchester in 1967, and a little white girl riding past in her mother's cart calls out excitedly, 'Oh look, Mommy, a baby maid!'" American culture often places the multicultural person in the place of a servant whose role is to placate the concerns of white Americans who increasingly rely of such support (Wong 1994).

Yet the harm of such marking is multifaceted. In the first place, it signals that marked people are better suited for care work, and thus, are not equals. This is a serious danger in a democratic society. Barbara Ehrenreich (2000, 70) observes that this has especially bad effects on children who learn that they do not need to learn to clean up after themselves:

> To be cleaned up after is to achieve a certain magical weightlessness and immateriality. Almost everyone complains about violent video games, but paid housecleaning has the same consequence-abolishing effect: you blast the villain into a mist of blood droplets and move right along; you drop the socks knowing they will eventually levitate, laundered and folded, back to their normal dwelling place. The result is a kind of virtual existence, in which the trail of litter that follows you seems to evaporate all by itself. . . . A servant economy breeds callousness and solipsism in the served, and it does so all the more effectively when the service is performed close up and routinely in the place where they live and reproduce.

One of the elements of this harm that Ehrenreich stresses is that it is exacerbated by being privatized and carried out in the household. As I have argued elsewhere (Tronto 2002), I also believe that the moral dimensions of exploitation of workers are worse in the household. This is so because household work is often not viewed as work at all, and household workers who do care work produce more intimate relationships than those produced in other kinds of work environments. Michael Walzer writes: "The principles that rule in the household are those of kinship and love. They establish the underlying pattern of mutuality and obligation, or authority and obedience. The servants have no proper place in that pattern, but they have to be assimilated to it" (1983, 52). What does it mean to assimilate servants to kinship and love? Feminist scholars have been more dubious than Walzer about the rule of kinship and love; nonetheless, the personalistic rule in the household makes this a distinctive work relationship. Insofar as domestic servants are conceived as substitutes for the wife in a traditional household, they are expected to conform to an account of their work that is only partly real "work." "You want someone who puts the children before herself," said a thirty-seven-year-old mother of two in Briarcliff Manor, New York, who works for a health insurance company. "But to find someone for the right amount of money is not so easy" (Rubenstein 1993, C1). As Pierrette Hondagneu-Sotelo (2001) observes, employers were often shocked to realize that their child-care workers were "only in it for the money." The solipsism that Ehrenreich describes is a kind of blindness that affects everyone in the employing household. One of the effects of such a self-referential view on other people is surely the diminishment of a sense of equality.

Having been treated in this manner, it is not surprising that the care workers themselves do not exercise the kind of equal voice that Anderson describes as necessary for democracy. If we return to Walker's view that proper moral judgment requires that everyone participate in the expressive-collaborative process of assigning responsibility, it is easy to see that there is a tradeoff when caregivers are included.

If we took the problems raised by servanthood for creating citizens who have equal standing with one another, we would address the problem of cleaned houses and watched-over children differently. But for now, we see ways in which unequal families produce unequal care, and unequal care produces great inequality in political life. That these inequalities reinforce and fall along the lines of race, class, and gender should not surprise us, but it should make us more eager to try to uproot them. As long as we give citizens passes for "taking-care-of-my-own," though, this question is not likely even to appear as a political question.

5

Can Markets Be Caring?

Markets, Care, and Justice

In 2009 a group of Massachusetts economists estimated the economic value of the care work done in that state. They added together the value of the twenty largest care industries, and discovered that $46.8 billion, or 13 percent, of Massachusetts' GDP (gross domestic product) was generated by care work. Using the average salary for care workers, they also calculated the value of unpaid care, which they defined as the primary care and supervision of children, the elderly, and the infirm, as well as education and household work. Their estimate is that adding together paid and unpaid care work, the economic value of care work in Massachusetts in 2007 was $151.6 billion, 36 percent of the state's GDP (Albelda, Duffy, and Folbre 2009).

These numbers are interesting in several ways. Unpaid care is worth more than double the amount of paid care. But why calculate "unpaid care" in economic terms anyway? Why does an economic value somehow make the care issue more tangible and real than the daily experience people have of trying to balance and meet all of their caring needs?

It has become routine in American society to try to calculate everything in economic terms: the value of an education, of an after-school program, of "the arts." Everything becomes measured, superficially, by the same metric, dollars, so that we can compare them. On another level, the turn to economic calculation reflects another answer about caring responsibilities. This chapter explores the final "passes" out of caring responsibilities that we will consider, the bootstrap pass (each for oneself) and the charity pass (helping others is an individual choice). By this account, the market (beyond the family) is the institution that best allocates care responsibilities, and allocates them well. Thus there is no need for government or other public institutions to reconsider the nature of caring responsibilities, since the market will do so with greater efficiency and more freedom. The lynchpin of contemporary neoliberalism is that the market creates the conditions for freedom and democracy, and that what is just is to allow the market to be guided by the invisible hand by which it allocates and distributes goods and services.

Can the market be caring? The answer to this question is: yes and no. Setting a market value on care is useful in order to show how extensive and central a part of human life it is. But thinking of care only in market terms also produces some serious distortions in how we think about caring responsibilities in society as a whole. Surely, care services and the work necessary to meet caring needs can be organized through a market. But markets, like other human institutions, serve purposes. The main purpose of the market in a capitalist economy is to produce profit, that is, wealth. Even capitalist markets, however, can also serve other ends. For example, were there no worker safety laws, companies could probably make more money. Nevertheless, it seems unconscionable to let corporations squeeze extra productivity and profit out of a workplace that is so dangerous that workers are harmed. The question about whether the market can be caring depends upon how members of a society think about the market and its purposes, and whether the market is accommodated to fit with other institutions. In this chapter, I shall argue that market fundamentalism— that is, the view that markets are sufficient to allocate everything, including caring responsibilities (cf. Ubel 2009)—ignores a number of problems with markets as tools to accomplish this end.

From an economist's standpoint, the limits of markets are twofold: markets are not good at pricing public goods, and markets cannot take into effect "externalities," that is, the costs and benefits that go beyond the transaction (Albelda, Duffy, and Folbre 2009; Folbre 2001). The social cost of neglected children, or the social good of well-raised children, for example, is not factored into the cost of child care. But markets could adjust for these problems by setting a "price" on public goods or on externalities. Environmentalists, for example, have argued that we can set a price for carbon dioxide released into the atmosphere that causes global warming in order to make the economy adjust to the cost of polluting the atmosphere.

But there are several reasons why markets still will not work to distribute care and care responsibilities well, even if it were possible to set a price on the public goods and the externalities of caring. These problems go more deeply to the starting assumptions of using markets as a means for distribution of caring responsibilities. They grow out of the nature of care itself, and out of the nature of market thinking. These are the concerns that I will take up in this chapter, considering, first, some incompatibilities between a "free market" and care, and second, that using market thinking obscures structural inequalities, which makes it impossible to allocate caring responsibilities adequately. I then consider how the use of market thinking in public education, exemplified by the "new public management" approach embedded in the No Child Left Behind legislation, illustrates these problems.

The Market as a Caring Institution

That markets are a defining quality of modernity was a thesis famously advanced by Karl Polanyi in *The Great Transformation* (2001 [1944]). Polanyi's sweeping work discussed changes in science as well as society, institutions as well as ideologies. One critical argument concerned how market relationships displaced feudal relationships in the early modern period and provided great freedom for individuals. The costs of such freedom, Polanyi argued, were some desirable features of feudal life, including a more connected type of society that was organized around different ways of sharing responsibilities. In 1977 Albert O. Hirschman published *The Passions and the Interests*, in which he described the positive effects that early advocates of capitalism saw flowing from the "one-dimensional" nature of market life. Following Hirschman's exegesis of Montesquieu, scholars identified this as the *doux commerce* thesis: commerce has the "sweet" or civilizing effect of substituting desires for goods in place of previous sensibilities of honor, pride, and so forth, which lead to frequent warfare and other forms of violence and disruption. As Adam Smith famously put it in *The Wealth of Nations* (1976 [1776]), English gentlemen were willing to surrender their private armies so that they could instead spend their monies on "a pair of diamond buckles, perhaps, or something as frivolous and useless as that" (III.iv.10; vol. 1, p. 331). As Hirschman put it, the alignment of the passions with the interests created a more peaceful social order. Insofar as care requires such a modicum of peace, the triumph of the market brought with it the conditions for greater economic development and the changing capacities of people and families to care for the young, the elderly, and the infirm. Modern forms of care would be inconceivable without a "market" that supported the creation of such institutions.

An extension of this argument is found in the work of Deirdre McCloskey (2006), who, against those who claim that capitalism reduces people to a single, amoral dimension, argues that capitalism fosters the development of virtues: "The tuition in scarcity, other-regarding, and liberal values of market society works as an ethical school" (413). She offers this list: "The bourgeois virtues, derivable from the seven virtues but viewable in business practice, might include enterprise, adaptability, imagination, optimism, integrity, prudence, thrift, trustworthiness, humor, affection, self-possession, consideration, responsibility, solicitude, decorum, patience, toleration, affability, peaceability, civility, neighborliness, obligingness, reputability, dependability, impartiality" (349–50; cf. Fourcade and Healy 2007). In this regard, McCloskey argues that capitalism's training in the bourgeois ethics is, like some accounts of an ethic of care, an appropriate virtue for living in the modern world. Far from being incompatible with an ethic of care, then, capitalism as a moral system is a cognate.

Finally, its advocates see capitalism as a necessary precondition for freedom and democracy. As Milton Friedman wrote, "Economic freedom is also an indispensable means toward the achievement of political freedom" (1962, 8). Because "empowering markets empowers people," write Marion Fourcade and Kieran Healy, "fettering the market prevents people from choosing what they really want. Consumer sovereignty is thus political freedom in another guise" (2007, 289). Insofar as democratic care is concerned to preserve and further human freedom, then, it seems compatible with the use of markets.

When people conceive of the market as providing care, they invoke two types of responsibility passes—two sides of the same coin, which fit together to lead to the view that the market wisely distributes care. On the one hand, there is the bootstrap pass. By this account, people meet their own caring needs by acting through the market. People should care for themselves or arrange for such care by creating families, buying insurance, or having enough resources to buy the care that they need on the market. On the other hand, some people do derive positive utility from helping others. For such people, there is the charity pass. There is no need to think more collectively or coercively about others' needs for care, because since everyone has the option to spend some of their money by giving it to charity, the needy can be helped. There is no need for a government, or government bureaucracy, to work this out.

Caring on the Market: Some Problems with Bootstraps and Charities

These are powerful defenses of markets, and indeed, markets do some things very well. Nevertheless, there are also a number of problems from the standpoint of care in using markets to allocate scarce goods. Care poses problems for the market that will be familiar to critics and supporters of markets alike. To think at the level of the market as a system for allocating scarce resources in which people pursue their own interests presumes that all people are capable of doing so. Like the assumptions of individual competence discussed in chapter 3 with regard to the "work ethic" individual, so too the individual who sells labor or other goods and consumes goods offered on the market is assumed to know his or her rational self-interest and to pursue it by the purchases made. An obvious problem with this view is that not every human being, at all phases of the life cycle, is capable of making such decisions. Young children, infirm individuals, some people with disabilities, and some frail elderly people, for example, cannot make such judgments. Historically, families stood in for such individuals in the market, and still the assumption was that markets made the right decisions for individuals *within* the families. This view is problematic, among other reasons, because it presumes that individuals within families can make correct judgments about the interests of others within the family (cf. Sen 1992). Perhaps this is the limiting condition for markets, a place where other institutions must join in.

Another serious problem is that the market assumes that the parties who meet to make an exchange do so from positions of relatively equal capacity. As noted in the first chapter, though, care settings are often settings of unequal power. If the person is being providing what Waerness (1984a, 1984b) called necessary care and cannot provide that care for the self, then the caregivers are in a somewhat more powerful position vis-à-vis the care receiver. Sometimes caregivers provide help that people cannot provide for themselves because the kind of knowledge or skill necessary to provide the care is not available to the person. This is true in most of health care. If the care is a kind of service, then often the care receiver can make alternative choices for caregivers, and the relative power of the caregiver is less. So something other than the amount of money being exchanged affects the quality of the exchange.

Another problem for care on the market is the way in which care is distinctive because of its intimate nature. To use the language of exchange also ignores the fact that care is highly intimate, often involving emotional attachments. In this way, care relationships are "sticky" and do not exhibit the freedom of the open market. People are not likely to throw over their care-giving spouses or assistants, for example, because they can find a cheaper model. Care will not respond only to market forces.

Another standard critique of markets is that they presume perfect information. The lack of perfect information is an especially serious concern in providing necessary and expert care. Indeed, given the vulnerabilities of people to being cheated in situations of necessary caring where imbalances of knowledge make a free, open, and rational exchange impossible, care areas have long been regulated markets. Not everyone can practice medicine, for example, or embalm a body. Licensing procedures are established by the states, which sometimes create regulations about, for example, the training of morticians. Generally, given how complicated such training is, states grant the power of licensing to associations, for example, the American Medical Association or bar associations. So in care there are no free markets. The question arises, though, what forms of regulations and restrictions should exist within the regulated care market? For example, in licensing doctors the state provides certain economic advantages to them. But the question of whether others might also be able to perform well as doctors is not open to debate or discussion. Thus, many groups do gain an economic benefit. But surely the alternative, having an absolutely free market, is not acceptable either. The question becomes, rather, whether such regulations are fair and match their purpose. But if the market is taken to be "free," then such questions never arise.

But there are two more serious problems from the perspective of a caring democracy that do not usually arise in economic conversations about the limits of markets. These are the relational qualities of human nature and the dimension of time.

The most familiar way to frame the question of relational ontology is to think about how markets respond to needs. The market sees needs as a result of individuals making decisions for themselves about the nature of their needs. When new needs emerge, some entrepreneur will see a new niche and provide some good or service to meet that need. Thus, needs are met when they arise.

From a care perspective, there are a few problems with this account. The view of human nature intrinsic to a caring democracy presumes that citizens are equal not by virtue of being declared equal, but through an elaborate social process through which they become equal. Learning the lessons of fair competition through the market (or in other ways) is a part of this process, as McCloskey rightly implies. Nevertheless, a caring democracy also requires that citizens understand their needs and wants within wider frameworks of responsibility. When scholars such as Friedman and McCloskey (and philosophers such as Robert Nozick and Ronald Dworkin) write about learning responsibility, they mean learning to take responsibility for one's own actions. Chapter 3 explored some problems with the nature of personal responsibility. Milton Friedman was unwilling to acknowledge that corporations, for example, had any "social responsibility" beyond maximizing profit, though others are willing to argue that corporations have social responsibilities and can foster responsibility in society (Lee 2008; Vives 2008; Frankental 2001). Friedman is, of course, correct: these forms of personal responsibility are vital. Nevertheless, caring requires that citizens think more broadly about other kinds of responsibility as well. If people do not understand where they come from, to whom and to what they are related, and how, then they will be incapable of making broader judgments about caring responsibilities. They will fall back into claims that "we should take care of ourselves" and ignore the ways in which this "we" who we are is the result of a confluence of circumstances as well as individual (or familial) initiative. Relying on one's bootstraps narrows, rather than broadens, one's ways of seeing and knowing about others.

Similarly, to rely upon the charity market is also problematic in meeting needs. When people decide to give charitable donations, they often donate to causes that are closest to their own interests. Thus, wealthy opera-goers are likely to give money to the opera, lower-middle-class churchgoers donate to their churches. The end result of such behavior is that wants and interests, and not necessarily needs, determine what gets met through charity (Bennett 2011; Piff et al. 2010). The existence of charity on the market does mean, then, that some caring responsibilities will be met. It does not, however, provide any reason to think that enough, or the right kinds, of charitable contributions will be made.

An atomistic, rather than a relational, conception of human nature fits best with the market, and in recent years economists and other scholars[1] have argued that scholarly study of other social institutions will improve if an essentially self-interested model of the self is used. For example, the economist Gary Becker (1976, 1991) has described the internal dynamics of family life using this model. Yet, as social theorists have noted, no real insight into actors' own senses of meaning in their activities can be learned from this model (Granovetter 1985). But does looking at the world from a self-interested perspective in the market necessarily require that people not look at themselves differently in other realms of life?

Nothing about the market says that market thinking must spread to other realms of life, but in fact the logic of the market does spread. Market fundamentalists insist that political life should follow the same logic as the market. While it is possible to argue that a different logic is necessary to make sense in other realms of life, it is becoming increasingly difficult to make this claim. Market claims now inform how one should parent, for example, with management companies offering advice to executives about how to be a better parent (Arlie Hochschild 2005). In the idea that market thinking should inform all realms of life, market fundamentalists actually share the view of Marxists, who also see the spread of a capitalist logic to all forms of life as inevitable,[2] and the spread of a "one-dimensional" human character as a quality of capitalist life (Marcuse 1964). A change like this can be controlled, and in a caring democracy such a limitation would be an important part of what democratic political institutions should do. But if there is no recognition of the insidious spread of market thinking—indeed, if it is held up as the only possible model for reasoning —then there is a great danger.

Nevertheless, there is one important vector along which the spread of market thinking poses real problems from the standpoint of care, that is, time.[3] The urgency of increased efficiency in providing care as a market commodity soon bumps into what Shahra Razavi (2007), following William Baumol (2012), calls care's "cost disease." Like Baumol's chamber music performance, no greater time efficiencies can be achieved in intimate caring, where spending time itself is a part of the activity. While some have begun to hope that robots will be able to replace some care activities (Graf, Hans, and Schraft 2004), an important aspect of care is simply spending time with another, listening to stories, observing care receivers.

Clare Stacey (2011) reports that home health aides understand that this part of their work with the elderly is vital for the clients' well-being.

Yet, as Arlie Hochschild (1997) has observed, the demands of the economy have placed care in a serious "time bind." Juliet Schor (1998, 2000) has explored why Americans work excessively and discovered that parents are so concerned with having money to spend on the "right" toys, vacations, and experiences for their children that they spend too much time working. The consumer market is highly adept at creating new wants (Lane 2000) that require more money for their satisfaction (meaning that workers must work more) and at finding new customers (very young children are now targets of marketing; Schor 2004). When looking at this situation from a perspective of care, an obvious question lurks: Isn't it counterproductive to work so hard, to spend so much time to raise money to buy things, in order to demonstrate that one cares? Wouldn't it be better to spend the time caring?

Finally, on a more philosophical level, we can raise the question of whether markets, which are organized to satisfy human wants, are the best institutions for meeting human needs, which is the basis for making judgments about care. While there are ways to translate needs into wants, it is well to remember the words of Robert E. Lane: "The market gratifies the wants of those with money, which already excludes the most miserable and impoverished individuals, and among those with money, it gratifies preferences according to the amount of money they have, not according to the urgency of different people's wants and certainly not according to needs" (1991, 497).

For many reasons, then, it seems that the market may not be the best way to provide care. The twin passes that market fundamentalists would approve, that given bootstraps and charity the market can meet caring needs, seems not to be deserved.

Structural Inequality and the Market

So far, this chapter has considered a number of ways in which markets provide an inadequate basis for allocating care and care responsibilities. On another level, there is a more serious, though less obvious, set of problems. Relying upon market thinking obscures the prospects of seeing how social structures create and perpetuate inequality. The "let the market do it" bootstrap and charity passes thus also deepen, rather than alleviate, problems of inequality.

In 1971, T. H. Julian published an article called "The Inverse Care Law" in the British medical journal *The Lancet*. Julian observed that the people with the worst health conditions received the least medical care in the United Kingdom, while those who were healthiest received the most care. Julian tied this finding to the perversity of using markets to distribute medical resources. He wrote, in defense of what was, at that time, the fairly young National Health Service:

> The availability of good medical care tends to vary inversely with the need for it in the population served. This inverse care law operates more completely where medical care is most exposed to market forces, and less so where such exposure is reduced. The market distribution of medical care is a primitive and historically outdated social form, and any return to it would further exaggerate the maldistribution of medical resources. (1971, 405)

In a recent survey of public health in the United States, a group of researchers formulated a parallel "inverse hazard law" that those who are least well-paid are most vulnerable to workplace hazards (Krieger et al. 2008). But in the past forty years, "market democracies" (as Robert Lane calls them) have experienced an ideological shift away from this understanding of markets as "primitive" in their distributional capabilities to increasing reliance on the market to distribute everything and to meet all forms of human needs in the name of freedom. The market is "flat" (cf. Friedman 2005), current thinking presumes, because individuals exercise their freedom by making their choices on the market. Compared to other ways of organizing life, in which someone else "tells" people what they want or what they should do, market life is synonymous with doing what one wishes, that is, with freedom.

Making this argument, though, requires both a partial account of freedom and an incapacity to understand how powerful social structures shape "choice." This section begins with an account of how market thinking operates to obscure social structure and power. Once this point is established, it becomes clear why the equation of choice on a market with freedom is erroneous.

I will follow an argument that I previously made to describe why "difference" is so confounding from the standpoint of moral theories of equal rights (Tronto 1993, 71–75). There, I described how Lawrence Kohlberg's theory of moral development, which rested upon the growth of thinkers from excluding others to a later stage in which they were universalist, could not take into account how those who excluded others at one time could not put themselves in those others' positions later in time. For example, having taken a racially biased position in the past, white children now saw the error of their ways. But Kohlberg's theory cannot explain how those *harmed* by the exclusionary taunts of racism should experience moral development beyond those harms. Indeed, a closer attention to the capacity of oppressed people to achieve moral virtues has shown that the condition of being oppressed often makes even seemingly simple virtues, such as the possession of hope, difficult and rare (Tessman 2000, 2005, 2009). How does this happen, and what bearing does it have on market thinking?

To continue to use this example, let us think about what moral development requires. Moral development, Kohlberg did establish, occurs over time. Kohlberg thought that as people outgrew their earlier, incomplete moral ideas, those ideas somehow disappeared. But acting or expressing those earlier moral views had an effect in the world, and may have already had deleterious effects on others. Only by returning to the past, by uncovering and renouncing those harms, can the objects of such mistaken views proceed. When Kohlberg's advanced moral thinkers could not understand why victims of racism did not stand up for themselves, they did not imagine themselves as perpetrators of the moral injuries that weakened minority members' capacities to "stand up for themselves." I called this two-step process "objectification" followed by "assimilation." First there is exclusion or some other exercise of power, then it is forgotten. Others are made different, then they are assumed to be just like the powerful.

A number of important lessons follow from this fact. We can generalize beyond moral development to other forms of development. People undergo many processes of development; they often leave behind (and do not consider the consequences of) what they did at earlier stages of development. The view that people are "born free," to take a current example of American political rhetoric, ignores the reality that people are born completely helpless and incapable of sustaining their own lives. To assert that one is free and able to make choices at birth says something absurd. Who would want to say such a thing? It actually says something very important, within this ideological construction, to oneself about oneself. It denies the fact that human infants are highly dependent. It denies that only through their relationships with others do humans become capable of making choices, and that the quality of those relationships will help or hinder one's capacities. It denies each person's vulnerability, and the centrality of caring in the formation of each person. Human autonomy is an *achievement*, not a starting premise, and it is an achievement that requires many years.[4]

There is an important type of denial that every person feels, then, in becoming adult and leaving behind being an infant and a child. But when such a pattern of denial repeats itself on a social level, it becomes deeply harmful. Individuals, as well as groups and societies, do not dwell upon the harms and incapacities of the past in order to move forward. But throughout history, we can see a similar process repeating itself. This two-step process—first, harm/exert power over others, and second, blame the powerless for their incapacity—is most effective when the first step of the process is erased. It has to be forgotten or somehow explained away.

Market thinking presumes that human societies consist of such fully formed, autonomous persons.[5] That they come to the market from somewhere else where their form was less complete is irrelevant from the standpoint of the market. That people are almost always going to come to the market, given their past life experiences, as unequal in some ways, is also irrelevant to the market.

But this point is not only, or even most importantly, about human nature. It is about time, and the place of the past in market thinking. Markets are not oriented to the past, they are oriented toward the future. Of course, future concerns affect present behavior and activity. As McCloskey observes, as a business person, one must create and maintain trust within one's circle. Market thinking can rely upon the past to learn about how to act in the present to achieve future goals. It does not look back to consider past injustices.

If the incentives to ignore past injustices are powerful, as I have suggested above, then they are even more powerful in the market. Looking beyond the formal equality of actors to make choices in the market would make a mess of the current market. Legal attempts to limit harms, for example, through tort law, allow some ways to correct for past injustices in the market, but to market fundamentalists, such intrusions in the "free market" threaten innovation. If there is a tug between reviewing past harms and encouraging future good, market thinking aims toward the future.

Among the most important forms of caring responsibilities are those that exist in close proximity, a spatial dimension, and those that exist through time, given the nature of caring and human vulnerabilities. While the market can contain these in another institution that operates along-side it, the family, market thinking itself is not good at making sense of how past (market) actions should affect current markets.

The reason that the exclusion of the past is a problem for marketing care is that care, both individually and collectively, always has a past. All individuals have been cared for in the past, and all societies, families, and institutions have cared in particular ways in the past. Indeed, much of people's perceptions about good and bad care grow out of judgments about their past care.

More importantly, many of the largest ethical questions that we currently face are about the ways in which we respond to past injustices. If we simply imagine that we are able to think about justice "from this moment forward," from the new deliberations in which we engage, then we are likely to bury or otherwise simply cover up the injustices that shape our world (cf. Walker 2006). But fixing past injustices requires more than just beginning de novo—it requires that we explore the nature of past injustices, assign responsibility for wrongful action in the past, and ameliorate the continuing effects of the injustice in whatever methods we can.

The more serious problem for markets as expressions of caring responsibilities arise from the fact that markets conceive of all interactions as between two parties making a contract with one another. This individualistic emphasis ignores the ways in which powerful consequences follow from the effects of unequal bargaining positions. When one is in a less powerful position the first time, say, an employment contract is made, one ends up with lower pay than one might otherwise have earned. Then, the next time one renegotiates, the inequality in power between the parties has not declined but may have increased, thereby weakening the bargaining power of the weaker party yet again. Multiplied over thousands of times, the end result is a structure of inequalities built into economic transactions. But the myth that each contract begins anew means that the existence of unequal bargaining power disappears each time the contract or conditions for agreement are re-determined. Relying upon, but effacing, past inequality allows this process to continue.

The end result is that the less well-off members of society become permanently less well off. But the question of responsibility cannot be addressed if every market transaction can appear to begin anew. This pattern of creating structural inequalities through past interactions and then declaring them formally irrelevant for the next transaction is one of the most important tools for neoliberal thinking. It is a sleight-of-hand that ignores past injustice by assuming that, from now on, we move forward with a clean slate.

This phenomenology of ignoring the past while benefiting from it cannot be made visible if market activity is so compartmentalized that each transaction is seen to be "free" from all others. Postcolonial writers often express rage at the kind of blindness that colonial powers have. But since the game is already rigged in their favor, it seems absurd (if not deceitful, or whining, or unjust) to such powers to look back rather than just going forward with this next transaction. The idea that past decisions and actions now affect the range of choices available, what political scientists call being "path dependent," does not apply if one presumes that every market transaction is, like every other one, an open and spontaneous bargaining between two parties. The market is, in this way, to use Thomas Friedman's term, "flat."

The erasure of the temporal dimensions of human life makes it much more difficult to discuss responsibility. Without a history, only proximity and family remain as grounds for responsibility. The enlarged sense of responsibility that emerged in chapter 2 cannot emerge under these circumstances.

There is no way to conceive of practices of care when hegemonic market thinking becomes the only way to think, when ongoing transactions and moving from the present to the future are all that matter. Given the initial starting point of humans as extremely vulnerable creatures, every person has a history of caring, whether it is a story of being well cared for or of being neglected (or more likely, some complex mixture of met and unmet needs). The problem is not only that it distorts reality and diminishes people's dignity to think that they are all guided by their given preferences or interests without recalling the relationship of these preferences and interests to their own unique pasts. The problem is also that those who have benefited from past injustice have a great incentive to forget that fact, whether they perpetrated injustice or were simply bystanders who benefited from the unjust acts of others. And those who have been so harmed cannot grasp how the world can go forward simply by ignoring or burying the past.

Social structures that neoliberals find obfuscating, such as "racism" or "sexism," are not just the actions or beliefs of individuals but are the result of patterns of actions in relationships that have had different effects on individuals within those relationships. Because those actions and relationships have had different impacts on the parties involved, they have affected their lives differently. Over time, the memories of those actions come to have different standing and significance in the lives of the people, in their future actions, and so on. Oppressors forget that they did oppressive things, while those who were oppressed still find it difficult to free themselves from the pressures of those actions. For the oppressors to say, "But we all have the same choices now," is an act of great irresponsibility. Yet, if one thinks only about the present, both the past actions and the structures of action that arose from them seem to be imaginary. Hence, we can now make more sense out of Margaret Thatcher's famous claim, "There is no such thing as society" (Casey 2009; Thatcher 1987).[6] For Thatcher, it is impossible to go beyond what is immediately before our eyes—in this case, families and individuals—to assign responsibility.

For people within a market, then, seeing only that institution before them, social structures might seem imaginary. To them, claims for justice based on past harms and unresolved responsibilities seem to be meaningless.

This discussion about how market thinking leads to an incapacity to think more deeply about the nature of caring responsibilities has been fairly abstract. It will become more clear in considering a case of using market thinking in public policy.

Marketing New Public Management

Each year *The Nation* conducts a contest and invites students to submit short articles in the style of the magazine. One of the winners in 2010 was an essay by Melissa Parnagian, who wrote about the effects of budget cuts on her high school in New Jersey. On the *Nation's* website, a reader, who did not question the accuracy of her account, chided her nonetheless: "so stop your whinning [sic] and hit the books and make enough to send your kids to private school when you are a parent instead of our crappy socialist public school system" (*The Nation* 2010). This comment sums up well a current view of American commitment to public goods such as education. Any public goods are "crappy" and "socialist." Anything that comes from the free market is good, and anybody with enough money will buy their way out of such "crappy socialist" alternatives. What explains this attitude about public schools and about public goods more generally?

One of the less widely discussed tenets of neoliberal ideology is how neoliberals view the transition from a state that has become too reliant upon the public provision of goods to a free market state. They argue,

simply, that public goods should be privatized because private entrepre-
neurs will devise new and more ingenious ways to provide public services.
The reality, as Naomi Klein explores in *The Shock Doctrine* (2007), is that
after public goods have been made private, after they are exploited for
what profit they might produce, the dregs of the public good will be re-
turned to the "public" in considerably weaker and less viable condition.
Part of what makes public goods "crappy" is that their better elements
have been carved off. Thus, with a smaller public to serve and fewer resources allocated, a downward spiral begins. Parents are advised, as the
commentator quoted above put it, to "hit the books and make enough to
send your kids to private school when you are a parent."

Many right-wing American political thinkers today start from the view
that if people no longer feel in control of their lives, the fault must lie with
the state. What they fail to appreciate is that the state is no longer the most
significant actor in shaping their lives: instead, the political economy
organized by and for large corporations and immensely wealthy people
(millions of them, but still a small percentage of the entire population)
has a more important effect. The people who organize the current political economy do not have the economic interests of everyone foremost in
their minds: they are much more interested in preserving and expanding
their own wealth (Madrick 2011; Winters 2010). And the role of the state
has been primarily to see the interests of such wealthy people, who hold
the keys to future investment and "economic growth," as paramount.[7]
Democrats have, since the New Deal, been more willing than Republicans
to constrain the activities of the wealthy and to try to pursue some redistributive economic policies. Nevertheless, both Democrats and Republicans share this view about the advantages to all of economic growth. Yet
when the market acts as the sole guide in a society, there is a pressure to
turn care into a service, and to presume that the best forms of care will be
those that are cheapest.

But since care is *not* the same thing as a standard market good, using
only market terms and values to understand its place in society distorts
its meaning. Virginia Held (2006) pointed out that the market has a legitimate scope of activity, though its scope will be circumscribed by needs
to care. My argument is different. I am not saying that the market distorts
care because care should be about feelings and the market is about rational calculation, as some have argued (cf. Nelson 1999). Nor am I saying
that it is a bad thing to use markets to provide care services. What I am
saying is this: The market is an institution that can further a variety of

ends. If, however, the market's ends are taken to be only those that fit with the neoliberal preferences for entrepreneurship, accumulation of wealth, driving prices for all goods as low as possible, then such a market will interfere with, rather than support, making just arrangements for care.

Market thinking suggests: If I can get it for you wholesale, so much the better. Paying less is good. But from the standpoint of a democratic society committed to caring well, the political question raised by using the market to distribute such goods as health care, education, and housing is the question of justice. How can a democratic society justify the unjust outcomes of unequal opportunity that arise from a market system?

Marketing Education

A thorough thinking about care and education has already consumed many books (Noddings 2002a, 2002b, 2005); in the remarks that follow I can touch upon only some of the issues involved here. But I hope that even this cursory account highlights some of the ways in which a democratic care approach allows us to see better the problems that face us than does the ideologically pure but simplistic account of personal responsibility.

Public schools have always been one of the hallmarks of equal opportunity. Children often find themselves in the same place in the social order as their parents (Bowles and Gintis 1977), but if there is a site of upward mobility in American society, it is in the schools. (Supreme Court Justice Sonia Sotomayor, who grew up in a public housing project in the Bronx, New York, is an example of this historic path.)

But public schools are also the ways in which communities sustain themselves. John Dewey's (1993) emphasis on the democratizing effects of education points to the role that schools play in a democratic society. Indeed, education can serve as a buffer against injustice. During segregation, African American schools provided care and a sense of justice to students (Siddle Walker and Snarey 2004; Siddle Walker and Tompkins 2004).

Education is one of the places where the "new public management" —that is, the increasing application of market concepts such as competition and customer satisfaction (Page 2005)—has been most thoroughly embraced. Arguing that school bureaucracies, teachers' unions, and other features of the status quo make good education impossible, a movement has swept through American education in the past twenty years to create "charter schools," standardize curricula, and reduce learning to a set of testable skills. This movement also affects current approaches to higher education in many ways. The market has become sovereign, in part because it replaces a "system" that seems no longer to work. Tests among the Organization for Economic Cooperation and Development (OECD) countries routinely show American children are at best mediocre compared to other children in such areas as reading, mathematics, and science (National Center for Education Statistics 2009). A popular television show invites contestants to answer the question, "Are You Smarter Than a Fifth Grader?" and the results are not always positive. In New York State, fewer than half of the students who graduated from high school were ready for college or a job in 2010, and in urban systems the percentage was lower, as low as 5% in Rochester (Otterman 2011). Jennifer Hochschild pointed out that prior to the 2000s, the perception was that urban public education was problematic, but not education more generally. Instead of targeted reform, though, the United States underwent a widespread reform aimed at "accountability." The term "accountability" seems to be a synonym for "responsibility," but as Debbie Epstein (1993) documented, it was conceived by conservative thinkers as a way to derail progressive educational policies in the United Kingdom, such as anti-racism education, while using a language that sounded, ostensibly, democratic and pro-student. As Hochschild writes, "School reform for accountability persists as a fascinating topic; by the usual political criteria it should not have gotten off the ground, and by the usual educational criteria it should not have met with much success" (2003a,120).

The policies adopted under the Bush administration, labeled "No Child Left Behind," used explicitly market-driven ways to think about education, including the ultimate solution for children who were receiving an inadequate or bad education: their parents were permitted to re-enroll them in another school. This legislation illustrates how neoliberals expect personal responsibility to replace or embody equal opportunity. By providing parents with "choices," neoliberals illuminate perfectly how the logic of personal responsibility masks the ways in which structural constraints can shape equal opportunity. A national testing system was created, and schools that failed to do as well as others were threatened with closure (like products that did not "sell" on the market). In addition, private companies sprang up to create charter schools, which promised to provide students with better education (though the evidence that they do so is, at best, mixed; Dean and Wolf 2010). There was no control for the differences in neighborhoods, parental background, poverty, or other factors that influence educational achievement. Schools that were already doing fairly well but did not improve were marked poorly. Nor was there any guarantee that a better school would be in the vicinity of the "failing" school. The presumption that if there is a need the market will meet it was taken as a truth. If any child fails, or is left behind, then the blame rests with the child's *parents* for failing to take advantage of "choices."

There are many problems with this approach. The one I want to point out here is about the historical situation in which public education finds itself in the twenty-first century. By focusing on the competition between school A and school B at the present moment, we fail to see that the entire system of public education has been systematically deprived of the two things it most needs for over a generation, and that the worst performance still occurs in urban public districts (Hochschild 2003b). Those two resources are outstanding teachers and sufficient resources such as books.

The 1970s brought two changes to education whose consequences cannot be understood in a market-based approach. The first is that the quality of teachers in the past was artificially inflated by an unjust caste system that allowed schools to attract great teachers at a low cost. Since the last century, when it became clear that women could be hired to teach for less than men, the teaching profession has been disproportionately female (Duffy 2011). When the only positions open to college-educated women were as teachers or housewives, the more adventurous among them chose to become teachers. Now that caste barriers have been removed, however, women who might have become teachers can become doctors, lawyers, physicists, mathematicians, or business executives.

I do not want to disparage the commitment and dedication of current teachers, but the fact is that under the caste system, there were more exceptional and outstanding teachers who were able to inspire and infuse a learnedness into public schools that is now lacking. Indeed, people who currently pursue teaching are not likely to be pioneers breaking the mold, but to be among the most conventional and traditional members of society in terms of such issues as breaking gender barriers. Teachers are now among the more conservative, not the more adventurous, members of society. (We can probably say the same thing for those who have remained in school administration.) Furthermore, the low pay that teachers receive (a legacy of a caste system) means that they are left behind in class standing compared to women who pursue careers in other professions. Injustice, then, had the unintended consequence of providing better teachers than we had any reason to expect in the past. Now, teachers are less likely to be adventurous and innovative, and they have considerably less incentive to do so, given changing ideas about what students are supposed to learn (i.e., to perform on standardized tests). Although there are now more teachers with advanced degrees (partly due to state requirements; Dee and Jacob 2010), with the exception of modest gains in mathematics, student learning has not increased since the mid-1990s and teachers now focus most of their energy on teaching reading and math (Dee and Jacob 2010; National Center for Education Statistics 2009).

The students who are now attracted to teaching as a profession are very different from the pioneering women who sought to work in an era in which middle-class, college-educated women were expected to remain at home and raise their children (Friedan 1963). Those women were pioneers who broke with social expectations. The current students attracted to education seem to be more timid. They (especially the students in elementary education) are often described as the worst students on a campus. Their test scores are lower than those entering other graduate schools. They are much less well-paid than other professionals with comparable training, and their work is viewed as less prestigious (Alcoff 2006). Arthur Levine (2006), former president of Teachers College, made the same call that many others have made in saying that the way to improve the quality of teaching is to raise teachers' salaries and prestige. But in a culture in which we think better management and competition will improve schools, there is little interest in recognizing our responsibility to pay teachers more and to attract "the best and the brightest" back to the classroom.

The second set of changes affected how schools are funded. In 1973, the U.S. Supreme Court overturned a lower court ruling that declared property taxes as the basis for state funding of education unconstitutional. The challengers had argued, in *San Antonio Independent School District v. Rodriguez* (411 U.S. 16 [1973]) that property taxes were an inherently unequal way to fund schools, since some districts were rich and others poor. In overturning that decision, the Supreme Court instead asserted that such inequalities were simply a result of factors beyond the government's reach; it is "inevitable that some localities are going to be blessed with more taxable assets than others" (at 54). As the costs of schools continued to rise and economic dislocations in the 1970s intensified, school budgets were voted down. Then, in 1978, California passed Proposition 13, which amended the state constitution to prohibit raising property taxes into the future. As if the availability of "taxable assets" did not already severely limit school budgets, this cap on taxes prevented the state schools from raising more revenue. California schools, among the most highly ranked state systems in the early 1970s, were ranked forty-seventh in 2006–7, according to Morgan-Quitno's ratings. In New Jersey, where the state Supreme Court interpreted the state constitution to require that state income tax revenues be used to equalize school costs across districts, the schools improved dramatically in quality; they are now ranked fourth, and more New Jersey students go on to pursue higher education than the graduates of any other state school system (Morgan-Quitno 2006–7)

Writing about the *Rodriguez* decision's effect on denying poor children an adequate education, J. A. Gross argued:

> The problems of education in this country and the proposed solutions are inextricably interconnected with issues of morality, justice and values. Fundamental issues of human rights, justice and morality must be addressed and resolved before any reconstruction of the educational system is attempted. What is excused as misfortune must be recognized as injustice and what has been dismissed as the status quo must be traced back to the action or inaction of the unjust. (Quoted in Strobl 2009, 951)

The "savage inequalities" (Brush and Vasupuram 2006) of the current school system cannot be addressed simply by creating market mechanisms for fostering competition among existing inadequate schools, or by creating a few good "charter schools" to serve as market models for the others (Phillips 2002). As Linda Darling-Hammond observed, there is an "enormous disparity in the provision of education offered in the United States. Unlike most countries that fund schools centrally and equally, the wealthiest U.S. public schools spend at least ten times more than the poorest schools—ranging from over $30,000 per pupil at the wealthy schools to only $3000 at the poorest. These disparities contribute to a wider achievement gap in this country than in virtually any other industrialized country in the world" (2004, 6).

Improving the quality of teachers would have another beneficial effect: it would improve the quality of education and allow schools to be less hierarchically and rigidly organized. When teachers unionized, they did so with the hope that they would therefore be able to control more of the conditions under which they work. But teachers are now so distrusted that they are monitored and checked constantly, not by seeing whether they actually inspire students and motivate them to learn, not by whether they promote understanding and curiosity in their classrooms, but based on the performance of students on standardized tests. One stunning example of school reform happened in a large urban high school in Brockton, Massachusetts, under impetus of the teacher's union (Dillon 2010). There, teachers committed themselves to improving writing throughout the curriculum, trained one another about how to accomplish this end, and produced much improvement. If we begin again from the question of what we want education to do, of what needs should be met in the schools, the results are likely to be quite different from what they are now.

What would good education look like from the perspective of a democratic caring society? First, we would begin with the purpose of education. Currently, education seems to meet the needs of "the economy" for workers (Bowles and Gintis 1977). A care approach would stress instead the need for individual development and developing the skills necessary both to care and to care about being a citizen in a democratic society.

Second, we would need to notice something peculiar about the need for education: it is a need that is often not obvious to the care receivers themselves. This is one reason why John Stanford writes that parents are an essential component of improving education: if parents do not communicate the importance of an education to their children, there is little hope that they will succeed (Stanford and Simons 1999).

Questions about class size, tailored needs, and being knowledgeable about students and their lives also need to be addressed in determining what the needs of particular students are. Teachers often feel inadequately prepared to enter the classroom; questions about the nature of authority should be addressed more clearly in training teachers. Most importantly, teachers should be evaluated not on the basis of preparing students to perform on tests, but on their students' substantive knowledge of the world, their curiosity about the world, and how well they have built a base for continued learning throughout their lives.

All of these factors can be spelled out in greater depth, of course, and with much greater intelligence. But unless we are willing to think about the responsibilities for education more broadly, the prospects improve for the next generation of Americans being the first generation to be less educated than their parents.

Critics often view calls for educational reform, and for reforming the funding for school education, as an attack on the efforts of individual parents and school districts to improve the quality of their own children. Chapter 4 considered the problem that caring well for one's own child comes at the cost of another child. But this view is wrong, because it sees greater levels of educational attainment as a threat, and thus a zero-sum game, rather than as a good for everyone. As Nancy Folbre argues, "Equality of opportunity does not imply that we should level down, imposing some strict standard of perfect equality that could easily be reached by cutting spending at all schools. It means that we should level up and spend enough on all our schools to develop fully our collective capabilities" (2001, 158).

Conclusion

This chapter has considered how the market passes of bootstraps and charity allow self-interested behavior to allocate care responsibilities. They do so, however, only by uneven processes where those with greater resources get more care. Furthermore, at the end of the day, given the way the market seems timeless, it becomes impossible to think structurally about past injustice in the face of market ideals. In these ways, the market passes undermine an underlying commitment to freedom, equality, and justice. It is possible to provide others ways to pursue caring in a democratic society. How to go forward is the task of the next and final section of this book.

PART III

Imagining Democratic Caring Practices and
Caring Democracies

6

Democratic Caring

We slowly learn that life consists of processes as well as results, and that failure may come quite as easily from ignoring the adequacy of one's method as from selfish or ignoble aims. We are thus brought to a conception of Democracy not merely as a sentiment which desires the well-being of all men, nor yet as a creed which believes in the essential dignity and equality of all men, but as that which affords a rule of living as well as a test of faith.
—Addams 1902, 6

So far this book has considered how market democracies, committed to prioritizing market values, have reached a point where they are unable to advance either the democratic goals of greater freedom, equality, and justice or the caring goals of ensuring that both care-giving and care-receiving have their proper place in society. How "we care now" misunderstands freedom as "choice" regardless of domination, perpetuates inequality, and makes it impossible to raise questions of care as issues of justice. This distortion happens in part because care is so thoroughly "backgrounded" as a critical part of human life that its role is hardly visible. And it happens in part because economic growth and production as the proper pursuit and concern of individuals, the state, and the market are so thoroughly foregrounded.

Caring is not only about the intimate and daily routines of hands-on care. Care also involves the larger structural questions of thinking about which institutions, people, and practices should be used to accomplish concrete and real caring tasks. This broad caring perspective on society differs in important ways from the perspective of a market, of individuals, or, for that matter, of most social sciences. To care well requires the recognition that care is *relational*: no judgment about whether care is good can be accomplished from a singular perspective, not that of caregivers or care receivers. In non-democratic settings, it is easy to assume that the kinds of care provided are fine by adopting the standpoint of the caregiver, or of care's patron, or somebody else. But in any form of care that is congruent with a democratic society, a democratic standard for judging the adequacy of care becomes important. "Nothing about us without us" (Charlton 2000), a rallying cry of the disability rights movement, captures this idea, and similar claims have been made since medieval re-readings of the Roman law dictum *Quod omnestangit, ab omnibus approbetur* (What touches all should be approved by all) through to contemporary theorists of democracy who similarly insist that people affected by decisions need to be included in those decisions (Gould 2004, 2008). In this way, caring in a democratic society is highly participatory, and, at the very least, depends upon honest inclusion of everyone's perspectives.[1] Thus, I claimed in chapter 1 that *democratic politics should center upon assigning responsibilities for care, and for ensuring that democratic citizens are as capable as possible of participating in this assignment of responsibilities for care.* The radical nature of this claim should now be clear. This task cannot be left to existing institutions and practices, not to families or households, systems of production and markets for consumption, nor existing government agencies and policies. Democratic citizens are all engaged in provided and need care together; this *caring with* is a political concern and one that needs to be resolved through politics.

Two forms of assigning responsibilities in democratic societies have limited the sharing of caring responsibilities. First, separations about who is competent to participate in decision-making from those who are not, such as the exclusion of women through the public/private split or of racial groups through assumptions about racial and ethnic hierarchies, limit any genuine discussion of caring roles and duties so that they only appear from the standpoint of those who have excluded others. Since those excluded "others" have historically been the people in society who do most of the care-giving, exclusion provides those who are excluding them with the advantage of receiving benefits of caring service. As Nancy Folbre put it, "Restrictions on women's rights were oppressive, but they lowered the cost of caring labor" (2001, xiv).

Second, some people have been able to exempt themselves from taking seriously the care responsibilities that all humans can assume. We have given some men free passes out of caring responsibilities because they protect and produce. We have given some middle-class women and men passes out of caring for others in the society because they engage in intensive parenting and invest so much in their own children. And we have given others, especially wealthier citizens, passes out of support for public institutions of care by allowing them to rely on the bootstrap and charity passes that arise out of the claim that the market covers and provides all of the care that is necessary.

It would be absurd to say that everyone has to share the care burdens of society equally. Such an imposition would interfere with people's liberty in unacceptable ways. It would impose a false form of equality. And, as Folbre has noted, it would probably make intimate caring relationships worse, as more of them were done out of duty. What should be shared is the duty to reflect upon the nature of care responsibilities, and the need for a generally acceptable way to allocate caring responsibilities—all of them—in a way that democratic citizens think best achieves the goals of freedom, equality, and justice.

In these next two chapters, the focus now shifts to describing two parts of the vision of a caring and democratic society. Here in chapter 6, the question to be considered is this: How can citizens care in a way that is more congruent with democratic life? That is, looking at practices and institutions, what is the nature of democratic caring? In chapter 7, the question to be addressed is: What are the goals of a caring democratic political order? This chapter proceeds by first drawing a rough sketch of what democratic caring practices entail. Then it considers some concerns about democratic caring. After those arguments, a section considers why democratic caring is better. Those ideas are then applied to how citizens can assess the adequacy of caring institutions. Finally, an argument about deepening democratic caring practices provides reasons to be optimistic about future prospects for this way of thinking.

If Caring Is Democratic Then It Must Be Inclusive

Democracy, Winston Churchill famously remarked, is the worst form of government, except for all the other forms (Rose and Mishler 1996). Yet democracy remains incomplete. The movements that produced remarkable social changes in the second half of the twentieth century—anticolonial, civil rights, feminist, queer, disability, and others—transformed the grounds of political inclusion. Yet a cursory examination of the status of the poor, people of color, women, the disabled, the colonized, and other excluded groups makes clear that these changes have not entirely succeeded. The great challenge of this new century remains how to create truly inclusive democracies.

Inclusion is not easy. Although it sounds good, there is no such thing as "simple justice." All social systems, even the most unjust, develop practices and ways of doing things that inform how people live their lives. Formal inclusion is rarely enough to undo deeply seated forms of oppression, or to change the patterns of life for those who lived under oppressive conditions. People who were part of a majority group do not even see these difficulties and struggles. To them, it simply looks as if those "others" were not as successful, not as committed, not as "good."

Feminists have offered a critique of formal forms of inclusion for over twenty years (Young 1990, 2000; Fraser 1989, 1997) and have proposed a variety of tentative solutions to this problem. Iris Marion Young (1990) in her earliest work proposed a break with formal inclusion by arguing that groups that had been excluded should be included on the basis of their group identity. Young's proposal was roundly criticized for being unworkable, and for reifying group membership (Fraser 1997). Insofar as Young's work was taken as an endorsement of "identity politics," many feminist scholars found it unsatisfying, among them Wendy Brown (1995), who argued that identity politics ran the risk of creating another form of perverse political association, the form of "wounded attachment." Others, such as Nancy Fraser (1997), proposed that adding the dimension of recognition to concerns about economic equality would help to alleviate the problem of identity politics becoming too fixed and artificial a remedy for exclusion. Others have suggested that recognition does not go far enough (Blum 1998).

From the standpoint of a democratic society that takes seriously rethinking responsibility in an expressive-collaborative morality, there may be another way to think through how formal change is not sufficient. From this standpoint, the change in legal or moral status is not a magic wand that transforms society, especially if we think of political life as the appropriate division of responsibilities. Feminists have long challenged the notion that inclusion is simply a matter of treating newcomers as if they were just like those who were there before. It is a problem because the ones added have been, among other things, constituted in important ways by their exclusion. If there is one thing that we should have learned from a generation of feminist scholarship, it is that the structural forms for devaluing some people (women and "others," including religious, linguistic, racial, ethnic, and sexual minorities) are very deep. Some call this point "Wollstonecraft's Dilemma" (Pateman 1989). One reason that feminists have insisted upon returning to a more "naturalistic" account of ethics is because these details—who one is, how one has lived one's life—are not irrelevant "facts" to bracket when one makes a moral judgment, but are at the heart of the judgment itself. Simply acknowledging that there has been sexism in the philosophical past (Tännsjö 2002) also does not dig out its roots deeply enough. Once those who have now acquired "moral status" join into "common morality," rethinking the nature of responsibilities turns out to be a much more radical project.

To take caring seriously as a kind of political concern upsets many of the starting premises of contemporary life in democratic societies. Because entrenched patterns of thought scripted care as a private matter, to include care as a public concern upsets the distinction between public and private life. Because contemporary society has historically relegated care as the concerns of women, working-class people, and racial and ethnic minorities, including care in public life forces a reconsideration of how to think about gender, race, class, and the treatment of "others." To be inclusive thus turns out to be more difficult than "add women and stir" (Bunch 1987).

The process of inclusion is also made more difficult by the emergence of neoliberal thinking. It is not surprising that this burden of greater inclusion produced a backlash. So a funny thing happened on the way to inclusion: neoliberalism. Although we are used to thinking about neoliberalism as an economic necessity of modern forms of capitalism, it is as well a *political reaction* against inclusion. Neoliberalism began in the mid-1980s in the face of the great successes of the civil rights movement and second-wave feminism. All movements for inclusion require that those who have previously held power now share it with those newly included. No wonder that people like Margaret Thatcher and Ronald Reagan were anxious to pronounce, as did Thatcher, that "there is no alternative." There was an alternative, but that alternative required a rethinking of social responsibilities that they found burdensome; hence, to those in power, there was no alternative. Following conservative economists, they argued that to make things previously private into public concerns had been disastrous as the power of the state expanded, failing to note that other institutions had, as well, usurped many of the "private" functions of the family. Indeed, they went further and advocated the return of many public concerns to the "private" sphere of the market. The reality of neoliberal practice belies the purity of this approach. But its ideological hostility to greater inclusion in public life, and its reduction of everything to the private sphere, labeling the latter as "freedom," created a worldview that persists today.

There is a logic and a reason why neoliberalism is so appealing that has to do with a desire not to move toward greater inclusion. But we have arrived at a fateful moment. As the global financial crisis continues, the people in the United States and other countries in the thrall of neoliberal policies need to decide what the future direction will be.

The first choice is to continue to follow the road of neoliberalism and its moral ideology of personal responsibility. On the one hand, it makes sense when newcomers to public life (women, people of color, poor people, migrants) make demands, neoliberals usually express the problem as an economic one: we will have to share our resources with those newcomers. On the other hand, personal responsibility as a *moral* ideology quickly runs into some serious limits. First, as a description of moral and economic life, personal responsibility does not really capture the reality of people's lives. It is, of course, possible to notice some people who are totally devoid of responsibility: they do not succeed as students, workers, parents, spouses, or friends. But even if one agrees that everyone must have some responsibility for his or her own actions, that does not lead to the magical view that if everyone only pursues their own responsibilities that everything will work out. Responsibility also requires power. Few people have much real control over their lives: they are beholden to those they work for and with, they depend upon conditions of economic growth, for example, if they want to sell their skills or goods on the market, or they depend upon the company that employs them for their job (and economic well-being) to continue. So to say that "personal responsibility" by itself will be the engine that runs how people should thrive in human societies ignores the reality that not everyone (in fact, probably no one) has the resources sufficient to operate on their own.

A second problem with personal responsibility is that it turns public provision for care into a dangerous form of care. It is not that there is no account of public care within neoliberalism, but rather that any form of private care is preferable to public care, because public care entails a harm to recipients. As noted in chapter 3, if neoliberalism presumes that everyone is capable of taking care of themselves, then by definition anyone who receives publicly provided advantages must be incapable of taking care of themselves, and indeed, must be incompetent. If they are incompetent, then it makes sense for the public to substitute its judgment for theirs. Welfare recipients, therefore, need to have their sexuality controlled by the state, which encourages them to marry (Smith 2007). State provision should remain barely adequate, lest it provoke the "moral hazard" of luring people to use more goods and services because they are available. Starting from such a framework, then, neoliberals can justify providing fewer benefits to people than their needs; to give them more (what they might see as "necessary") is harmful to them. In this way, the neoliberal state cares for the least well off by preventing them from becoming "too dependent" upon the state (Mead 2001).

The end result of a neoliberal starting point is a vicious circle by which all forms of inclusion become more difficult. All groups become more parochial. More and more public services become privatized or "crappy." People are thrown back on their own resources, but their resources are increasingly strained by the need to buy more and more of what they require on the private market. As the "rich grow richer and the poor stay poorer," there is still less trust, less equality, and for those without a lot of money, less ability to do things—that is, less freedom. Being less well off becomes a sign of one's lack of worth. The vicious circles spins more tightly: those "others" become "irresponsible" by their economic failure, and citizens become more angry, distrustful, and resentful. Politics becomes increasingly punitive. The cycle repeats. Citizens become increasingly resentful and unhappy about public life. A future lies ahead in which those who can afford it will live inside gated communities and organize their lives so that they never need to meet the people who live elsewhere. At that point, the capacity to trust those "others" becomes more remote. Democratic citizens may come to have only the equal power to loathe and fear those who are not like them. How can people think of those others as their equals? It is reminiscent of life on Bellamy's carriage, comfortable for some moments, but even the people atop the carriage are always afraid —in this case, afraid of falling and of losing their status.

Here is a different possibility. Let's take seriously the importance of care. People will have to make some transitions as caring responsibilities are debated and reallocated. It will require thinking more broadly about caring responsibilities. People who have been given a pass and have exercised privileged irresponsibility will need to step up and assume greater roles in direct and intimate caring. This is not easy. Some will object that not everyone is cut out for caring for others. Caring is often frustrating and difficult. It requires balancing competing needs, it requires sacrifice, and it is not always successful. On the other hand, care also brings joy and success. And to become more caring is to become more attentive and more capable of making judgments about responsibility. For everyone to become more caring requires the adoption of a moral framework that guards against moral dangers of acting paternalistically, which reduces other's freedom, and parochially, which makes equality more difficult to achieve (Tronto 1993).

To divide up caring responsibilities in society differently requires a shift in values away from the notion that the only things that matter are economic gains. There is an alternative: the more people share responsibilities for care publicly, the less they have to fear and the more easily they can trust others. From such positions of trust, the world becomes more open: more free, more equal, more just. Changing the way we think is hard, but the choice is real, and neoliberalism's promise is a false one. Humans can organize society so that they are not only and always in constant and vicious competition with one another.

Being Inclusive Requires Rethinking Ourselves as Care Receivers

The first step that citizens need to take, and the one that requires considerable bravery, is for each person to admit human vulnerability. *We are care receivers, all.* This is certainly true when people are infants, infirm, and frail in old age. But all people have needs, all of the time. If citizens are willing to recognize their own needs, then they can also recognize that others have needs as well. Once people recognize their own self-care, they also see how much of their time and energy are devoted to caring for themselves and others.

Once people recognize their vulnerability, they need also to reflect upon the care practices of those around them. Even people in the same family and other intimates, such as friends and neighbors, have different ideas about the best way to care. Deepen these differences across space, cultural background, and economic condition, and it becomes clear that all citizens have particular caring needs and ways of caring for themselves and others. Rethinking needs requires that citizens think differently. In the complicated roles of citizen caregiver and care receiver, citizens cannot judge one another using the false abstractions that now inform their judgments of others. Seyla Benhabib (1986) long ago criticized abstract philosophical discussion of the "generalized other" instead of the "concrete other." There is an equally serious danger, though, when citizens think they "know" about others but in fact do not. Martin Gilens's argument about why Americans hate welfare (1999), discussed in chapter 4, is an example of this problem. He discovered that Americans do not object to welfare, only to welfare for those who are "lazy." But most white Americans mistakenly believed that most recipients of welfare are African American, and that African Americans are "lazy." Hence, their racist attitudes were covered up. In light of the continued housing segregation in the lives of white Americans (more than 75 percent of whites still live in neighborhoods in which there are few people of color), there will be little opportunity on a daily basis to change people's perceived attitudes. A report based on the 2010 U.S. Census concluded, after describing the persistence of racial segregation, that despite demographic changes, "diversity is experienced very differently in the daily lives of whites, blacks, Hispanics, and Asians" (Logan and Stults 2011, 2). The demand for expressive-collaborate morality will require people to rethink many assumptions that they make in order to rethink caring responsibilities.

How will such decisions get made? "Caring with" requires the transformation of both democratic caring practices and democratic caring institutions.

Democratic Caring Practices

What would democratic caring practices require? Because people are familiar with caring for themselves and intimate others, it might seem that expanding care would not be so difficult; one need only "scale up" to care for others. But the truth is that to care for others requires knowledge about their lives. Citizens would need to spend time learning about the lives of others, and not simply accepting the views of others that they expect are true.[2] There would need to be practices that allowed people to meet beyond their homes, workplaces (where segregation also persists; see Hellerstein and Neumark 2008), and schools. To take on the task of learning about other citizens in order to understand caring responsibilities thoroughly will require, in itself, a large investment of time and energy.

Beyond this task of learning about others, or creating the conditions within which the views of others could be heard so that any expressive-collaborative process was genuinely expressive and collaborative, this book has also suggested a number of other dimensions of caring that will inform caring democratic practices. At a minimum, the following elements seem to be crucial. First, care is multidimensional, and so any democratic caring practice must make provision for this complexity. There are the four dimensions of care that Berenice Fisher and I identified (Fisher and Tronto 1990): *caring about*, or recognizing caring needs in the first place; *caring for*, or assuming responsibility for caring; *care-giving*, or the hands-on work of caring; and *care-receiving*, that is, being responsive to the ways in which the caring processes either have or have not met the initial needs. A further dimension, *caring with*, or thinking about the effects of multiple care processes on trust and respect, makes these processes more complex. In contemporary societies, these complex processes are often divided among institutions and among different ranks within institutions. Charting the flow of caring through these processes is a first step toward making them more democratic. To what extent do practices of care permit caregivers and care receivers to understand the entire process?

Furthermore, care always occurs in a context, and among the most important elements of the context Fisher and I identified is the unequal distribution of power that usually is found in care practices. Consider some simple and familiar examples: needs are defined by more powerful members of the society, rather than those who have the needs themselves. Consider, as an example, the logic of the welfare reform movement in the United States in the 1990s, where lack of proper family structure, sexual mores, and work were taken to be problems to be solved.[3] Adequate resources for care-giving can be absent after responsibilities for care are assigned, as frequently happens in public education. As disabilities advocates often point out, caring for disabled people often slips into a paternalistic discourse in which the views of the disabled people themselves are muted or muffled (Scully 2008; Beckett 2007; Silvers 1995). As many have noted, care workers are disproportionately concentrated at the bottom of the economic scale, lacking basic benefits, and many of these workers are also marginalized by race and migration status. So a democratic rethinking of caring practices would also require close attention to the dynamics of power in different caring settings. Furthermore, the chances are good that no single set of care institutions can meet the needs of everyone; flexibility and innovative policies have to be included to allow for exceptions, for people whose life experiences do not fit the usual patterns, and so forth.

Finally, expressive-collaborative processes of assigning responsibilities in the first place, before actual care-giving begins, require a rethinking of the separation of the "spiritual" and "menial" aspects of caring (Roberts 1997), a separation that all too often marginalizes those who are already most marginal in the society. No process of assigning caring responsibilities that is abstract and removed from the actual practices of caring, and that fails to explore these processes down to the level of "who is doing what caring, for whom, and why," will be adequate to instill democratic caring.

This account of how to begin to make caring practices more democratic is, of necessity, fairly abstract. This is so not only because the institutions to carry out such practices will have to evolve, but also because the aim of this book is not to impose my point of view on democratic citizens, but to spell out the ways in which such citizens can proceed.

Some Concerns about Democratic Caring

Nevertheless, some obvious and difficult questions arise that challenge the whole presumption that caring can be more democratic. Three are considered here: that since caring often happens among unequals, it cannot be democratic; that caring is dyadic and must therefore remain on an intimate and private level; and that to focus so much on caring undermines a more politically important emphasis on rights and human rights. Each objection is considered in turn.

How Can Unequal Care Be Democratic?

Care creates an obvious problem from the standpoint of democracy: many care relationships are not relationships of equality and therefore seem to be a threat to the very idea of democracy. Humans are not equal in their capacities within the society—especially those who are too young, too infirm, or too frail. Historically, democratic theorists and democratic practices solved this problem by excluding those who were "dependent" or not fully rational from being citizens. For the ancients, these exclusions extended to slaves and women. In the modern period, the struggles in democratic societies have been aimed at expanding who gets included as full citizens; propertyless and working-class men, and eventually women, were added to the franchise. In a democratic future, this problem needs to be considered.

Care is often about the needs of dependents; in having "needs," dependents are often framed as less than equal to other citizens. As scholars have shown, throughout the twentieth century notions of "dependency" shifted from the general condition of being less well off to a kind of pathology possessed by individuals. Such "dependency" makes it possible for others in the society to make judgments about the adequacy of these citizens' capacities to be citizens (Fraser and Gordon 1994).

Citizens prefer to think of themselves as autonomous, that is, as capable of making decisions for themselves. Since the eighteenth century, to be dependent and to be autonomous have been viewed as incompatible (Tronto 2010). Furthermore, the division of "autonomous" actor and "dependent" recipient operates intellectually to transform the care-receiver into "the other" (Beauvoir 1968). As Simone de Beauvoir and others have demonstrated, this process of making someone into an "other" interferes with an ability to analyze the "other's" situation, to make judgments, and to see what is going on for them. Autonomous actors, who think of themselves primarily as caregivers rather than as care receivers, are thus apt to misunderstand the nature of their own situation and to project their loathing about dependency onto care-receivers. The result is to misconstrue both care and its place in society.

Almost all discussions of care start from the perspective of the caregiver, not the care receiver. It is perhaps a necessary intellectual trend, in a society in which the lives of autonomous actors are taken as the norm for human action, that care will be discounted as an aspect of human life. Care receivers may need necessary care, but their need for care does not make them incompetent to participate in the processes by which care needs are set, met, and assessed. Indeed, care receivers are often better sources about the adequacy of care. In this way, too, care is more equal than it might appear to be solely from the standpoint of the autonomous caregiver.

Michel Foucault's late work on "care for the self" was an important break in the understanding of care as simply an act of passivity. Foucault's earlier work emphasized the ways in which social practices and capillary-like modes of power literally constitute individuals (indeed, the very notion of an "individual" or "subject"). In writing about the care of the self as an ethical category, Foucault (1997) sought to challenge the view that being cared for is necessarily a kind of passive activity. The capacity to see oneself as vulnerable is not highly valued in our culture. Until we recognize that we are "care receivers, all," there can be no change in the ways that we think about care or in the fact that it is undervalued.

Two effects follow once all actors are willing to view themselves as recipients of care. First, the view of the self as a receiver, and not only an actor, becomes normalized. This change may seem small, but it undermines completely the presumption that people are only rational actors able to compete in a marketplace, and forces us to recognize the limits of market life as the metaphor for all human actions. Second, care recipients cease to be viewed as "others." Once people can begin to make judgments about these "others" as if they were making judgments about themselves, a different social psychological process of more genuine empathy will be necessary. That people can exercise such empathy is well established, though its scope is limited. Changing our understanding of care allows the scope of empathy to be expanded. Recognizing our own vulnerability undercuts these processes.

Every day many have taken the responsibility to make certain that citizens are cared for well enough so that they can go about their daily lives. As able-bodied adults, many people can give themselves much of the basic care, and even additional care, that they need. Nonetheless, this work, too, is caring. Over the course of a lifetime, then, those who are cared for and those who give care turn out to be the same people. In trying to care, and to assign care responsibilities throughout a society, inequality is a problem that must be kept in mind, but people's constant roles as caregiver and care receiver make the prospect of thinking about care and equality less of a problem than it might at first seem to be.

Caring Involves Breaking Hierarchies: The Problem with Caring Dyads

A second objection to making care a large-scale democratic project is the assumption that care relationships are primarily dyadic, and therefore to try to think about them on a larger scale destroys the intimacy of care itself. On the one hand, such an argument misunderstands the claim for democratic caring practices as a way of understanding how care responsibilities, not actual care-giving work, will be organized in a society. But it is also worth considering some of the pitfalls of the automatic assumption that care is dyadic.

Nel Noddings (1984) famously described care as a dyad between caregiver and care receiver, and for Noddings, no care existed unless the care receiver acknowledged the care received. The problem is that, while the image of care as the babe in its mother's arms has a strong hold on the imagination, it is a distortion of care. There is no such thing as "Robinson

Crusoe" care in which one person cares for one other, and that is the end of the situation. In the first case, care receivers often try to reciprocate the care that they receive; even small infants try to return care to their caregivers (Bråten 2003). Despite our attachment to the dyadic relationship as a model of care, it is hardly ever an accurate description. Think of some cases of supposedly dyadic care: the doctor/patient relationship, the mother/child relationship, a student/teacher relationship. Doctors do not provide health care alone; they are increasingly involved in a complex set of social relationships of care. Families provide much of the health care that people receive. But other professionals, insurance companies, government agencies, hospital administrators, and so on, are also involved in care relations. To think of this as dyadic is obviously inaccurate. The same holds true with mother/child relationships. Although there is often a particularly strong bond between mothers and children, the ideological construction of this as the primary relationship of life is relatively new. Among other primates, the feminist primatologist Sarah Hrdy has discovered, infants are hardly ever left to the care of the mother alone; a complex set of "allomothers" help to raise infants (Else 2006; Henry 2006; Hrdy 1999). In centuries past in Western societies, children were sent to wet-nurses who might be some distance from their mother. The doula, described by Eva Kittay (1999), is a helper who is present in the home early in the child's life. Nursemaids, fathers, siblings, grandparents, and other adults in the family are often significant influences in children's lives. The idea that only the mother cares for a child helps to create a misimpression about the nature of care. Similarly, while students learn from teachers, they do not only learn from teachers, nor do they mainly do so dyadically. So, for example, at the college level, research suggests that if students conceive of their learning as isolated, without connection to other students, they are less likely to persist and complete college (Tinto 2000).

The dualism image is not only inaccurate, it has bad consequences. Plumwood's (1993) warning about "backgrounding" applies as well to the dualism of caregiver and care receiver. The dyad caregiver / care receiver is not simply an analytical tool. It also functions, as does the dualism reason/emotion, as a way to avoid recognizing some qualities of the caregiver and the overall relationship. Here, backgrounding obscures that caregivers too are vulnerable, needy, and sometimes incompetent. These qualities are cut out of the self and made qualities of the care receiver only. Thus, the dyadic model of care serves to heighten our sense of "dis-ease" and discomfort about asymmetries of care.

Within the framework of the dyad, the problems of asymmetries of necessary care are simply irresolvable. Even Noddings seems to notice this, stipulating that the care receiver must acknowledge the support, that is, must be grateful. But the problem with this model is that it begins to import into the very nature of care its inequality. From the standpoint of democratic societies, such inequality can serve as a justification for continuing to exclude and not think about care receivers and their close caregivers as full, participating citizens. Shortly, I consider the claim that an important part of democratic caring concerns the breaking down of hierarchical relationships. One starting point for doing so is to undermine the logic of care as dyadic. Care rarely happens between two people, only. And to create opportunities to "triangulate" care also creates opportunities to break up a relentless hierarchy of power.

Needs and Rights and Care

Another possible objection to relying upon caring practices to allocate responsibilities for caring is that it may undo an approach to providing care that is based in rights.

Care receivers have needs. They also have rights. It is important to think about both their needs and their rights. The danger is that democratizing care may lead to a competition among needs, rather than a commitment on the part of society to address all the needs that are most urgent. In recent years, conservative governments have often used rhetoric to cut back on support for public forms of care that makes such changes sound more democratic. Hence, in the United Kingdom and the United States, conservative regimes have demanded "accountability" in education (Epstein 1993) and "personalization" in caring for the elderly (Barnes 2011) while cutting resources for care. Although proponents describe these moves as "more democratic," from the standpoint of the allocating of care responsibilities they look very different. Advocates for care cannot allow such pitting of care needs against one another; this is the point at which a discourse of rights becomes vital.

Are there rights to care? Clearly there are at least three.[4] If we believe that there is good reason to take care seriously as a public value, then we will need to make three presumptions to provide such care. First, we need to presume that everyone is entitled to receive adequate care throughout their lives; we can even call this "the right to receive care." Second, there is a "right to care": everyone is entitled to participate in relationships of care

that give meaning to their lives. Third, everyone is entitled to participate
in the public process by which judgments are made about how society
should ensure these first two premises.

The first premise seems to be a restatement of a classic "social right,"
as T. H. Marshall (1981) asserted. My claims, however, require that we understand care as an ongoing social process, not as an entity that can be
granted or withheld from citizens. The model of social rights often presumes a one-sided relationship in which the state provides a concrete
benefit. Marshall himself described the model of seeing citizens as holders
of social rights (i.e., as people who make claims on the state by asserting a
right to social welfare benefits) as ultimately disempowering:

> As for social rights—the rights to welfare in the broadest sense of the
> term—they are not designed for the exercise of power at all. They re-
> flect, as I pointed out many years ago, the strong individualist element
> in mass society, but it refers to individuals as consumers, not as actors.
> There is little that consumers can do except imitate Oliver Twist and
> "ask for more," and the influence politicians can exert over the public
> by promising to give it is generally greater than the influence of citizens
> —or those who care about these things—can exercise over politicians
> by demanding it. (141)

For these reasons, it is not enough to assert any entitlement to care as
if it were a good to be distributed. Instead, we have to see care as *caring
with*, that is, as an activity in which citizens are constantly engaged. The
change advocated here is not that the state should become the provider of
such services, but that the state's role in supporting or hindering ongoing
activities of care needs to become a central part of the public debate.

The second right is critical because people's views of good care do vary
by race, class, ethnicity, religion, region, ideology, and even personality.
Thus, the notion that one model of care will work for everyone is absurd.
Asserting that every frail elderly person should be confined to a nursing
home, or that every family should take care of its own, violates the ways
in which humans vary in their abilities to give and receive care. Just as no
one should be forced to receive care of a type that they find demeaning,
neither in a good society would we insist that family members, for example, must provide care; Janet Finch (1996) calls this "a right not to care."

The third right is critical because simply to say that people will think
of "others" when they are acting in altruistic ways (Kelman 1988) is not to

say that they will genuinely reflect upon the needs of others, as opposed to imposing their own sense of those needs onto care provision. We have earlier seen how the practice of presuming that everyone's needs and desires are like one's own causes people to act in ways that perpetuate vicious circles of care. Such a posture can only be turned around through reflection upon people's real accounts of their needs. Democratic processes are required to assure that the voices of all people, not just the powerful, middle class, and so forth, are heard.

This requirement for democratic process may seem unrealistic given how unrepresentative most political institutions in the United States are (Winters 2010). While that is true, the levels at which to intervene and begin processes of democratic caring are myriad. What needs to change is a set of ideas about how democracy and care fit together. Once that task is accomplished, locations for democratic care practices will become obvious.

Democratic Caring Is Better Caring

In looking at after-school programs for children, Julie White has demonstrated that in specific care settings, those that are organized more democratically succeed more thoroughly (White 2000). The next concern of this chapter is to generalize this finding: democratic caring is not only better because it is more democratic, it is better because it provides better care.

Earlier in this book I argued that care as a concept contains within itself some "ways of thinking," some logics of care (cf. Mol 2008). But in order fully to appreciate care, any concept of it needs to be placed within a political theory, a complete "way of seeing" a society. After all, feudalism had a conception of care, as did colonialism, but those are not concepts of care that we would want to endorse. Throughout this book, I have argued that to understand care as an alternative approach to morality requires it to be understood in the context of democratic life. Only democratic institutions are capable of guaranteeing the kind of "expressive-collaborative" practices that Margaret Walker described as necessary for properly allocating responsibility in a society (cf. Card 2002); that is, only in democratic societies is "caring with" possible.

At the end of this thinking about care and democracy, we now find ourselves in the position to make an even more dramatic claim. Not only is democratic care better care, but caring forms of democratic life result in better democracies. By this account, democracy is the best form of political regime because it is the kind of political arrangement that best permits humans to care for one another, for other animals and things in the world, and for the world itself. Thus, the acceptance of democracy as the best framework within which to argue for better care is not only a result of the contextual fact that most governments in the world are democratic today. Instead, another, second-order argument explains why democracy is preferable: If people care about living in a world where people, things, and the planet can be well cared for, then they should favor democracy because democratic care is better care.

At first, this point must seem counterintuitive. Why should it be better to turn care over to a democratic majority, rather than to leave it in the hands of experts? After all, it has been extremely difficult to get majorities in existing democratic countries to agree to take action that is in the common good. Consider, as an example, the reluctance of democratic majorities to restrict their greenhouse gas emissions. Thomas Friedman (2008), the *New York Times* columnist on global affairs, writes that when he sees how easily the communist regime in China can adopt environmentally friendly policies, it makes him wish that he could be an autocrat for just a few minutes. Care has been well studied, and scholars have made excellent policy proposals for the improvement of care.[5] Why, then, would democracies care better?

Recall that the key problem with current democracies is not that they are democratic, but that they set the value of economic production higher than any other value. Were democracies to become more caring—which would, among other things, entail a greater value to caring itself—then democratic caring would come to inform all of the myriad caring practices in society. Under those conditions, not only would democracies be less corrupt, more responsive, and so forth, they would also be more caring.

First we should observe that care is better when done democratically. "Two heads are better than one," goes the saying. "Triangulation" is a more effective form of navigation and of research. The dyadic model of care is not only inaccurate, it is also normatively not a good model of care. Care, like other aspects of human life, benefits from being done by more people. While there is a limit to how large any given circle of care might expand, there are ways to try to ensure that the circles of care are wide enough to guarantee that quality care will be provided.

Second, solidarity, as a social value, creates the conditions for caring among people and for greater responsiveness to democratic values

(Schwartz 2009; Gould 2004; Sevenhuijsen 1998). Citizens who share a sense of common purpose with others are more likely to care for others, and are more likely to feel committed to other citizens by virtue of their own caring acts. Furthermore, such solidarity creates a virtuous circle: since people are more attuned to others' needs, they are likely to be better at caring for them.

Third, insofar as democratic caring flattens hierarchy, it improves the quality of caring. This argument is derived from a reading of the accounts of social capital offered by Robert Putnam and others. Putnam (1993) and his colleagues discovered in Italy that when hierarchies of authority exist, those who are beholden to higher-ups in the social structure are less likely to share information with them. The result is a social system that is unable to respond to problems, in part, because the problems are unclear. Less hierarchical authority patterns were more likely to produce shared views, and those shared views were more likely to result in social capital and wise action. This principle, though it flies in the face of the presumed rationality of bureaucratic hierarchy, is becoming more widely accepted.

Undermining hierarchy seems to improve function when it requires people to work together as a team. Consider the comparison of doctors and pilots. Robert Helmreich and his team of researchers compared how pilots and doctors are trained. They discovered that doctors are still trained more hierarchically, and are more likely to think of errors as a personal responsibility. The doctors believed that there was clear communication in, for example, operating rooms, while the nurses who were their subordinates found communication incomplete (Sexton, Thomas, and Helmreich 2000). On the other hand, after carefully studying plane crashes, the trainers of pilots realized that if members of a crew deferred to the pilot's understanding of the situation, they were often unable to correct a mistake. Once pilots were trained to recognize that crews make mistakes, that mistakes are not a sign of weakness but are natural, they were able to work within a more flattened hierarchy to resolve problems more effectively. Of course, doctors must ultimately take responsibility for exercising their medical judgment, but they do so in a situation in which errors are considered normal. After making sure that everyone else has expressed their views, they are less likely to make mistakes. When Captain Chesley Sullenberger successfully landed a jet that had lost all of its engine power in the Hudson River in 2009, people hailed him as a hero. He responded by saying that he and his crew were only following the training that they had received. After assessing the situation, the transcripts of the conversation with air traffic controllers show, he then asserted that he was in control of the plane, made his decision, and followed the established procedures.

Another example from medicine comes from the creation of "the checklist." Helmreich's team found that when doctors and nurses who worked in a neonatal intensive care unit were asked, the doctors were all sure that the level of communication among the various members of the medical staff was excellent, while the nurses saw it as poor. How could people in the same room have such different experiences? The doctors were at the top of the hierarchy and thus did not know what they did not hear. The nurses, who found themselves not speaking, had the different experience of their own hesitations to speak. Doctor Atul Gawande (2010), who frequently writes about his role as a surgeon, wanted to design a checklist that would allow surgical teams everywhere in the world to make fewer medical mistakes. Although it was devised for use everywhere, Gawande thought it would have the greatest impact in less well-resourced hospitals around the globe. Within a few weeks of using it in his own surgeries, he discovered that it prevented medical mistakes even in his own practice. From these examples, we should conclude that flattening out hierarchies provides better opportunities for teams of workers to prevent serious errors.

The examples of doctors and pilots help us to realize why lessened hierarchies, and democracies in general, are better. This is akin to the argument made by political scientist Robert Putnam and his associates in writing about "social capital." So, too, in societies where there is less fear, less hierarchy, and more cooperation, levels of trust are higher. What Waerness called "spontaneous care" (Waerness 1984a, 1984b) is more visible in countries where there are greater levels of social trust.

Caring practices can be made more democratic, and making caring practices more democratic also is likely to make them better practices of care. Institutions can also be made more caring in similar ways.

Democratic Caring Institutions

Can Institutions Care?

The family, as an institution, was the classical locus of care. As care moves from the family to other institutions, people become suspicious that the care received from more social and communal settings can be as good as the care received at home. Can institutions care well?

To begin from the family: What is it that makes family care so desirable? First, it is that care seems somewhat automatic. In fact, family care rests upon clearly understood lines of power and obligation: children and parents, spouses, aunts and uncles, and servants all know what they owe to one another. Second, care in the family is highly particularistic: each family evolves its own ways of doing certain things, and part of the pleasure in being cared for by someone in one's own family is that the family member is more likely to understand and act to accommodate those peculiarities. Third, care in the family has a clear purpose: it is taken to be an expression of love (at least since the family ceased to be primarily a unit of production, in which one's relation was also that of producers to one another).

The family was not such a paradise, perhaps, but it was the realm where caring work was done. We should not be too nostalgic for the family, however. While changes in care through the growth of public institutions correspond to the diminishment of the family as the primary institution of care, these changes are also tied to many other changes in the nature of modern life. Until professional health structures grew, for example, people expected to live and die in their homes. Until antibiotics, death was often caused by fast-moving infections as well as by long-term chronic illness. Until recently, children of all but the most privileged classes were expected not to be educated but to become workers, often at a very early age. The field, mine, or workhouse served as day care and school. Whether earlier modes of care are more desirable is not such an easy question.

Leaving aside sentimental views of the family, the challenge is: Can institutions be similarly arranged so that they provide the same elements of care that the family ideally provided? I will suggest that the same three elements can be present, but not in the same way. While the beauty of relationships in the mythic, glorified family was that they did not need discussion, they could be taken for granted; in any other institution these aspects of care need to be worked out consciously. This does not make these elements less achievable, but it does mean that they become more visible and require a deliberate, political process to enact them. These three elements are: first, a clear account of power in the care relationship and, thus a recognition of the need for a *politics* of care at every level; second, a way for care to remain *particularistic and pluralistic*; and third, for care to have clear, defined, acceptable *purposes*.

A Little Utopian Thinking

Although utopian thinking cannot be the end point for any analysis, it is often a good starting point. One place to start is to ask: What kind of care would each person wish for him- or herself? Such care would probably include some of these elements. First, we would want those who were caring for us to be happy about the fact that they were giving us care. They would find care rewarding, on both personal and, if necessary, economic grounds (either by the amount they were paid, or by some alternative means of economic provision so that they were not concerned about the "opportunity cost" of caring). Second, we would not want to be cared for according to some set model of standardization. That is, we would want care to rest upon a thick model of our own sensibilities (for example, respectful of our senses of physical modesty, propriety, spiritual life, etc.), and our real needs. Third, we would want some way to acknowledge both the pleasures and the frustrations of receiving both good and bad care, and we would want to share our judgments with people who would understand them.

As simple as these premises seem, they could entail a somewhat thick account of conditions for caring in a good society. First, no one's social opportunities or "life chances" would be constrained by gender, sexual orientation, race, or imposed creed. Such a view incorporates the wishes of the goals of inclusive citizenship and social cohesion. Second, people would be free to live with and to affiliate with others in intimate arrangements of their own choosing (at least beyond a minimal age; Marge Piercy suggested in her utopian *Woman on the Edge of Time* [1976] that children at thirteen be permitted to choose their own names and mothers). Some of the caring work in society would be organized so that intimates could share such arrangements, but other possible arrangements would also exist. Tamara Metz (2010a, 2010b) has recently called for the creation of "intimate caregiving units" to replace families. While the name is not elegant, the point she makes—that families are not the only institutions that can provide intimate care—is an accurate one. Third, all personal service work would be well paid, so that no class distinctions marked the necessity to do caring work or the privilege of receiving it (cf. Waerness 1990). Fourth, social institutions and practices would be organized so that vulnerable people, as well as able-bodied, strong, healthy, normative adults, can be accommodated. People think about the needs of others, but everyone also has the capacity to state what their own needs are (Fraser 1989). There are multiple ways to meet needs; in a good society, people would have choices about which way their needs would be met. Further, people would want the caring work that they did to have these same qualities of being rewarding, fulfilling, and well received, and they would want the chance to share their judgments and experiences with others. Finally, no one should be asked to do so much caring work that there was no space in that person's life outside of the circles of care.

Incomplete as this list is, it does make clear that it is both possible and crucial to articulate the ends of care. Along with care, other values need to be included. In democratic societies, these other values would include such concerns as freedom (understood, as discussed earlier, as freedom from domination) and genuine equality. In pluralistic democratic societies, citizens need to think about freedom and equality in ways that "engage across differences" (Hancock 2011, 22).

If it is possible to articulate what caring institutions should take as their purposes, it is also possible to assess institutions based on how well they achieve these ends. It is possible to create responsive institutions that are staffed by people who are themselves attentive, responsible, competent, and responsive.

Absent such a change in institutions, those who engage in caring often face what Nancy Folbre (2001) calls the "Nice Person's Dilemma." This nice person is someone who makes a contribution to caring for others, but whose sacrifices are never reciprocated. As a result of this treatment, the nice person ends up having been cheated, or deciding not to be "nice" in the future. That many thinkers are conceiving of care in terms of dilemmas suggests that "dilemma" captures some essential problem with the way care is organized. Sometimes the care dilemmas are intensely personal, sometimes they directly reflect larger social and political choices.

Caring Institutions: Some Practical Moral/Political Criteria

Although I usually describe attentiveness, responsibility, competence, and responsiveness as moral aspects of the ethic of caring (Tronto 1993, 1995), they—and a fifth standard, solidarity and trust—are also criteria by which we can judge care itself. The complication is that in institutions of care, there are many sets and levels of needs. This possibility of conflicting ends within institutions is a long-established problem with viewing institutions as single-purposed and single-minded. Just as all individuals have many ends, so too organizations and the individuals within them have many different ends.

Furthermore, "needs" change (cf. Fraser 1989). They change over time for particular individuals; they change as techniques of medical intervention change; they change as societies expand their sense of what should be cared for; they change as groups make new, expanded or diminished demands on the political order. The demands placed upon institutions change. As the particular individuals within the institution change, they have different needs. Workers within institutions have their own needs. Scholars have considered how elaborate are the processes by which professionals create and assess needs (Culpitt 1992). Determining needs is complicated.

The process of determining needs is one of the foremost political struggles of any account of care (cf. Fraser 1989), and the key point of democratic caring practices will be to embrace this struggle as an intrinsic part of democratic life. Needs-talk is rarely taken as seriously as rights-talk. Michael Ignatieff (1984), for example, argued against replacing rights with needs, though his argument presumes that it is easy to discern the meaning of rights in specific situations. Needs, which are much more contested and unclear conceptually, raise many questions (Reader 2007). Who should determine the needs of those who "need" care? On one level, we expect people to be able to determine their own needs. On another level, though, professional expertise may be necessary to make certain determinations of needs. Sometimes experts disagree with each other and with care receivers about how to proceed in caring. Further, sometimes professionals might have their own agendas in determining others' needs. Who then should be entrusted with such determinations? How can these different assessments of needs be resolved? Can there be "impartial observers" in these situations?

The question of trying to define and to specify "needs" is a difficult problem, both politically and philosophically. Others have tried to articulate another approach that avoids "needs" and focuses instead on "basic human capabilities." Philosophers Martha Nussbaum (Nussbaum 2000, 2004) and Amartya Sen (2009) have relied upon a notion of "basic human capabilities" in order to begin the discussion about the nature of needs and justice. Whatever approach is taken, however, a democratic practice of revisiting this question will be a key part of a democratic caring practice.

A number of feminist authors have supported some version of a "communicative ethics" to guarantee that such needs interpretations will go on well (Sevenhuijsen 1998). Nevertheless, even such a commitment is no guarantee that the process will be workable (Bickford 1996). Further, the "needs" expressed by less-advantaged people may be manipulated or distorted (Cruikshank 1994). So, the task of thinking about and reassessing needs is an ongoing and complicated process.

No caring institution in a democratic society can function well without an explicit locus for the needs-interpretation struggle—that is, without a "rhetorical space" (Code 1995), a "moral space" (Walker 1998), or a *political space* within which this essential part of caring can occur. Thus, some important criteria for investigating institutions are: How does the institution come to understand its needs? How does it negotiate needs within itself? Which needs are taken as legitimate? How are responsibilities within the organization allocated? Who actually gives the care? How is the reception and effectiveness of care work evaluated?

One danger is that all caring institutions will be marked as undemocratic because they concern dependency. In the minds of most people, care is a concern for those who are vulnerable (Goodin 1985) or dependent. In truth, all human beings require care, all the time. Some are able to care better for themselves. Some are able to command the caring labor of others as "personal service," so while they could clean up after themselves, for example, they hire others to do that work for them so that they can do something less tedious (cf. Waerness 1990). As long as the image of the "autonomous career man" (Walker 1999) continues to exist, then those who are perceived as needing care are marginalized. It is, as many have observed (Knijn and Kremer 1997), quite remarkable that this image of "man" so dominates the way that we conceive of citizens because it so obviously does not describe how humans live their lives.

Another danger for caring in a democratic society is that market-like criteria may come to inform care. Ungerson (1997) has written extensively about the problem of the commodification of care, which is usually associated with a certain degree of dissatisfaction with the way that care is provided. Here, as in the classic Marxist framework, the problem with commodification is that it is alienating. However, there is an analytical difference between providing cash within care relationships and the problem of alienation, though Ungerson is probably correct that the danger of alienation is great when money is introduced in the framework of a capitalist society. Nevertheless, it is possible to imagine a system in which alienation does not occur even though money has entered the equation. Diemut Bubeck's (1995) work describing care in terms of exploitation points to some of the ways that care is different from other commodities.

There is a greater danger, though, in thinking of care as a commodity, as purchased services, rather than as a process. Talking about care in terms of commodification begins to slip into thinking of the concomitant notion of *scarcity* (Xenos 1989). The usual view that arises from thinking of care as a commodity is to see any increase in caring time as a cut in time for another activity. If activities such as paid work can be arranged flexibly, then it may be possible to increase both care and other activities. But to do so requires flexibility, creative thinking, and going beyond the zero-sum model.

The complexity of care requires political space within which to make such decisions. Everywhere, men and women have to be willing to take on caring responsibilities and to discuss the resolution of these problems. The most pressing political discussions for us to have require us to surrender the "model of man" as a robust, autonomous, self-contained actor. But having come to some resolution about our own views of care requires the greatest courageous act of solidarity: to treat others with respect in their choices as people. Any system of care that avoids the plurality of people will probably be inadequate. Hierarchies pose a threat to care: they divide up the process of responsibility and separate it from the actual work and response to care. Thus, democratic caring will try as much as possible to flatten out hierarchies. Being interdependent does not deny people freedom, though being dependent may do so, and being inside a hierarchical order may do so as well. And once again, the demand is that everyone must be able to participate in such discussions. When we have arrived at such values, when institutions are flexible enough to have several ways to meet people's needs, when no one acts out of neglect or abuse, then we will be able to say that we live in a caring society.

These steps are not esoteric, and many engaged in care practices are already trying to accomplish some of them. In nursing homes, a growing number of institutions and scholars have begun to think about starting from a "person-centered" model for organization (Groombridge 2010). They call this the culture-change model, and it includes such ideas as allowing residents choices, creating a homelike atmosphere, building relationships among particular caregivers and residents, and empowering staff (Koren 2010).

Another example of a democratizing of caring practices occurs in the family. John Stuart Mill wrote, "The true virtue of human beings is fitness to live together as equals" (1998 [1869], 518). Political scientists have long argued that authority patterns in families are repeated in political life. Non-authoritarian families are more likely to produce citizens who are capable of dealing with the give-and-take of democratic politics (Eckstein and Gurr 1975). Supported by UNICEF, a group of social workers in Argentina have been working to democratize family structures (Di Marco 2005, 2006; Di Marco and Palomino 2004). Linda McClain (2006) made an extended argument for making American families more responsive to the concerns of living in a democratic society. She argued that if liberal governments are committed to democratic values, they must make three concerns their central "family values": fostering individual capacity for self-government, fostering equality, and fostering responsibility. As she examines recent policies that seem to be aimed at one or another of these three goals (for example, the favoring of marriage incorporated into welfare reform, as a way of fostering responsibility), many recent policies seem to run afoul of the other two goals while trying to uphold one of them. McClain insists that liberal policies toward families must promote all three goals. Adherence to *all three* of these values provides very clear guidance about which kinds of government policies toward families are acceptable and which are not.

Thus, McClain seems to share with communitarians a concern that governments foster individuals' growth and development in the family, that families are the "seedbeds of virtue." Having agreed with that position, she then insists that government policies that do not respect different sexual orientations, for example, cannot meet the test of serving as a "seedbed of virtue" because they are intolerant. McClain thus argues for a number of seemingly controversial family proposals: same-sex marriage, kinship registration, equality in sharing housework and caring duties, and comprehensive (rather than abstinence-only) sex education in schools.

Other scholars have proposed additional democratic institutions that might be used. The "citizen jury" is one such idea (Fishkin 2009; Barnes 1999, 2007). Providing procedures for citizen input, as in the participatory budgeting process adopted in Porto Alegre, Brazil, is another (see Gret and Sintomer 2005). Many similar ways of involving citizens in local, regional, national, and international political arenas can be imagined.

These examples are meant only to be illustrative. It would obviously take entire books to argue for the ways in which each part of social life can be more fully democratized through caring democratic practices. Even these quick examples demonstrate that it would be possible to arrive at arrangements that were more likely to accommodate our goals of creating just institutions that treat their members fairly, and that enhance their members' capacities to participate in the public life of democracy.

Time for Democratic Caring

One final point needs to be reiterated. At the heart of change toward democratic caring is this critical fact: care is about relationships. And relationships require, more than anything else, two things: sufficient time and proximity. Among the most important considerations in rethinking society from a caring perspective, then, is creating time and space for care.

In Italy, feminists have agitated to change the *tempi della città* (city times).[6] That official government offices are open during the hours when women have had other responsibilities that tied them to the household has meant that women have been effectively unable to take advantage of public offices or to conduct public business. The resulting movement has produced a change in opening and closing hours of government businesses so that women's lives could be more easily arranged.

We might think about how to extend the idea of "city times" so that its impact on men's and women's lives might be less disruptive to every culture and setting. Consider, for example, the fact that in the United States, elementary and high school hours do not match work schedules. The burden of arranging for children's care when they are not in school but parents are still at work falls disproportionately on women and especially women in lower classes (Heymann 2000). Surely, political force could be brought to bear to make schools, businesses, shops, and other public service schedules coincide more accurately with one another.[7] Certain configurations of time serve the interests of capitalism best, it is true. Nevertheless, as Marx argued in describing the struggle for a shorter work week, the political power of a democratic majority can outweigh capitalism's temporal imperatives.

The example of *tempi della città* demonstrates that feminists can resist thinking of time only as the product of the productive speed-up and flux of the moment. As Kerry Daly observed, "A new paradigm of time must begin with the idea that decisions about time are decisions about values. When people experience time conflicts, not only are there competing demands placed on that time, but divergent underlying values shape how the time is spent" (1996, 211). Time can be reordered around people's lives in ways that make it possible to live better. Both time and space can be reordered so that they make it easier, rather than more difficult, for care. Fiona Williams expressed this concern clearly:

> If work/life balance is actually to mean balance, then instead of paid work being the starting point and the question being how, as a society we are to fit our life around our paid work, we put it the other way round and ask: how do we fit our work around our life? Balancing these two ethics, of work and care, enables us to think about how we organise time and our environment—our space—differently. Rather than care needs being fitted in with the traditional requirements of work, we can start by asking what is important for the following areas of our lives. (2004, 77)

Around a decade ago, Deborah Stone (2000) called for a "care movement" that would relieve the pressures on families who have members who need care, the care workers who provide their care, and the people who receive care. While Stone's hoped-for social movement has not yet arisen, it is worth following Daniel Engster's (2010) advice to repeat and extend this call. All people living in democratic societies stand to gain a great deal if they think more about the care they need, and how badly organized our societies are to provide us with such care, and to allow us to provide that care to ourselves and others. Stone's call is still unanswered.

In placing a higher value on care, people would need to lessen their single-minded commitment to the individual pursuit of economic wealth. Reorganizing time and thinking about proximity and care might produce new ways of thinking about how best to live. This is not an easy process; the fears and anxieties that are part of the contemporary moment—fears about economic livelihood, safety, and the encroachment of "others"—are difficult problems that will inform any rethinking of social life. Nevertheless, putting care at the center of a system of values has the good effect of mitigating, or at least changing perceptions of, some fears. From that perspective, more difficult challenges might become easier to consider. Contemporary democracies might be able to embody "a pluralistic conception of shared citizenship" (Schwartz 2009, 178).

Bootstrapping Democratic Care

One last point about democratic caring practices and institutions deserves to be made. Because such practices and institutions reflect a fundamental change in values, they will undoubtedly begin tentatively. Nevertheless, as practices emerge in one sphere of caring, lessons that can be applied elsewhere will become more clear, just as methods for training pilots are now aiding in the training of doctors. Making care responsive to changing needs does not mean that every caring need will be met or that controversy, conflict, and disagreement will disappear. It may mean, however, that people in institutions and in public discourse about caring will become more adept at thinking about caring. Just as vicious circles reproduce themselves, so too do virtuous circles. Beginning to care better in society will likely yield new conflicts, but it will also likely yield better-cared-for citizens who will themselves become more adept at caring for others.

This chapter has explored some ways in which caring life can be made more democratic. Present experience suggests that there is much to be gained from making caring more democratic. A future in which democratic caring practices become more routine will help to replace the vicious circle of unequal privatized care with a virtuous circle in which caring becomes an expectation and the danger of falling from the top of Bellamy's carriage less of a fear.

7

Caring Democracy

With the emergence of democratic ideas during the seventeenth
and eighteenth centuries, it fell to the citizen to assume responsibility for taking care of political and social arrangements, not
only operating institutions but "cultivating" them, caring for
them, improving them, and, ultimately, defending them.
—Wolin 2008, 138

How do we do it? How do we go from a society that is primarily concerned with economic production to one that also emphasizes care? How
do we change our concepts about humans so that instead of thinking of
them as autonomous, we also recognize them as vulnerable and interdependent? How do we think about freedom as the absence of domination, about equality as the condition of equal voice, about justice as an
ongoing process of assigning and reassigning caring and other responsibilities in a framework of non-dominated inclusion? To do so, we have to
re-imagine democratic life as ongoing practices and institutions in which
all citizens are engaged. This engagement presumes that relational selves,
who need ongoing participation as both receivers and givers of care, will
be central in making judgments about responsibility.

So, metaphorically, the first thing that we need to do is to collect all of
those free passes out of taking care responsibilities seriously. No one automatically receives a pass out of caring for themselves or others because

they are involved in protection, production, or taking care of their own, or are sufficiently wealthy to lift themselves by their own bootstraps or to give to charity. Everyone, from the richest to the poorest, from the most self-reliant to the most dependent, has to sit down at the table and be involved in the renegotiation of caring responsibilities.

The starting principle with which this renegotiation must take place is this: We have got things backwards now. The key to living well, for all people, is to live a care-filled life, a life in which one is well cared for by others when one needs it, cares well for oneself, and has room to provide for the caring—for other people, animals, institutions, and ideals—that gives one's life its particular meaning. A truly free society makes people free to care. A truly equal society gives people equal chances to be well cared for, and to engage in caring relationships. A truly just society does not use the market to hide current and past injustices. The purpose of economic life is to support care, not the other way around. Production is not an end in itself, it is a means to the end of living as well as we can. And in a democratic society, this means everyone can live well, not just the few.

These simple principles are easier to state than to imagine in practice, and simpler to state than to implement. It will be no simple task to turn society around, but from this compelling vision, it is possible to begin to sketch in some dimensions of the task ahead. In order to begin this work, several avenues for concrete change are clear. We need to begin to rethink the nature of protection; to rethink the nature of production and the place of the market; to think about how to ensure that people receive the direct care that they need, often through the family but through other institutions as well; and to think about how values of caring suggest that we rethink the relationship of the market and the democratic state. To do so will also require changes in institutions and in how time is spent.

In the rest of this chapter, I explore each of these areas of change. The goal here is not to arrive at many specific policies. That task is, after all, the work of caring democratic citizens. Nor would it fit with the model of expressive-collaborative morality and politics for an author to propose all of the solutions to intractable problems that everyone must address and feel comfortable with the arrived-upon solutions. My goal is simply to suggest some of the directions of thought and action that will make an idea of caring more familiar. After all, caring responsibilities have been obscured for so long that some account of where to begin to return them to their rightful central place is useful.

Collecting the Passes

This book has argued that contemporary liberal democratic societies start from the premise, still, that care is contained in the private sphere and is of secondary concern to the state. I have argued that, given any commitment to including those who have been previously relegated to the private sphere in order to carry out caring duties, this model is no longer consistent with a commitment to democratic inclusion. Interestingly, the pattern of caring needs described here also reflects traditional gendered conceptions of care. What has counted ideologically as (dominant group) men's care—protection and production—has received public support. What has counted ideologically as women's (and oppressed men's) care —care in the family and the purchasing on the market of such care (e.g., originally such concerns as household help but later more products such as food and clothing)—has been accounted as private.

That there is now, and always has been, a public commitment to certain kinds of caring needs to be acknowledged. Furthermore, these realms of public commitment have to be expanded. The involvement of public institutions in caring goes beyond those of protection and production, and needs to go beyond the gendered, class-laden, and racialized divisions of care responsibilities that divides such responsibilities into public and private ones. Specifically, there has to be a public concern to ensure that the direct caring that could be assumed to occur in the household—that is, care for children, the infirm, and the elderly—is adequately supported in society. The public can no longer allow some, especially migrant workers of color, to bear the burdens of doing society's dirty work at exploitative rates (cf. Duffy 2011; Glenn 2010; Sarvasy and Longo 2004). It will not longer suffice to allow families and the market to bear these burdens without recognizing that these institutions are shaped by, legitimated by, and intertwined with public life and values as well.

So collecting these passes and creating political processes that will offer different ways to allocate these caring responsibilities is necessary to make democratic society inclusive. While the state in contemporary democratic societies has begun to assume these roles, it has usually been done in the name of a paternalistic principle that extends the concerns of protection and production. Rarely have democratic states expanded their caring roles with any explicit acknowledgment of the change in the nature of the state's relationship to public and private life, to women and to those marked as inferiors. But if democratic societies are to be honest about the ways in which they reconfigure care responsibilities, a commitment to inclusion, and thus a reorganizing of public and private concerns, is essential.

How will genuinely inclusive democratic societies approach the tasks of reallocating caring responsibilities? Let us consider briefly some possibilities for reworking responsibilities after the passes we have described are removed.

1. Protection without the Protection Pass

Without the protection pass, citizens can see that the military, "homeland security," police and police powers, and the prison system are caring tasks. Viewed from the standpoint of democratic care, the inadequacies of current ways of organizing these forms of protection are obvious and serious.

Historically, participation in the military was the mark of citizenship. With the advent of the volunteer army, the burden has fallen disproportionately on the less-well-to-do. If citizens actually organized this responsibility with a commitment to inclusion and equal voice, it would probably be obvious that it is not fair that some bear these burdens while others do not. Perhaps the result would be a re-implementation of a draft, or of some form of national service. It is also likely that requiring everyone who is eighteen, for example, to serve for a year in a protective caring role (such as in the military or police, in conservationist efforts, or in other police duties, such as guaranteeing protections of air or water quality or of the food supply) would also address another problem in American society, namely, the ways in which residential and occupational segregation keep people from meeting others who are not like them. While such a program is costly, it also has the advantage of directly engaging all citizens in the use of the military's power, so the military will be more accountable to a wider range of citizens.

On the other side of the protection system, to recognize prisons as a system not only for punishment but also for care would force a reconsideration of a myriad of care responsibilities. The injustices of the current system of incarceration are often mixed up with the problems of racism, violence, use of illegal drugs, inadequate opportunities for education and jobs, the desire of states to provide employment in rural areas by building prisons far away from the urban areas where most prisoners come from, and so on (Sim 2009; James 2007; Hallett 2006; Siddle Walker and Tompkins 2004). Why is the U.S. prison population so large? Why are prisoners disproportionately men of color? Why are those who find themselves in prison so poorly educated? Thinking about prisons from a care perspective would force these questions into a broader public focus.

Finally, to think differently about the place of "protection" in society will also require a rethinking of the nature and place of violence in human life. While it may be impossible to eliminate violence, there is strong evidence that when violence appears normal, it is more likely to happen. While it is true that "accidents happen," keeping loved ones out of harm's way is more difficult for those who have less space, fewer resources, and inadequate time (Frenkel 2008; Heymann 2006). Care has long been associated with nonviolence, both in Charlotte Perkins Gilman's *Herland* (1979) and in the peace practices of such care thinkers as Jane Addams (Fischer 2006; Ross-Sheriff and Swigonski 2006; Addams 1907) and Sara Ruddick (1989). If we understand violence as a type of domination, furthermore, then the commitments to equal care and freedom, and the exposure of how domination functions by making itself invisible (see chapter 5), should make it more possible for a caring democracy to address questions of violence.

2. Production without the Production Pass

In the twentieth century, having a job and contributing to economic production replaced military service as the mark of citizenship. In making this contribution to the collective good, workers (conceived of as male, though women also worked in paid employment, especially below the middle-class level) were conceived to have fulfilled their care-giving roles. This breadwinner-homemaker model of the household informed many of the social welfare policies of the twentieth century (Kilkey and Perrons 2010; Weir 2005; Pascall and Lewis 2004; Mahon 2002; Lister 2001; Knijn and Kremer 1997; Lister 1997; Ungerson 1997).

To make the claim that working is no longer sufficient for receiving a pass out of more direct forms of care, and to call into question ways in which working is a public contribution at all, raises very large questions about what citizens do and should do. There are two sides to rethinking this pass. First, is it valuable for citizens to receive this pass in the first place, and second, if there is a reallocation of care duties around this idea, what would that entail?

One of the difficult issues of the modern political economy is that it does not require so many *workers* for economic growth. In the United

States in the past decades, the economy and corporate profits have grown while workers' salaries have remained stagnant. The economy has grown while the numbers of workers employed has declined. Partly this is a result of shifting more and more manufacturing positions overseas. But throughout the global political economy there is a problem of unemployed and underemployed workers. Has capitalism succeeded to such an extent that "the wealth of nations" no longer derives from the power of labor?

But the more interesting question is this: If we think of the production responsibility as an equal responsibility of citizens, how would we allocate it? Among the many arguments for a basic income is the view that there is no longer enough "work" in the globalized political economy for everyone to earn enough to live. Perhaps it makes sense to give people a basic income; perhaps it makes sense to give people a job. But to approach this question as a systematic concern would mark a great change in the way that the political economy is now managed.

Were citizens' duties around production to be reorganized, this would also require a rethinking of other pieces of responsibility as well. For example, as we saw in chapter 3, there is much inequality currently in the ways in which the "ideal workers" rely upon others in the private sphere so that they can be ready to come to work tomorrow. Unequal benefits such as sick days, personal days, and provisions of various forms of care on the jobsite have the effect of making the production pass one of widely different value.

At the very least, it seems, rethinking the production pass from the standpoint of trying to equalize caring responsibilities would create a floor below which workers would not be permitted to fall. Higher minimum wage laws and required personal and sick days would go a long way toward making the production passes that do exist more equal (Heymann 2000).

An obvious objection to this point is that in a globalized political economy, it would be nice to provide greater benefits to workers, but if one is in competition with workers around the world, this is not possible. It is certainly true that the problems of raising the care capacities of citizens cannot be solved within one economy alone. But that argues for a greater degree of cooperation among citizens around the world in guaranteeing that basic caring needs can be met at the same time that individuals can work in the political economy. The same dangers confront families around the world that face inadequate working and living conditions (Heymann 2006).

3. Direct Care without the "Only My Own" Pass

Chapter 4 demonstrated that caring in current democratic societies often continues a vicious circle of unequal care. When the requirements of intensive mothering make it imperative that upper-middle-class and middle-class women invest many resources to make certain that their children have a competitive advantage over others, those children gain their advantage at the expense of other children. Such unequal caring has the deleterious effects not only of making some children advantaged because they are born into wealthier families, but of making it desirable for the intensive mothers to keep wages and working conditions for those who provide services as low as possible. The end result is that caring well for one status group of children requires exploiting family members of other children, who end up receiving much less care.

Ending the "only my own" pass would require rethinking the ways in which public provision of care, through schools, preschools, and day-care, might make it possible for all children to experience childhoods that taught them that they were special and able to develop their talents. Working-class parents already try to do so for their children, but they often lack the resources available to middle-class parents.

Another effect of reorganizing responsibility away from "only my own" is that it would make the "winner-take-all" society less appealing to the relatively affluent. It is already not an appealing view of society for those who are less well off. Raising the minimum wage and improving access to such basic benefits as sick days and personal days would make it more likely that all parents could help their children more. Of course, some will still be better parents than others; people have divergent views about the nature and meaning of good care. But the proper reasons for such differences should not be the parents' resources, but rather the parents' and children's hopes and aspirations.

A further effect of ending the "only my own" pass is that it would provide incentives to reevaluate some time misallocations that currently occur in care work. As noted in chapter 6, the difference between "school time" and "work time" turns out to produce difficulties for parents and children alike. Children are at greater risk in the hours after school. While it would change a long-lasting set of cultural practices, to make the school day and the work day last for the same time would have the beneficial effect of allowing parents more time to spend with their children, and children more time to learn and play in school.

Children learn to live in a diverse world by experiencing greater diversity among their peers. While residential segregation continues to affect the diversity of schools, the diversity that does exist in classrooms and in society could be more thoroughly explored in a longer school day. Alternatively, rather than lengthening the school day, the work day could be shortened. Some scholars have argued that a shorter work week would force employers to pay workers more in overtime or to hire more workers, increasing economic demand for workers (Bruzalski 2004, 147). Once again, out of such an adjustment, many positive benefits in terms of broader care for diverse individuals might result.

Similarly, if caring responsibilities for the infirm and elderly were rethought, creative solutions to the problems of overburdened caregivers could emerge. At present, the amount of time spent in caring for the elderly and infirm increases each year. While people benefit greatly from providing such care, they also often feel burdened by it. In a caring democracy, provisions would be made to permit family caregivers time to care, but also time to take off from their caring duties. While it would be an additional expense to provide for such care services, it would also generate additional jobs.

It is now clear that one key feature of any reorganization of caring responsibilities in society is that it can no longer take advantage of the unequal pay gap that has, until now, characterized most work in the care sector. From teachers to child-care workers, sanitation workers to home health aides, the current depression of economic benefits for care workers happens in part because of the market's historically low pay for these positions, in part because the work is taken to be "easy" or "low-skilled" for the women who take these positions, and in part because there is an incentive for individuals who employ such workers to pay them as little as possible. Nevertheless, "Justice for Janitors" would describe the reality that, in order for vicious circles of unequal care to become more virtuous circles of equal care, the wages and economic circumstances of the working poor would need to be substantially improved.

Furthermore, insofar as many of those who currently do this low-paid and low-status caring work are migrant workers, any real solution to the problems of care imbalances within households would also need to consider the needs and aspirations of such global care workers as well.

As long as the myth of the "she does it all" mother remains intact, some of the worst inequalities that exist in society remain invisible and no opportunity for thinking creatively about solutions to them is possible. Were there to be an expressive and collaborative process for addressing these questions, the fears that one's own children would be left behind could be assuaged and honest discussion about the needs of all children, infirm, and elderly people could realize more robust forms of care.

4. Economic Life without the "Market Is Wise" Passes of the Bootstrap and Charity

Chapter 5 offered a critique of the market mechanism as a way to distribute care. Since markets do not begin from equality, there is no reason to believe that they will produce more or less equal levels of care, nor is there any reason to think that charity will make up this difference. A more serious consequence, though, was also discussed: The assumption that the market is free and equal produces the result that, over time, injustices that cannot be redressed by the market become invisible.

As has already been clear in thinking about each of the other passes, economic inequality produces good care for some and inadequate care for others. This is not a condemnation of capitalism or markets per se, but it is a critique of markets in which no value is permitted to count except increasing the profits of companies and individuals. Market mechanisms can be useful in distributing care. Given equal starting points, using a market mechanism to distribute some types of health care, provision for the elderly, or child care is a good idea, since there is a plurality of views about the proper forms for such care. What markets do best is to make choice available. But such choices have to be constrained by the needs of a democratic society. If the choices of some are made only under conditions of domination, then their choices are not free. Using policies such as taxation and subsidies, it would be possible to allow care markets to flourish that would provide variety in forms of care without permitting some to have such superior care and others such inferior care.

In order for a market to be regulated in such a way, though, there would also need to be political reform of a large magnitude. Who cares about the market, at present, except those who stand to benefit from its operations? If the market is directed only by those who seek to maximize their own profit, they have few incentives to put controls in place. Thus, a caring democracy would also need to create mechanisms whereby citizens without personal interests in the regulation of markets would become involved in such regulation. Financing campaigns out of funds that cannot be traced back to particular donors, for example, might make it less likely

for candidates and public officials to accept the views of particular corporations as the wisest public policy (Ackerman and Ayres 2006).

One final issue needs to be considered here. The argument made here
flies in the face of neoliberal ideology, not only on the terms of defining
freedom and democracy as market choice, but in the paean to the globalization of the political economy. For neoliberals, the capacity of the economic order to transcend the state is one of the ways in which it makes
us free. But as other scholars have noted, especially those writing about
"global cities" (Sassen 2001), the advent of globalization produces some
new opportunities for wealth, but also a demand for many low-paying,
low-skilled, undesirable jobs. The Australian scholar Ghassan Hage has
put the point in this provocative way:

> The global/transcendental corporation needs the state, but does not
> need the nation. National and sub-national (such as state or provincial)
> governments all over the world are transformed from being primarily
> the managers of a national society to being the managers of the aesthet-
> ics of investment space. Among the many questions that guide govern-
> ment policy, one becomes increasingly paramount: how are we to make
> ourselves *attractive* enough to entice this transcendental capital hover-
> ing above us to land in our nation?" (2003, 19)

Hage's point, that in a neoliberal, globalized economy, citizens have
to make themselves attractive to capital, captures the ways in which
neoliberal globalization has its ends and means backwards. The goal of
economic life is not for citizens to comply with capital, but for capital to
provide for the needs of people. If states compete to be attractive to capital, then people end up losing the world over. It is not clear that any one
state can "stand up" to global capital; indeed, economic conditions in the
past decade suggest the opposite. But if any states have the leverage to
try to turn this situation around, it has to be those states where capital
feels rather at home. Making capital caring will not happen until citizens
begin to demand it. Even then, it is not clear that it will happen. But it is
certainly so that unless such demands are made, they can never be met.

Whether or not particular policy recommendations above are worthy
of adoption, it is clear now that making caring a central value in democratic life will require a rethinking of many existing social institutions,
political institutions, and practices. Not only will money need to be redis-
tributed and the relationship of work and care rethought, there will also

be a need to reconsider how citizens spend their time. The end result of such rethinking, though, will be greater levels of equality, freedom, and justice, and therefore a more democratic society.

What Will Caring Democratic Citizens Do?

So, let's take seriously the idea that democratic citizens care. What is it that they do, precisely, while engaged in practices of caring with? In the first instance, they promote care. This means that they try to find ways to value care work in society. One way to accomplish this end is to use the market incentives that exist to convince more people to enter care work. Caring democratic citizens would support higher wages and salaries for necessary care workers.

In a recent book about the care workforce, Claire Cameron and Peter Moss (2007) describe their views of how to improve care work and to attract more men to it. Their solutions, though, include creating more managerial care work and reducing the amount of "low-skill" care work. While their logic matches perfectly the current logic of the market, they miss entirely that much of the care work that is done through the market is, by its very nature, "low skill" if we use current economic measures. Care-giving is irreducibly personal. Nonetheless, care workers, like everyone else, can benefit from better training and education, and in a caring society, not only would workers be better paid, they would also be better trained at the expense of their companies. More importantly, though, care workers would have, as part of their jobs, the opportunities necessary to reflect upon their practices as caregivers. Home health aides in the Netherlands, for example, used to have a part of their work week set aside for them to meet, discuss their work, compare notes, and decompress. Ray Oldenburg (1989) has argued that everyone needs a "third place," separate from work and home, where they can make meaning in their lives; in a democratic society, we might use the market and regulation of work to try to ensure that care workers have such options.

Finally, those concerned with care would notice how the market provides unequal access now to the benefits of support for people's private caring. As a result, they would provide family-friendly workforce policies so that family members can do much of the care work required by children, adolescents, infirm people, and the elderly, as well as the care work that they require for themselves.

In the second instance, citizens promote *democratic* forms of care. The basic keys to making care practices more democratic will require that people think about the democratic ends of their caring practices. To this end, for example, people should think about the diversity of caring needs and practices and try to create social institutions congruent with that diversity. Here again, the market is an aid. One of the qualities of the market is that it does produce new goods to meet newly perceived demands. Not everyone wishes to be cared for in the same way. Using markets to provide a myriad of ways, for example, to organize care for the elderly, will make it more likely that everyone finds a kind of care that is suitable to him or her.

Third, democratic citizens care enough about care to organize and to act on their commitments to freedom, equality, and justice. Heroic acts of care occur everyday all over the globe. Here is one remarkable case: In April 2008, dockworkers in Durban, South Africa, refused to unload cargo from an approaching Chinese ship. The ship carried ammunition —seventy-seven tons—for the government of Zimbabwe, described by Chinese Foreign Ministry spokesperson Jiang Yu as "perfectly normal trade in military goods between China and Zimbabwe." Given the unwillingness of the Mugabe government to release weeks-old election results, though, the labor federation and dockworkers in South Africa did not see this cargo as simply a part of international trade, but as a deliberate threat to the human rights of neighboring Zimbabweans. Despite Chinese appeals not to "politicize" this normal trade, these dockworkers and, later, other dockworkers supported by their governments throughout East Africa, refused to unload the ship. The *An Yue Jiang* carried the cargo back to China (Baldauf and Ford 2008; Dugger 2008). The solidarity with Zimbabweans that these dockworkers acted upon requires the existence of knowledge about the circumstances of others, a willingness to act, and the capacity to act without doing too much harm to oneself. If such acts are praiseworthy, then in a caring democracy citizens would engage in such actions themselves. Furthermore, they would seek to organize their own polity, and the world, so that such actions become more possible. The capacity of workers and citizens to organize in their own best interests, and to understand the centrality of care within those interests, will make the world a considerably safer and more caring place.

A final point needs to be made: the process of evaluating how well society meets its caring responsibilities is not a one-time decision. As a reiterative process in which citizens will need to monitor and to revisit their decisions, we can expect that, just as people become more adept at caring once they have become attentive to needs, citizens will become more adept in thinking about the consequences of their collective actions and decisions. Because "government" will be closer to the kinds of issues that motivate and concern real citizens every day, the gap between government and citizens will diminish. As citizens with different views struggle to express themselves, no one will be the winner. As politics comes closer to the bone, as the stakes become more clear, citizens will be able to appreciate their interdependence at the same time that they pursue their own interests. In such a setting, it is possible that citizens will become, as Aristotle once described them, those who rule and are ruled in turn, and, as a result, will be moderate and thoughtful about the effects that their actions have on others.

Conclusion

I began this book by arguing, perhaps counter-intuitively, that the care deficit and the democratic deficit were two sides of the same coin. What I hope is now more clear is my claim that by turning in this deficient coin and taking instead one that begins with adequate levels of care, it will be possible to arrive at more adequate levels of democratic participation and life.

This is a real choice, perhaps the most important choice that contemporary societies face. Up until now, as Robert Lane has observed, market democracies have been able to generate a great deal of economic wealth, which has produced abundance. But Lane's careful reading of the signs of human satisfaction show that citizens in industrialized countries have now reached a point where future economic gain does not produce more happiness, and that what humans crave instead is what he calls "companionship," and what I have called here "care": that is, an understanding of the irreducibly relational nature of human existence. As Lane warned,

[T]he belief that more money and goods will make us happy is a product of cultural lag. Like other successful societies, market democracies must, by the logic of their own success, continue to emphasize the themes that have brought them to their current eminent positions. In these circumstances, individuals are not, in any practical sense, free to go against the culture that nurtures them. . . . Market economies present the kind of learning situation familiar to all learning theorists: the immediate rewards (reinforcements) of more income are persuasive, even captivating, so much so that they discourage a peek over the wall of the maze to see what else is there. (2000, 60).

What we see if we peek over the wall is the possibility of a world in which our capacities to care for ourselves and others will increase only if we have the courage to admit that we need, and will benefit from, recognizing the large web of caring relationships within which our lives gain meaning.

There is a way to turn our world around. It requires us to recommit to caring for ourselves and others by accepting and rethinking our caring responsibilities and providing sufficient resources for care. If we are able to do this, then we will be able to enhance levels of trust, reduce levels of inequality, and provide real freedom for all. In such a society, we would have to conclude, with Giambattista Vico (1990 [1709], 67): "What is justice? It is the constant care for the common good."

NOTES

NOTES TO THE INTRODUCTION

1. It is difficult to know if Bush was being sincere or cynical in this call for an "ownership society" at a time when economic inequality had grown to pre–New Deal levels. Drawing upon the Federal Reserve Bank's Survey of Consumer Finances data, Zhu Xiao Di (2007) pointed out that "in 2004, the top quartile of the household net wealth distribution held the lion's share—87 percent (or $43. 6 trillion) while the bottom quartile of households had nothing. The upper and lower middle quartiles combined held $6. 5 trillion, or 13 percent of total household net wealth."
2. The idea that care can be cultivated will be discussed in Chapter 1. See also Mann 2010; Ruddick 1989.

NOTES TO CHAPTER 1

1. One reason why the public/private split seemed to be an important target of early feminists was that it not only created the divide that kept women out of political life, but also provided a rationale for that division: someone had to "take care" at home. In dividing up the realms of life, thinkers from Aristotle through Rousseau justified this strict separation in the ways that they characterized the two realms differently.
2. Within feminist theory, there was an early discussion about whether "maternal thinking" should play a role in public life. While some drew analogies between feminine thinking and appropriate political behavior—see, for example, Jean Elshtain in her essay "Antigone's Daughters" (1982)—others argued that since politics was a distinctive realm of political life, it required a different set of values, rationalities, and practices (see, e.g., Dietz 1985). While for some readers, the compelling arguments against Elshtain's position seemed to make any political argument for care a nonstarter, later thinkers showed how one could take Dietz's critique seriously and still argue for care's role in politics. For a good account of the development of this discussion, see Hankivsky 2004.
3. See, among others, Raghuram, Madge, and Noxolo 2009; M. Robinson 2007; Sander-Staudt 2006; Di Marco 2005; Paperman and Laugier 2005; Engster 2004, 2005, 2007; Gould 2004; Hankivsky 2004, 2006; Verkerk et al. 2004; Gornick and Meyers 2003; Lareau 2003; Kittay and Feder 2002;

Hondagneu-Sotelo 2001; Cancian and Oliker 2000; Glenn 2000; Koziak 2000; Meyer 2000; Stone 2000; Harrington 1999; Kittay 1999; Moore 1999; F. Robinson 1999; Verkerk 1999; Koehn 1998; Koggel 1998; Sevenhuijsen 1998; Knijn and Kremer 1997; Clement 1996; Schwarzenbach 1996; Bubeck 1995; Van Parijs 1995; Folbre 1994, 2001; Glenn, Chang, and Forcey 1994; Held 1993, 1995, 2006; Larrabee 1993; Manning 1992; Romero 1992; Sarvasy 1992; Collins 1990; Hochschild 1989; Ruddick 1989; Cannon 1988; Tronto 1987, 1993, 1995, 2001, 2006; Noddings 1984, 2002b; Gilligan 1982.

4. One prominent account of contemporary democratic theory retells the old public/private split in terms of various forms of recognition (Honneth 1996). But recognition is not a solution to problems of inequality; it is simply an attempt after the fact to mitigate such inequality.

5. Those who have not followed the debate closely may be surprised that I have not referenced the care-justice debate and that I am using the language of justice to discuss public care. Does that mean that justice "won" that debate?

   There are two responses to that question. First, care theorists no longer argue that there is no need for a concept of justice that also informs care practices (see, e.g., Engster 2007; Noddings 2002b; Held 1995, 1996, 2006). So-called justice theorists, on the other hand, have not been as ecumenical in observing that there is a realm of care whose goods need also to be considered in any form of social justice.

   Second, some care theorists and others argue that the critical issue between care theory and justice theory is now more a methodological one: no one discusses care from the standpoint of ideal theory, and there are now more theorists of justice who work from non-ideal theory and are more likely to include elements of care. But for some care theorists, including me, the distinction goes further still, to a different ontology and epistemology. To view care as part of the "relational revolution" is to move it further away from standard theories of justice, which start from the premise of competing separate parties. The claims made about the nature of a feminist democratic ethic of care later in this chapter spell out these differences.

6. As Anita Allen succinctly put it: "Modes of privacy and private choice make us all—male and female—morally and psychologically more fit for responsible social participation" (2003, 39).

7. See, among others, Vazquez-Arroyo 2008; Brown 2005; Harvey 2005.

NOTES TO CHAPTER 2

1. Rights to care are considered in chapter 6.

2. Ethan J. Leib (2006) suggests "four central grounds" of responsibility: what an agent causes, what she chooses, what she identifies with, what sort of character she has. Reader's (2007) account might fall into category three, but not all of Reader's identifications are voluntary. Or, consider William

Rowe's view: "There are logical connections among the three concepts: moral responsibility, agent-causation, and freedom. The logical connections are centered in the concept of a person's actions. If you are morally responsible for your action then you must have played a role in causing your action and the action must have been done freely. I take this claim to be widely accepted, if not self-evident" (Rowe 1991, 237).

3. One example she uses is of a stranger who falls right in front of another —presence creates a relationship. Now, whether presence does create a relationship in this situation is actually a *political question*, too. In places where presence on the street marks being a member of a community, the resolution of this point might be different than those in which the "street" is an expected site of danger.

4. For example, liberals often place confidence in an independent judiciary to interpret laws so that "the rule of law" and appropriate legal protections are in place (see, e.g., Dworkin 2000; Nussbaum 2000, 2004, 2007).

5. Ruth Groenhout (2004) has also recognized in a somewhat different way that the moral quality of responsibility is, in some ways, the most public quality of care. Groenhout does not use the language of responsibility, but her description of "finitude and interdependence" as elements of care that determine "all those who are capable of responsible action" (46–47) is parallel..

6. See also Adam Hochschild 2005.

7. Peter French (1992) described a different "Responsibility Barter Game." I am indebted to Walker (2007, 101) for this reference.

8. Charles Mills writes in *The Racial Contract* (1997) about an old African American saying, "When white people say 'justice,' they mean 'just us.'"

NOTES TO CHAPTER 3

1. On intersectionality, see, among others: Duffy 2011; Mattis et al. 2008; Hancock 2007, 2011; Simien 2007; White 2007; Weldon 2006; Collins 2005; McCall 2005; Hankivsky 2004; Roberts 1997; Glenn 1992, 2000.

2. Some critics have read my claim in earlier work that caring is a concern that goes beyond "women's morality" as an incapacity to understand that there is a "linkage between caring and women." As I argue in this chapter, this linkage is more complex. Women still do most of the work that people in contemporary Western societies label as care. Yet men care, and the intersections of race/ethnicity and class influence how men and women care. Men care, though their practices are hardly ever labeled as such, and understandings about the social categories of "care" change with men's changing roles. For one such critic, see Williams (2000, 197f). My position is actually closer to Williams's, and I draw upon her account of domesticity later in this chapter.

3. Consider, for a moment, the class dynamic at work in *Ma Vie en Rose*. Ludovic's father is fired from his upper-middle-class job because the son is

an embarrassment. It seems a disaster for the family; they lose their income, status, and even their house. When they move to a working-class neighborhood, the neighbors turn out to be much more accepting of Ludovic; that's just the way he is. The film is thus not only about a boy who imagines himself in pink, but of the differential policing of gender across class lines. Perhaps boys who like pink will not find this an accurate account of the relationship between gender and the class dynamic, but the film shows how class and conceptions of masculinity cannot be separated.

4. To quote R. W. Connell: "Hegemonic masculinity can be defined as the configuration of gender practice which embodies the currently accepted answer to the problem of the legitimacy of patriarchy, which guarantees (or is taken to guarantee) the dominant position of men and the subordination of women" (2005, 77). Connell also emphasizes the importance of understanding different types of masculinities and, more importantly, the relationship among them (37). She mentions, as an example: "Black sports stars become exemplars of masculine toughness; while the fantasy figure of the black rapist plays an important role in sexual politics among whites, a role much exploited by right-wing politics in the United States. Conversely, hegemonic masculinity among whites sustains the institutional oppression and physical terror that have framed the making of masculinities in black communities" (80). On the status of black males, see also bell hooks: "Sadly, the real truth, which is a taboo to speak, is that this is a culture that does not love black males, that they are not loved by white men, white women, black women, or girls and boys. And that especially most black men do not love themselves. How could they, how could they be expected to love surrounded by so much envy, desire, hate? Black males in the culture of imperialist white supremacist capitalist patriarchy are feared but they are not loved. Of course part of the brainwashing that takes place in the cultural domination is the confusion of the two. Thriving on sadomasochistic bonds, cultures of domination make desire for that which is despised take on the appearance of care, of love. If black males were loved they could hope for more than a life locked down, caged, confined; they could imagine themselves beyond containment" (2004, ix).

5. In identifying the protection and production passes, I do not mean to suggest that there are no other forms of passes out of caring responsibilities that men disproportionately receive. In some religious communities, men serving as religious leaders receive such passes out of daily caring work so that they can attend to the spiritual needs of others (a different kind of care); in other religious communities (e.g., a monastery), sharing all caring duties is a part of the religious practice. Once again, the account here is not meant to be definitive or inclusive, but rather illustrative of the way in which thinking about

caring responsibilities allows new insights into inequality and constraints on freedom in democratic societies.

6. This passage would read differently if the crime under discussion were rape rather than robbery.

7. For a parallel argument about the recipient of welfare assistance, see Barbara Nelson (1986), who distinguished mother's aid grants from workman's compensation grants.

8. It is important to recall that the ideological construction of separate spheres, in which women were only at work nurturing their domestic homes, never matched the reality of most migrants, women of color, and working-class women. Indeed, such women often worked away from their own families providing what Mignon Duffy called "nonnurturant care"—clean clothing and homes, edible food, and so on—for those in the middle-class women's homes, constructing their domestic worlds. See Duffy 2011.

9. The legal scholar Joan Williams (2000) has called this person the "ideal worker."

10. For example, after women's suffrage was achieved in the United States, a struggle continued until 1934 for a woman's citizenship status not to be affected by marriage. See Bredbenner 1998.

11. There is a huge and burgeoning literature on this topic of citizenship. See, among others, the journal *Citizenship Studies*, launched in 1997; and Lister 1997; Turner 1997; Vogel 1994.

12. For some early discussions of public/private distinctions, see, e.g., Pateman 1988; Elshtain 1981; Okin 1979. This category remains fundamental to feminist readings of political theory until the present.

13. This is one reason why the "opt-out" revolution and other discussions, primarily among upper-middle-class women, about the need for care givers and women who choose to assume that role distract our attention from the real debate in care. The real debate is not about whether women should have the "choice" to become stay-at-home mothers. The real choice is to resist a social structure that creates these alternatives in the first place.

14. Here I draw upon the work I did with my colleague, Stephen Leonard (Leonard and Tronto 2007).

NOTES TO CHAPTER 4

1. Heymann's example that government agencies have been slow to respond to the different temporal needs of citizens who engage in care is a powerful one. In Italy, feminists have worked to reform local governments so that *tempi della città* (urban time policies) are sensitive to the needs of care; see Mareggi 2002. This topic is discussed again in chapters 6 and 7.

2. Arlie Hochschild (2005) has called this phenomenon "the empathy squeeze."

3. Incidentally, as Shapiro notes, Adam Smith (1981) had noted a similar
   tendency and worried about its consequences for republican virtues in *The
   Theory of Moral Sentiments.*
4. I prefer not to use the language of "global care chain" because this language
   restricts and naturalizes our views of the women and men in the "chain" as
   mothers.
5. It would be possible to create a long list of examples of such marking. Consider, for example, the stigma among American teenagers in working with
   food (D. Johnson 2001). This pattern of marking and its consequences may
   be more severe for the least qualified care workers, but it also affects doctors
   and nurses. One in six British health-care workers reported being bullied,
   especially by immediate supervisors, but among ethnic minorities the number increased to three in ten (International Centre for Human Resources in
   Nursing 2008).

NOTES TO CHAPTER 5

1. The classic critique of such approaches in political science is Green and
   Shapiro 1996.
2. "The bourgeoisie, historically, has played a most revolutionary part. . . . The
   bourgeoisie, wherever it has got the upper hand, has put an end to all feudal,
   patriarchal, idyllic relations. It has pitilessly torn asunder the motley feudal
   ties that bound man to his 'natural superiors,' and has left no other nexus
   between people than naked self-interest, than callous 'cash payment.' It has
   drowned out the most heavenly ecstasies of religious fervor, of chivalrous
   enthusiasm, of philistine sentimentalism, in the icy water of egotistical calculation. It has resolved personal worth into exchange value, and in place of the
   numberless indefeasible chartered freedoms, has set up that single, unconscionable freedom—Free Trade." Marx and Engels, *The Communist Manifesto,*
   in Tucker 1977, 337.
3. Feminist scholars have explored the dimensions of this topic; see, among
   others, Folbre and Bittman 2004; Bittman et al. 2003; Tronto 2003; Phipps,
   Burton, and Osberg 2001; Hochschild 1997, 2005; Daly 1996; Adam 1995;
   Bonfiglioli 1990; Kristeva 1982).
4. This more relational account of development also helps us to make sense out
   of the "wounded attachments" associated with identity politics (Brown 1995).
   If people think of an "identity" as a thing, then they are likely to miss the loci
   of responsibility for its formation and what is needed to undo its harms.
5. Market thinking may so assume, though market practice does not. Juliet
   Schor (2004) ha shown that infants can be drawn to the market, and the
   existence of child labor, from the nineteenth century until today, shows that
   children's choice to join the workforce happens before their maturity. See,
   e.g., Bales 2007.

6. Here is the longer quotation: "Who is society? There is no such thing! There are individual men and women and there are families and no government can do anything except through people and people look to themselves first. . . . If children have a problem, it is society that is at fault. There is no such thing as society." Corey Robin (2011), in his blog, points out that in returning to the *family*, Thatcher reveals that her neoliberal market politics rest upon a hierarchical institution. Even if other neoliberals have a different view of family, Thatcher's is clearly one about families that teach children personal responsibility. I am grateful to Robin for this insight into this famous passage.

7. "Struggles around the wages-share and state mechanisms of distribution have been conceived within an economic discourse that privileges a centered conception of the economic totality. One key flow of surplus value, that which is ultimately distributed toward increasing the stock of productive capital . . . is privileged with greater influence over economic futures than others" (Gibson-Graham 1996, 180).

NOTES TO CHAPTER 6

1. Hans Agné (2006) argues that the condition "nothing about us without us," i.e., full participation, is too demanding and unrealistic. This critique is an important one. The suggestion to use empirical evidence as an alternative is not quite so clear cut. How can one guarantee that the evidence collected represents the complexity of the relationships considered, and that bias has not entered into these data?

2. This notion is parallel in some ways with Nancy Hirschmann's (2002) view of equality within her feminist theory of freedom; her account of equality also requires that the particular context of people's lives be a part of the ongoing judgments about freedom and equality. See the discussion above in Chapter 3.

3. There is a voluminous literature on this subject; see, among others, Pulkingham, Fuller, and Kershaw 2010; Monnat and Bunyan 2008; Smith 2007; McCluskey 2003; Weaver 2000; Seccombe 1999; Gault and Hartmann 1998; Mink 1998.

4. For a different and useful account of the nature of caring rights, see Kershaw 2005.

5. This list of scholars who have proposed thoughtful schemes for care giving is immense; consider only a few: Stacey 2011; Engster 2007; Hankivsky 2004; Eriksen 2003; Gornick and Meyers 2003; Folbre 2001; Goodin 2001; Gerstel 2000; White 2000; J. Williams 2000; Kittay 1999; Uttal 1999, 2006; F. Williams 1999, 2001; Sevenhuijsen 1998, 2000, 2003; Fineman 1995.

6. I am indebted to Christel Eckart, Universität Gesamthochschule Kassel, for introducing me to this concept and to the work of Sandra Bonfiglioli. For the theoretical work behind the reconsideration of time in Italy, see Bonfiglioli 1990.

7. Furthermore, the brunt of such incongruities are borne by the less well off. Lower-income people are less likely to have jobs that provide them with time flexibility, paid vacation, and sick or personal days. See Heymann 2000, chaps. 2–3).

BIBLIOGRAPHY

Ackerman, Bruce A., and Ian Ayres. 2006. *Voting with Dollars: A Paradigm for Campaign Finance*. New Haven: Yale University Press.

Adam, Barbara. 1995. *Timewatch: The Social Analysis of Time*. Cambridge, UK: Polity.

Addams, Jane. 1902. *Democracy and Social Ethics*. New York: Macmillan.

———. 1907. *Newer Ideals of Peace*. New York: Macmillan.

Agné, Hans. 2006. "A Dogma of Democratic Theory and Globalization: Why Politics Need Not Include Everyone It Affects." *European Journal of International Relations* 12 (3): 433–58.

Albelda, Randy, Mignon Duffy, and Nancy Folbre. 2009. "Counting on Care Work: Human Infrastructure in Massachusetts." Amherst: Center for Social Policy, University of Massachusetts.

Alcoff, Linda Martin. 2006. *Visible Identities: Race, Gender, and the Self*. New York: Oxford University Press.

Allen, Anita. 2003. *Why Privacy Isn't Everything: Feminist Reflections on Personal Accountability*. Lanham, MD: Rowman and Littlefield.

Anderson, Bridget Jane. 2000. *Doing the Dirty Work? The Global Politics of Domestic Labour*. New York: Palgrave Macmillan.

Anderson, Elizabeth S. 1999. "What Is the Point of Equality?" *Ethics* 109 (2): 287.

Anker, Richard. 1998. *Gender and Jobs: Sex Segregation of Occupations in the World*. Geneva: International Labour Organisation Press.

Arendt, Hannah. 1958. *The Human Condition*. Chicago: University of Chicago Press.

———. 1970. *On Violence*. New York: Harcourt Brace Jovanovich.

———. 2005. *The Promise of Politics*. New York: Schocken.

Aristotle. 1981. *The Politics*. Translated by T. Saunders. New York: Penguin.

Baldauf, Scott, and Peter Ford. 2008. "China Slammed for Arming Zimbabwe's Mugabe." *Christian Science Monitor*, April 23.

Bales, Kevin. 2007. *Ending Slavery: How We Free Today's Slaves*. Berkeley: University of California Press.

Barnes, Marian. 1999. *Building a Deliberative Democracy: An Evaluation of Two Citizens' Juries*. London: Institute for Public Policy Research.

———. 2007. "Participation, Citizenship and a Feminist Ethic of Care." In *Care Community and Citizenship*, ed. S. Balloch and M. Hill. Bristol, UK: Policy.

———. 2011. "Abandoning Care? A Critical Perspective on Personalisation from an Ethic of Care." *Ethics and Social Welfare* 5 (2): 153–67.

Baron-Cohen, Simon. 2011. *The Science of Evil: On Empathy and the Origins of Cruelty*. New York: Basic Books.

Baumol, William. 2012. *The Cost Disease*. New Haven: Yale University Press.

Beauvoir, Simone de. 1968. *The Second Sex*. New York: Modern Library.

Becker, Gary S. 1976. *The Economic Approach to Human Behavior*. Chicago: University of Chicago Press.

———. 1991. *A Treatise on the Family*. Enlarged ed. Cambridge: Harvard University Press.

Beckett, Clare. 2007. "Women, Disability, Care: Good Neighbours or Uneasy Bedfellows?" *Critical Social Policy* 27: 360–80.

Bellamy, Edward. 1888. *Looking Backward, 2000–1887*. Boston: Houghton Mifflin.

Benhabib, Seyla. 1986. "The Generalized and the Concrete Other: The Kohlberg-Gilligan Controversy and Feminist Theory." *Praxis International* 5: 402–24.

Benjamin, Jessica. 1988. *The Bonds of Love: Psychoanalysis, Feminism, and the Problem of Domination*. New York: Pantheon Books.

Bennett, Roger. 2011. "Why Urban Poor Donate: A Study of Low-Income Charitable Giving in London." *Nonprofit and Voluntary Sector Quarterly*, published online August 15, doi: 10.1177/0899764011419518.

Bennhold, Katrin. 2011. "From Afar, Moneymaker and Mother." *New York Times*, March 7.

Berlin, Isaiah. 1969. *Four Essays on Liberty*. New York: Oxford University Press.

Bickford, Susan. 1996. *The Dissonance of Democracy: Listening, Conflict, and Citizenship*. Ithaca: Cornell University Press.

Bittman, Michael, Paula England, Nancy Folbre, Liana Sayer, and George Matheson. 2003. "When Does Gender Trump Money? Bargaining and Time in Household Work." *American Journal of Sociology* 109: 186–214.

Blakemore, Judith, and Renee Centers. 2005. "Characteristics of Boys' and Girls' Toys." *Sex Roles* 53 (9): 619–33.

Blum, Lawrence. 1998. "Recognition, Value, and Equality: A Critique of Charles Taylor's and Nancy Fraser's Accounts of Multiculturalism." *Constellations: An International Journal of Critical and Democratic Theory* 5: 52.

Bologh, Roslyn Wallach. 1990. *Love or Greatness: Max Weber and Masculine Thinking—A Feminist Inquiry*. London: Unwin Hyman.

Bone, John, and Karen O'Reilly. 2010. "No Place Called Home: The Causes And Social Consequences of the UK Housing 'Bubble.'" *British Journal of Sociology* 61 (2): 231–55.

Bonfiglioli, Sandra. 1990. *L'architettura del tempo. La città multimediale*. Naples, Italy: Liguori.

Borooah, Vani K., and Martin Paldam. 2007. "Why Is the World Short of Democracy? A Cross-Country Analysis of Barriers to Representative Government." *European Journal of Political Economy* 23 (3): 582–604.

Bowles, Samuel, and Herbert Gintis. 1977. *Schooling in Capitalist America: Edu-*

cational Reform and the Contradictions of Economic Life. New York: Basic Books.

Boyte, Harry. 2004. Everyday Politics: Reconnecting Citizens and Public Life. Philadelphia: University of Pennsylvania Press.

———. 2011. "Constructive Politics as Public Work." Political Theory 39 (5): 630–60.

Bråten, Stein. 2003. "Participant Perception of Others' Acts: Virtual Otherness in Infants and Adults." Culture and Psychology 9 (3): 261–76.

Bridges, Amy. 1979. "The Other Side of the Paycheck." In Capitalist Patriarchy and the Case for Socialist Feminism, ed. Z. Eisenstein. New York: Monthly Review Press.

Brown, Wendy. 1995. States of Injury: Power and Freedom in Late Modernity. Princeton: Princeton University Press.

———. 2005. Edgework: Critical Essays on Knowledge and Politics. Princeton: Princeton University Press.

Brush, B. L., and R. Vasupuram. 2006. "Nurses, Nannies and Caring Work: Importation, Visibility and Marketability." Nursing Inquiry 13 (3): 181–85.

Bruzalski, Bart. 2004. "Mitigating the Consumption of the US Living Standard." In Philosophy and Its Public Role, ed. W. Aitken and J. Haldane. Charlottesville, VA: Imprint Academic.

Bubeck, Diemut. 1995. Care, Justice and Gender. Oxford: Oxford University Press.

Bufacchi, Vittorio. 2007. Violence and Social Justice. Basingstoke, UK: Palgrave Macmillan.

Bunch, Charlotte. 1987. Passionate Politics: Feminist Theory in Action: Essays, 1968–1986. New York: St. Martin's.

Bush, George W. 2001. "First Inaugural Address." January 20, http://www.bartleby.com/124/pres66.html.

Bussemaker, Jet, and Kees van Kersbergen. 1994. "Gender and Welfare States: Some Theoretical Reflections." In Gendering Welfare States, ed. D. Sainsbury. London: Sage.

Cameron, Claire, and Peter Moss. 2007. Care Work in Europe: Current Understandings and Future Directions. London: Routledge.

Campbell, Lori D., and Michael P. Carroll. 2007. "The Incomplete Revolution." Men and Masculinities 9: 491–508.

Cancian, Francesca M., and Stacey J. Oliker. 2000. Caring and Gender. Thousand Oaks, CA: Sage.

Cannon, Katie G. 1988. Black Womanist Ethics. Atlanta: Scholars.

Card, Claudia. 1996. The Unnatural Lottery: Character and Moral Luck. Philadelphia: Temple University Press.

———. 2002. "Responsibility Ethics, Shared Understandings, and Moral Communities." Hypatia 17 (1): 141–55.

Casey, Catherine. 2009. "Organizations, Workers, and Learning: New Prospects for Citizenship at Work?" Citizenship Studies 13 (2): 171–85.

Charlton, J. I. 2000. *Nothing about Us without Us: Disability Oppression and Empowerment*. Berkeley: University of California Press.

Chicago Sun Times. 2008. "'I Know Why Kids Are Killing. They're Hurting.'" September 4, 23.

Chodorow, Nancy. 1978a. "Mothering, Object-Relations, and the Female Oedipal Configuration." *Feminist Studies* 4 (1): 137–58.

———. 1978b. *The Reproduction of Mothering: Psychoanalysis and the Sociology of Gender*. Berkeley: University of California Press.

———. 2004. "Psychoanalysis and Women." *Annual of Psychoanalysis* 32: 101–29.

Clement, Grace. 1996. *Care, Autonomy, and Justice: Feminism and the Ethic of Care*. Boulder, CO: Westview.

Code, Lorraine. 1995. *Rhetorical Spaces: Essays on Gendered Locations*. New York: Routledge.

———. 2002. "Narratives of Responsibility and Agency: Reading Margaret Walker's *Moral Understandings*." *Hypatia* 17 (1): 156–73.

Cokley, Kevin, Meera Komarraju, Rachel Pickett, Frances Shen, Nima Patel, Vinetha Belur, and Rocio Rosales. 2007. "Ethnic Differences in Endorsement of the Protestant Work Ethic: The Role of Ethnic Identity and Perceptions of Social Class." *Journal of Social Psychology* 147 (1): 75–89.

Collins, Patricia Hill. 1990. *Black Feminist Thought: Knowledge, Consciousness, and the Politics of Empowerment*. Boston: Unwin Hyman.

———. 2005. "An Entirely Different World? Challenges for the Sociology of Race and Ethnicity." In *The Sage Handbook of Sociology*, ed. C. Calhoun, C. Rojek, and B. S. Turner. Thousand Oaks, CA: Sage.

Congressional Budget Office. 2012. *Comparing the Compensation of Federal and Private-Sector Employees*. A CBO Report. U.S. Congress, January 30, 2012, http://cbo.gov/sites/default/files/cbofiles/attachments/01-30-FedPay.pdf.

Connell, R. W. 2005. *Masculinities*. 2nd ed. London: Polity.

Connolly, William E. 1999. *Why I Am Not a Secularist*. Minneapolis: University of Minnesota Press.

Cott, Nancy. 1977. *The Bonds of Womanhood: "Woman's Sphere" in New England, 1780–1835*. New Haven: Yale University Press.

Cruikshank, Barbara. 1994. "The Will to Power: Technologies of Citizenship and the War on Poverty." *Socialist Review* 23 (4): 29–35.

Culpitt, Ian. 1992. "Citizenship and 'Moral Generosity': Social Needs, Privatization and Social Service Contracting." In *Welfare and Citizenship: Beyond the Crisis of the Welfare State?*, ed. I. Culpitt. London: Sage.

Daly, Kerry. 1996. *Families and Time: Keeping Pace in a Hurried Culture*. Beverly Hills, CA: Sage.

Darling-Hammond, Linda. 2004. "From 'Separate but Equal' to 'No Child Left Behind': The Collision of New Standards and Old Inequalities." In *Many*

Children Left Behind: How the No Child Left Behind Act Is Damaging Our Children and Our Schools, ed. D. Meier and G. H. Wood. Boston: Beacon.

Davenport, Rick D. 2005. "Robotics." In *Smart Technology for Aging, Disability and Independence: The State of the Science*, ed. W. C. Mann. Hoboken, NJ: Wiley.

Dean, Jeffery R., and Patrick J. Wolf. 2010. "Milwaukee Longitudinal School Choice Evaulation: Annual School Testing Summary Report 2008–09." In *SCDP Milwaukee Evaulation*. Fayetteville: University of Arkansas.

Dee, Thomas S., and Brian A. Jacob. 2010. "The Impact of No Child Left Behind on Students, Teachers, and Schools." *Brookings Papers on Economic Activity* 2010 (2): 149–94.

Dewey, John. 1993. *Political Writings*. Indianapolis: Hackett.

Di, Zhu Xiao. 2007. "Growing Wealth, Inequality, and Housing in the United States." Cambridge: Joint Center for Housing Studies, Harvard University.

Di Marco, Graciela. 2005. *Democratización en las familias: estrategias y alternativas para la implementación de programas sociales*. Buenos Aires: Jorge Buadino, Universidad Nacional de General San Martín.

———. 2006. "Movimientos sociales y democratización en Argentina." In *De lo privado a lo público: 30 años de lucha ciudadana de las mujeres en América Latina*, ed. E. Maier and N. Lebon. Mexico City: Siglo XXI.

Di Marco, Graciela, and Héctor Palomino, eds. 2004. *Construyendo sociedad y política: Los proyectos de los movintos socialies en acción*. Buenos Aires: Jorge Baudino Ediciones.

Diedrich, W. Wolf, Roger Burggraeve, and Chris Gastmans. 2006. "Towards a Levinasian Care Ethic: A Dialogue between the Thoughts of Joan Tronto and Emmanuel Levinas." *Ethical Perspectives: Journal of the European Ethics Network* 13 (1): 33–61.

Dietz, Mary G. 1985. "Citizenship with a Feminist Face: The Problem with Maternal Thinking." *Poltical Theory* 13 (1): 19–37.

Dillon, Sam. 2010. "4,100 Students Prove 'Small Is Better'Rule Wrong." *New York Times*, September 27, A1.

Douglas, Ulester, Dick Bathrick, and Phyllis Alesia Perry. 2008. "Deconstructing Male Violence against Women." *Violence against Women* 14 (2): 247–61.

Dubber, Markus D. 2005. *The Police Power: Patriarchy and the Foundations of American Government*. New York: Columbia University Press.

Duffy, Mignon. 2007. "Doing the Dirty Work: Gender, Race, and Reproductive Labor in Historical Perspective." *Gender and Society* 21 (3): 313–36.

———. 2011. *Making Care Count: A Century of Gender, Race, and Paid Care Work*. New Brunswick: Rutgers University Press.

Dugger, Celia W. 2008. "Zimbabwe Arms Shipped by China Spark an Uproar." *New York Times*, April 19.

Durant, Robert F. 1995. "The Democratic Deficit in America." *Political Science Quarterly* 110 (1): 25.

Dworkin, Ronald. 2000. *Sovereign Virtue: the Theory and Practice of Equality.* Cambridge: Harvard University Press.

Eckstein, Harry, and Ted Gurr. 1975. *Patterns of Authority: A Structural Basis for Political Inquiry.* New York: Wiley.

Ehrenreich, Barbara. 2000. "Maid to Order: The Politics of Other Women's Work." *Harper's*: 59–70.

Else, Liz. 2006. "Meet the Alloparents." *New Scientist* (109): 50–51.

Elshtain, Jean Bethke. 1981. *Public Man, Private Woman: Women in Social and Political Thought.* Princeton: Princeton University Press.

———. 1982. "Antigone's Daughters." *Democracy* 2 (2): 46–59.

Engster, Daniel. 2004. "Care Ethics and Natural Law Theory: Toward an Institutional Political Theory of Caring." *Journal of Politics* 66: 113.

———. 2005. "Rethinking Care Theory: The Practice of Caring and the Obligation to Care." *Hypatia* 20 (3): 50–74.

———. 2007. *The Heart of Justice: Care Ethics and Political Theory.* New York: Oxford University Press.

———. 2010. "Strategies for Building and Sustaining a New Care Movement." *Journal of Women, Politics and Policy* 31 (4): 289–312.

Epstein, Debbie. 1993. "Defining Accountability in Education." *British Educational Research Journal* 19 (3): 243–57.

Eriksen, John. 2003. "Public Payment for Informal Care of Disabled Children." *European Societies* 5 (4): 445.

Eshleman, Andrew. 2009. "Moral Responsibility." *Stanford Encyclopedia of Philosophy*, http://plato.stanford.edu/entries/moral-responsibility/.

Esquith, Stephen 2010. *The Political Responsibilities of Everyday Bystanders.* College Park: Penn State University Press.

Ewen, Stuart. 1996. *PR! A Social History of Spin.* New York: Basic Books.

Faludi, Susan. 1999. *Stiffed: The Betrayal of the American Man.* New York: HarperCollins.

Feinberg, Joel. 1970. *Doing and Deserving: Essays in the Theory of Responsibility.* Princeton: Princeton University Press.

Ferguson, Adam. 1995 [1767]. *An Essay on the History of Civil Society,* ed. Fania Oz-Salzbereger. Cambridge: Cambridge University Press.

Ferguson, Ann Arnett. 2001. *Bad Boys: Public Schools in the Making of Black Masculinity.* Ann Arbor: University of Michigan Press.

Fergusson, David M., L. John Horwood, and Joseph M. Boden. 2008. "The Transmission of Social Inequality: Examination of the Linkages between Family Socioeconomic Status in Childhood and Educational Achievement in Young Adulthood." *Research in Social Stratification and Mobility* 26 (3): 277–95.

Finch, Janet. 1996. "Family Responsibilities and Rights." In *Citizenship Today: The*

Contemporary Relevance of T. H. Marshall, ed. M. Bulmer and A. M. Rees. London: University College of London Press.

Fineman, Martha S., ed. 1995. *The Neutered Mother, the Sexual Family and Other Twentieth-Century Tragedies*. New York: Routledge.

Fischer, Marilyn. 2006. "Addams's Internationalist Pacifism and the Rhetoric of Maternalism." *NWSA Journal* 18 (Fall): 1–19.

Fischer, Marilyn, Carol Nackenoff, and Wendy Chmielewski, eds. 2009. *Jane Addams and the Practice of Democracy*. Urbana: University of Illinois Press.

Fisher, Berenice, and Joan C. Tronto. 1990. "Toward a Feminist Theory of Caring." In *Circles of Care*, ed. E. K. Abel and M. Nelson. Albany: SUNY Press.

Fishkin, James. 2009. *When the People Speak: Deliberative Democracy and Public Consultation*. Oxford: Oxford University Press.

Folbre, Nancy. 1994. *Who Pays for the Kids? Gender and the Structure of Constraint*. London: Routledge.

———. 2001. *The Invisible Heart: Economics and Family Values*. New York: New Press.

———. 2009. *Greed, Lust and Gender: A History of Economic Ideas*. New York: Oxford University Press.

Folbre, Nancy, and Michael Bittman, eds. 2004. *Family Time: The Social Organization of Care*. New York: Routledge.

Foucault, Michel. 1997. "The Ethics of the Concern of the Self as a Practice of Freedom." In *Ethics: Subjectivity and Truth*, ed. P. Rabinow. Harmondsworth, UK: Penguin.

———. 2007. *Security, Territory, Population*. Translated by G. Burchell. New York: Picador.

Fourcade, Marion, and Kieran Healy. 2007. "Moral Views of Market Society." *Annual Review of Sociology* 33 (1): 285–311.

Frankental, Peter. 2001. "Corporate Social Responsibility—a PR Invention?" *Corporate Communications: An International Journal* 6 (1): 18–23.

Frankfurt, Harry. 1988. *The Importance of What We Care About: Philosophical Essays*. Cambridge: Cambridge University Press.

Fraser, Nancy. 1989. *Unruly Practices: Power, Discourse, and Gender in Contemporary Social Theory*. Minneapolis: University of Minnesota Press.

———. 1997. *Justice Interruptus: Critical Reflections on the "Postsocialist" Condition*. New York: Routlege.

———. 2009. *Scales of Justice*. New York: Columbia University Press.

Fraser, Nancy, and Linda Gordon. 1994. "A Genealogy of Dependency: Tracing a Keyword of the U.S. Welfare State." *Signs* 19 (2): 309–36.

French, Peter. 1992. *Responsibility Matters*. Lawrence: University of Kansas Press.

Frenkel, Louise. 2008. "A Support Group for Parents of Burned Children: A South African Children's Hospital Burns Unit." *Burns* 34: 565–69.

Freud, Sigmund. 1958. *Civilization and Its Discontents*. Garden City, NY: Doubleday.

Friedan, Betty. 1963. *The Feminine Mystique*. New York: Norton.

Friedman, Milton. 1962. *Capitalism and Freedom*. Chicago: University of Chicago Press.

Friedman, Thomas L. 2005. *The World Is Flat: A Brief History of the Globalized World in the Twenty-First Century*. New York: Allen Lane.

———. 2008. *Hot, Flat and Crowded: Why We Need a Green Revolution—And How It Can Renew America*. New York: Farrar, Straus and Giroux.

Frost, Robert. 1969. "The Death of the Hired Man." In *The Poetry of Robert Frost*, ed. E. C. Lathem. New York: Holt.

Garey, Anita Ilta. 1999. *Weaving Work and Motherhood*. Philadelphia: Temple University Press.

Gault, Barbara, and Heidi Hartmann. 1998. "Prospects for Low-Income Mothers'Economic Survival Under Welfare Reform." *Publius* 28 (3): 175.

Gawande, Atul. 2010. *The Checklist Manifesto: How to Get Things Done Right*. New York: Metropolitan Books.

Gerstel, Naomi. 2000. "The Third Shift: Gender and Care Work outside the Home." *Qualitative Sociology* 23: 467–83.

Gibson-Graham, J. K. 1996. *The End of Capitalism (As We Knew It): A Feminist Critique of Political Economy*. Minneapolis: University of Minnesota Press.

Gilens, Martin. 1999. *Why Americans Hate Welfare: Race, Media, and the Politics of Antipoverty Policy*. Chicago: University of Chicago Press.

Gilligan, Carol. 1982. *In a Different Voice: Psychological Theory and Women's Development*. Cambridge: Harvard University Press.

———. 1996. "The Centrality of Relationship in Human Development: A Puzzle, Some Evidence, and a Theory." In *Development and Vulnerability in Close Relationships*, ed. G. G. Noam and K. W. Fischer. Mahwah, NJ: Erlbaum.

———. 2002. *The Birth of Pleasure*. New York: Knopf.

———. 2004. "Recovering Psyche." *Annual of Psychoanalysis* 32: 131–47.

Gilligan, Carol, and David A. J. Richards. 2009. *The Deepening Darkness: Patriarchy, Resistance, and Democracy's Future*. New York: Cambridge University Press.

Gilman, Charlotte Perkins. 1979. *Herland*. New York: Pantheon Books.

Glenn, Evelyn Nakano. 1992. "From Servitude to Service Work: Historical Continuities in the Racial Division of Paid Reproductive Labor." *Signs: Journal of Women in Culture and Society* 18 (1): 1–43.

———. 2000. "Creating a Caring Society." *Contemporary Sociology* 29 (1): 84–95.

———. 2010. *Forced to Care*. Cambridge: Harvard University Press.

Glenn, Evelyn Nakano, Grace Chang, and Linda Rennie Forcey, eds. 1994. *Mothering: Ideology, Experience and Agency*. New York: Routledge.

Goodin, Robert E. 1985. *Protecting the Vulnerable: A Reanalysis of Our Social Responsibilities*. Chicago: University of Chicago Press.

———. 2001. "Work and Welfare: Towards a Post-Productivist Welfare Regime." *British Journal of Political Science* 31 (01): 13–39.

Gornick, Janet C., and Marcia K. Meyers. 2005. *Families That Work: Policies for Reconciling Parenthood and Employment*. New York: Russell Sage.

Gould, Carol. 2004. *Globalizing Democracy and Human Rights*. New York: Cambridge University Press.

———. 2008. "Negotiating the Global and the Local: Situating Transnational Democracy and Human Rights." In *Democracy in a Global World: Human Rights and Political Participation in the Twenty-First Century*, ed. D. K. Chatterjee. Lanham, MD: Rowman and Littlefield.

Graf, B., M. Hans, and R. D. Schraft. 2004. "Mobile Robot Assistants." *Robotics and Automation Magazine, IEEE* 11 (2): 67–77.

Granovetter, Mark. 1985. "Economic Action and Social Structure: The Problem of Embeddedness." *American Journal of Sociology* 91 (3): 481–510.

Green, Donald P., and Ian Shapiro. 1996. *Pathologies of Rational Choice*. New Haven: Yale University Press.

Gret, Marion, and Yves Sintomer. 2005. *The Porto Alegre Experiment*. New York: Zed Books.

Groenhout, Ruth E. 2004. *Connected Lives: Human Nature and an Ethics of Care*. Lanham, MD: Rowman and Littlefield.

Groombridge, Brian. 2010. "Better Government with Older Citizens: A Test of Democracy." *Political Quarterly* 81 (1): 131–40.

Hage, Ghassan. 2003. *Against Paranoid Nationalism*. Annandale, NSW: Pluto Australia.

Hallett, Michael A. 2006. *Private Prisons in America: A Critical Race Perspective*. Urbana: University of Illinois Press.

Hamilton, Alexander, John Jay, and James Madison. 1787. *The Federalist Papers*. Library of Congress, http://thomas.loc.gov/home/histdox/fedpapers.html.

Hancock, Ange-Marie. 2007. "Intersectionality as a Normative and Empirical Paradigm." *Politics and Gender* 3 (2): 248–54.

———. 2011. *Solidarity Politics for Millennials: A Guide to Ending the Oppression Olympics*. New York: Palgrave Macmillan.

Hankivsky, Olena. 2004. *Social Policy and the Ethic of Care*. Vancouver: University of British Columbia Press.

———. 2006. "Imagining Ethical Globalization: The Contributions of a Care Ethic." *Journal of Global Ethics* 2 (1): 91–110.

Harrington, Mona. 1999. *Care and Equality*. New York: Knopf.

Harvey, David. 2005. *A Brief History of Neoliberalism*. New York: Oxford University Press.

Haskell, Thomas L. 1998. *Objectivity Is Not Neutrality: Explanatory Schemes in History*. Baltimore: Johns Hopkins University Press.

Hays, Sharon. 1996. *The Cultural Contradictions of Motherhood*. New Haven: Yale University Press.

Hearn, Jeff, and David L. Collinson. 1994. "Theorizing Unities and Differences between Men and between Masculinities." In *Theorizing Masculinities*, ed. H. Brod and M. Kaufman. Thousand Oaks, CA: Sage.

Heidegger, Martin. 1996 *Being and Time*. Translated by J. Stambaugh. Albany: SUNY Press.

Held, Virginia. 1993. *Feminist Morality: Transforming Culture, Society and Politics*. Chicago: University of Chicago Press.

———. 1995. *Justice and Care: Essential Readings in Feminist Ethics*. Boulder, CO: Westview.

———, ed. 1996. *Care and Justice*. Boulder, CO: Westview.

———. 2006. *The Ethics of Care: Personal, Political, and Global*. New York: Oxford University Press.

Hellerstein, Judith K., and David Neumark. 2008. "Workplace Segregation in the United States: Race, Ethnicity, and Skill." *Review of Economics and Statistics* 90 (3): 459–77.

Henry, Michael S. 2006. "Uncertainty, Responsibility, and the Evolution of the Physician/Patient Relationship." *Journal of Medical Ethics* 32: 3.

Herr, Ranjoo Seodu. 2003. "Is Confucianism Compatible with Care Ethics? A Critique." *Philosophy East and West* 53 (4): 471–89.

Heymann, Jody. 2000. *The Widening Gap: Why America's Working Families Are in Jeopardy and What Can Be Done about It*. New York: Basic Books.

———. 2006. *Forgotten Families: Ending the Growing Crisis Confronting Children and Working Parents in the Global Economy*. New York: Oxford University Press.

Hirschman, Albert O. 1977. *The Passions and the Interests: Political Arguments for Capitalism Before Its Triumph*. Princeton: Princeton University Press.

Hirschmann, Nancy J. 1996. "Toward a Feminist Theory of Freedom." *Political Theory* 24 (1): 46–67.

———. 2002. *The Subject of Liberty: Toward a Feminist Theory of Freedom*. Princeton: Princeton University Press.

———. 2010. "Mothers Who Care Too Much." *Boston Review*. July–August, http://bostonreview.net/BR35.4/hirschmann.php [accessed April 15, 2012].

Hobgood, Mary Elizabeth. 2000. *Dismantling Privilege: An Ethics of Accountability*. Cleveland: Pilgrim.

Hochschild, Adam. 2005. *Bury the Chains: Prophets and Rebels in the Fight to Free an Empire's Slaves*. New York: Houghton Mifflin.

Hochschild, Arlie Russell. 1989. *The Second Shift*. New York: Avon.

———. 1997. *The Time Bind: When Work Becomes Home and Home Becomes Work*. New York: Metropolitan Books.

———. 2005. "On the Edge of the Time Bind: Time and Market Culture." *Social Research* 72 (2): 339–54.

———. 2012. *The Outsourced Self: Intimate Life in Market Times*. New York: Holt.

Hochschild, Jennifer. 1981. *What's Fair: American Beliefs about Distributive Justice*. Cambridge: Harvard University Press.

———. 2003a. "Rethinking Accountability Politics." In *No Child Left Behind? The Politics and Practice of School Accountability*, ed. P. E. Peterson and M. E. West. Washington, DC: Brookings Institution Press.

———. 2003b. "Social Class in Public Schools." *Journal of Social Issues* 59 (4): 821.

Hondagneu-Sotelo, Pierrette. 2001. *Doméstica: Immigrant Workers Cleaning and Caring in the Shadows of Affluence*. Berkeley: University of California Press.

Honneth, Axel. 1996. *The Struggle for Recognition: The Moral Grammar of Social Conflicts*. Translated by J. Anderson. Cambridge: MIT Press.

hooks, bell. 2004. *We Real Cool: Black Men and Masculinity*. New York: Routledge.

Hrdy, Sarah Blaffer. 1999. *Mother Nature: A History of Mothers, Infants, and Natural Selection*. New York: Pantheon Books.

Huggins, Martha K., Mika Haritos-Fatouros, and Philip G. Zimardo. 2002. *Violence Workers: Police Torturers and Murderers Reconstruct Brazilian Atrocities*. Berkeley: University of California Press.

Ignatieff, Michael. 1984. *The Needs of Strangers*. New York: Penguin.

International Centre for Human Resources in Nursing. 2008. "Workplace Bullying in the Health Sector." Geneva: International Centre for Human Resources in Nursing.

Isin, Engin F. 1997. "Who Is the New Citizen? Towards a Genealogy." *Citizenship Studies* 1 (1): 115–32.

James, Joy, ed. 2007. *Warfare in the American Homeland: Policing and Prison in a Penal Democracy*. Durham: Duke University Press.

Johnson, Allan G. 2001. *Privilege, Power and Difference*. Mountain View, CA: Mayfield.

Johnson, Dirk. 2001. "For Teenagers, Fast Food Is a Snack, Not a Job." *New York Times*, January 8, 2001, A1, A13.

Julian, Tudor Hart. 1971. "The Inverse Care Law." *The Lancet* 297 (7696): 405–12.

Kelman, Steven. 1988. "Why Public Ideas Matter." In *The Power of Public Ideas*, ed. R. B. Reich. Cambridge, MA: Ballinger.

Kershaw, Paul. 2005. *Carefair: Rethinking the Responsibilities and Rights of Citizenship*. Vancouver: University of British Columbia Press.

Kershaw, Paul, Jane Pulkingham, and Sylvia Fuller. 2008. "Expanding the Subject: Violence, Care, and (In)Active Male Citizenship." *Social Politics* 15 (2): 182–206.

Keynes, John Maynard. 1971 [1923]. *The Collected Writings of John Maynard Keynes*, vol. 4, *A Tract on Monetary Reform*. London: Macmillan for the Royal Economic Society.

Kilkey, Majella, and Diane Perrons. 2010. "Gendered Divisions in Domestic Work Time." *Time and Society* 19 (2): 239–64.

Kilminster, S., J. Downes, B. Gough, D. Murdoch-Eaton, and T. Roberts. 2007. "Women in Medicine—Is There a Problem? A Literature Review of the Changing Gender Composition, Structures and Occupational Cultures in Medicine." *Medical Education* 41 (1): 39–49.

Kimbrell, Andrew. 1995. *The Masculine Mystique: The Politics of Masculinity.* New York: Ballantine Books.

Kimmel, Michael S. 1996. *Manhood in America: A Cultural History.* New York: Free Press.

Kittay, Eva Feder. 1999. *Love's Labor: Essays on Women, Equality and Dependency.* New York: Routledge.

———. 2001. "A Feminist Public Ethic of Care Meets the New Communitarian Family Policy." *Ethics* 111 (3): 523–47.

Kittay, Eva Feder, and Ellen K. Feder. 2002. *The Subject of Care: Feminist Perspectives on Dependency.* Lanham, MD: Rowman and Littlefield.

Klein, Naomi. 2007. *The Shock Doctrine: The Rise of Disaster Capitalism.* New York: Holt.

Klyza, Christopher McGrory. 2002. "The United States Army, Natural Resources, and Political Development in the Nineteenth Century." *Polity* 35 (1): 1–28.

Knijn, Trudie, and Monique Kremer. 1997. "Gender and the Caring Dimension of Welfare States: Toward Inclusive Citizenship." *Social Politics* 4 (3): 328–61.

Koehn, Daryl. 1998. *Rethinking Feminist Ethics: Care, Trust and Empathy.* London: Routledge.

Koggel, Christine M. 1998. *Perspectives on Equality: Constructing a Relational Theory.* Latham, MD: Rowman and Littlefield.

———, ed. 2006. *Moral Issues in Global Perspective: Human Diversity and Equality.* 2d ed., vol. 2. Toronto: Broadview.

Koren, Mary Jane. 2010. "Person-Centered Care for Nursing Home Residents: The Culture-Change Movement." *Health Affairs* 29 (2): 312–17.

Koziak, Barbara. 2000. *Retrieving Political Emotion: Thumos, Aristotle, and Gender.* University Park: Penn State University Press.

Krieger, Nancy, Jarvis T. Chen, Pamela D. Waterman, Cathy Hartman, Anne M. Stoddard, Margaret M. Quinn, Glorian Sorensen, and Elizabeth M. Barbeau. 2008. "The Inverse Hazard Law: Blood Pressure, Sexual Harassment, Racial Discrimination, Workplace Abuse and Occupational Exposures in US Low-Income Black, White and Latino Workers." *Social Science and Medicine* 67 (12): 1970–81.

Kristeva, Julia. 1982. "Women's Time." In *Feminist Theory: A Critique of Ideology,* ed. N. Keohane, M. Rosaldo, and B. Gelpi. Chicago: University of Chicago Press.

Kyle, Jess. 2011. "Protecting the World: The Problem of Military Humanitarian Intervention for an Ethic of Care." Conference Paper Presented at the IDEA Conference, Bryn Mawr, PA.

Lane, Robert E. 1991. *The Market Experience.* New Haven: Yale University Press.

———. 2000. *The Loss of Happiness in Market Democracies.* New Haven: Yale University Press.

Lareau, Annette. 2003. *Unequal Childhoods: Class, Race, and Family Life*. Berkeley: University of California Press.

Larrabee, Mary Jeanne. 1993. *An Ethic of Care: Feminist and Interdisciplinary Perspectives*. New York: Routledge.

Lasch, Christopher. 1995. *Haven in a Heartless World: The Family Besieged*. New York: Norton.

Lasswell, Harold D. 1936. *Politics: Who Gets What, When and How*. New York: Peter Smith.

Lee, Min-Dong Paul. 2008. "A Review of the Theories of Corporate Social Responsibility: Its Evolutionary Path and the Road Ahead." *International Journal of Management Reviews* 10 (1): 53–73.

Leeder, Elaine J. 2004. *The Family in Global Perspective: A Gendered Journey*. Thousand Oaks, CA: Sage.

Leib, Ethan J. 2006. "Responsibility and Social/Political Choices about Choice; or, One Way to Be a True Non-Voluntarist." *Law and Philosophy* 25 (4): 453–88.

Leonard, Stephen T., and Joan C. Tronto. 2007. "The Genders of Citizenship." *American Political Science Review* 101 (1): 33–46.

Lévinas, E. 1996. *Emmanuel Lévinas: Basic Philosophical Writings*. ed. A. Peperzak, S. Critchley, and R. Bernasconi. Bloomington: Indiana University Press.

Levine, Arthur. 2006. "Educating School Teachers." Princeton, NJ: Education Schools Project.

Lister, Ruth. 1995. "Dilemmas in Engendering Citizenship." *Economy and Society* 24 (1): 1–40.

———. 1997. *Citizenship: Feminist Perspectives*. London: Macmillan.

Llana, Sara Miller. 2006. "Global Stopgap for US Nurse Deficit." *Christian Science Monitor*, March 6.

Logan, John R., and Brian Stults. 2011. "The Persistence of Segregation in the Metropolis: New Findings from the 2010 Census." Census Brief prepared for Project US2010, http://www.s4.brown.edu/us2010/Data/Report/report2.pdf.

Lorde, Audre. 1984. *Sister Outsider: Essays and Speeches*. Trumansburg, NY: Crossing.

Madrick, Jeff. 2011. *Age of Greed: The Triumph of Finance and the Decline of America, 1970 to the Present*. New York: Knopf.

Mahon, Rianne. 2002. "Gender and Welfare State Restructuring: Through the Lens of Child Care." In *Child Care Policy at the Crossroads: Gender and Welfare State Restructuring*, ed. S. Michel and R. Mahon. New York: Routledge.

Mann, Hollie Sue. 2010. "Politics, Human Flourishing, and Bodily Knowing: A Critical Theory of Embodied Care." PhD dissertation, University of North Carolina, Chapel Hill.

Manning, Rita C. 1992. *Speaking from the Heart: A Feminist Perspective on Ethics*. Lanham, MD: Rowman and Littlefield.

Marcuse, H. 1964. *One Dimensional Man: Studies in the Ideology of Advanced Industrial Society.* Boston: Beacon.

Mareggi, Marco. 2002. "Innovation in Urban Policy: The Experience of Italian Urban Time Policies." *Planning Theory and Practice* 3: 173–94.

Marshall, T. H. 1981. *The Right to Welfare and Other Essays.* New York: Free Press.

Marshall, T. H., and Tom Bottomore. 1992 [1950]. *Citizenship and Social Class.* Concord, MA: Pluto.

Mattis, Jacqueline, Nyasha Grayman, Sheri-Ann Cowie, Cynthia Winston, Carolyn Watson, and Daisy Jackson. 2008. "Intersectional Identities and the Politics of Altruistic Care in a Low-Income, Urban Community." *Sex Roles* 59 (5–6): 418–28.

Maume, D. J. 2006. "Gender Differences in Restricting Work Efforts Because of Family Responsibilities." *Journal of Marriage and Family* 68 (4): 859–69.

McCall, Leslie. 2005. "The Complexity of Intersectionality." *Signs: Journal of Women in Culture and Society* 30 (3): 1771–1800.

McClain, Linda C. 2006. *The Place of Families: Fostering Capacity, Equality and Responsibility.* Cambridge: Harvard University Press.

McCloskey, Deirdre. 2006. *The Bourgeois Virtues: Ethics for an Age of Commerce.* Chicago: University of Chicago Press.

McCluskey, Martha T. 2003. "Efficiency and Social Citizenship: Challenging the Neoliberal Attack on the Welfare State." *Indiana Law Journal* 78 (2): 783–876.

McDowell, Linda. 2007. "Spaces of the Home: Absence Presence, New Connections and New Anxieties." *Home Cultures* 4 (2): 129–46.

McGregor, Joann. 2007. " 'Joining the BBC (British Bottom Cleaners)': Zimbabwean Migrants and the UK Care Industry." *Journal of Ethnic and Migration Studies* 33 (5): 801–24.

McIntosh, Peggy. 1988. *White Privilege and Male Privilege: A Personal Account of Coming to See Correspondences through Work in Women's Studies.* Wellesley, MA: Wellesley College Center for Research on Women.

Mead, Lawrence M. 2001. *Beyond Entitlement: The Social Obligations of Citizenship.* New York: Simon and Schuster.

Meriac, John P., Taylor L. Poling, and David J. Woehr. 2009. "Are There Gender Differences in Work Ethic? An Examination of the Measurement Equivalence of the Multidimensional Work Ethic Profile." *Personality and Individual Differences* 47 (3): 209–13.

Metz, Tamara. 2010a. "Demands of Care and Dilemmas of Freedom: What We Really Ought to Be Worried About." *Politics and Gender* 6 (1): 120–28.

———. 2010b. *Untying the Knot: Marriage, the State, and the Case for Their Divorce.* Princeton: Princeton University Press.

Meyer, Madonna Harrington. 2000. *Care Work: Gender, Class, and Welfare States.* New York: Routledge.

Mill, John Stuart. 1998 [1869]. *On Liberty and Other Essays.* New York: Oxford University Press.

Mills, Charles. 1997. *The Racial Contract.* Ithaca: Cornell University Press.

Mink, Gwendolyn. 1998. *Welfare's End.* Ithaca: Cornell University Press.

Miraftab, Faranak. 2004. "Invited and Invented Spaces of Participation." *Wagadu* 1: 1–7.

Mol, Annemarie. 2008. *The Logic of Care: Health and the Problem of Patient Choice.* Abingdon, UK: Routledge.

Monkkonen, Eric H. 1981. *Police in Urban America, 1860–1920.* Cambridge: Cambridge University Press.

Monnat, Shannon M., and Laura A. Bunyan. 2008. "Capitalism and Welfare Reform: Who Really Benefits from Welfare-to-Work Policies?" *Race, Gender and Class* 15 (1–2): 115–33.

Moore, Margaret. 1999. "The Ethics of Care and Justice." *Women and Politics* 20 (2): 1–16.

More, Thomas. 1965 [1516]. *Utopia.* Translated by P. Turner. New York: Penguin.

Morgan-Quitno. 2006–7. "Results of the 2006 Smartest State Award: Which State Is Smartest?" http://www.morganquitno.com/edrank06.htm.

Morrison, Andrew R., and Maurice Schiff. 2007. "Looking Ahead: Future Directions for Research and Policy." In *The International Migration of Women*, ed. A. R. Morrison, M. Schiff, and M. Sjöblom. Washington, DC: World Bank.

Moskowitz, Andrew. 2004. "Dissociation and Violence." *Trauma, Violence and Abuse* 5 (1): 21–46.

Mullin, Amy. 2005. "Trust, Social Norms, and Motherhood." *Journal of Social Philosophy* 36 (3): 316–30.

Murray, Jillian. 2010. Discussion of *Mihi cura futuri*, Hunter College Listserv, January 9, 2003, http://urban.hunter.cuny.edu/~mkuechle/Hunter_Motto.html.

Myers, Ella. 2012. *Between Selves and Others: Worldly Ethics and Democratic Politics:* Durham: Duke University Press.

Narayan, Uma. 1995. "Colonialism and Its Others: Considerations on Rights and Care Discourses." *Hypatia* 10 (2): 133–40.

Nation, The. 2010. Reader comment to "Failing New Jersey's Schools" by Melissa Parnagian, September 20, http://www.thenation.com/article/154902/failing-new-jerseys-schools#.

National Center for Education Statistics. 2009. "U.S. Performance across International Assessments of Student Achievement: Special Supplement to the Condition of Education." Jessup, MD: NCES.

Nelson, Barbara J. 1986. *Making an Issue of Child Abuse: Political Agenda Setting for Social Problems.* Chicago: University of Chicago Press.

Nelson, Julie A. 1999. "Of Markets and Martyrs: Is It OK to Pay Well for Care?" *Feminist Economics* 5 (3): 43–59.

Neocleous, Mark. 1998. "Policing and Pin-Making: Adam Smith, Police and the State of Prosperity." *Policing and Society* 8 (4): 425–49.

New Statesman. 2000. "America's Democratic Deficit." *New Statesman*, November 20, 5.

Noddings, Nel. 1984. *Caring: A Feminine Approach to Ethics and Moral Education.* Berkeley: University of California Press.

———. 2002a. *Educating Moral People: A Caring Alternative to Character Education.* New York: Teachers College Press.

———. 2002b. *Starting at Home: Caring and Social Policy.* Berkeley: University of California Press.

———. 2005. *The Challenge to Care in Schools: An Alternative Approach to Education.* 2nd ed. New York: Teachers College Press.

Nussbaum, Martha Craven. 2000. *Women and Human Development: The Capabilities Approach.* Cambridge: Cambridge University Press.

———. 2004. "Beyond the Social Contract: Capabilities and Global Justice." *Oxford Development Studies* 32 (1): 3–18.

———. 2007. "The Supreme Court 2006 Term; Foreword: Constitutions and Capabilities: 'Perception' against Lofty Formalism." *Harvard Law Review* 121 (4): 5–97.

Nye, Joseph S., Jr. 2001. "Globalization's Democratic Deficit." *Foreign Affairs* 80 (4): 2–6.

Oberman, Michelle. 2004–5. "Mothers Who Kill: Coming to Terms with Modern American Infanticide." *Depaul Journal of Health Care Law* 8 (3): 3–107.

Okin, Susan Moller. 1979. *Women in Western Political Thought.* Princeton: Princeton University Press.

———. 1989. *Justice, Gender and the Family.* New York: Basic Books.

Oldenburg, Ray. 1989. *The Great Good Place: Cafes, Coffee Shops, Bookstores, Bars, Hair Salons, and Other Hangouts at the Heart of a Community.* New York: Paragon.

Omolade, Barbara. 1994. *The Rising Song of African American Women.* New York: Routledge.

Otterman, Charon. 2011. "Most New York Students Are Not College-Ready." *New York Times*, February 8.

Page, S. 2005. "What's New about the New Public Management? Administrative Change in the Human Services." *Public Administration Review* 65 (6): 713–27.

Paley, John. 2000. "Heidegger and the Ethics of Care." *Nursing Philosophy* 1: 64.

Paperman, Patricia, and Sandra Laugier, eds. 2005. *Le Souci des Autres: Éthique et politique du Care.* Vol. 16. Paris: Éditions de l'École des Hautes Études en Sciences Sociales.

Parreñas, Rhacel Salazar. 2001. *Servants of Globalization: Women, Migration, and Domestic Work.* Stanford: Stanford University Press.

Pascall, Gillian, and Jane Lewis. 2004. "Emerging Gender Regimes and Policies for Gender Equality in a Wider Europe." *Journal of Social Policy* 33 (3): 373–94.

Pascoe, C. J. 2007. *Dude You're a Fag: Masculinity and Sexuality in High School*. Berkeley: University of California Press.

Pasquino, Pasquale. 1991. "Theatrum Politicum: The Genealogy of Capital: Police and the State of Prosperity." In *The Foucault Effect: Studies in Governmentality, with Two Lectures by and an Interview with Michel Foucault*, ed. M. Foucault, G. Burchell and C. Gordon. Chicago: University of Chicago Press.

Pateman, Carole. 1988. *The Sexual Contract*. Stanford: Stanford University Press.

———. 1989. *The Disorder of Women: Democracy, Feminism, and Political Theory*. Stanford: Stanford University Press.

Pateman, Carole, and Charles W. Mills. 2007. *Contract and Domination*. Malden, MA: Polity.

Peltz, Rachael. 2008. "Learning from History: An Interview with Robert Jay Lifton." *Psychoanalytic Dialogues* 18 (5): 710–34.

Pettit, Philip. 2002. "Keeping Republican Freedom Simple: On a Difference with Quentin Skinner." *Political Theory* 30 (3): 339–56.

———. 2007. "Responsibility, Inc." *Ethics* 117 (1): 171–201.

Phillips, Anne. 2002. "Feminism and the Politics of Difference: Or, Where Have All the Women Gone?" In *Visible Women: Essays on Feminist Legal Theory and Political Philosophy*, ed. S. James and S. Palmer. Oxford, UK: Hart.

Phipps, Shelley, Peter Burton, and Lars Osberg. 2001. "Time as a Source of Inequality within Marriage: Are Husbands More Satisfied with Time for Themselves Than Wives?" *Feminist Economics* 7: 1–21.

Piercy, Marge. 1976. *Woman on the Edge of Time*. New York: Knopf.

Piff, P. K., M. W. Kraus, S. Côté, B. H. Cheng, and D. Keltner. 2010. "Having Less, Giving More: The Influence of Social Class on Prosocial Behavior." *Journal of Personality and Social Psychology* 99: 771–84.

Plumwood, Val. 1993. *Feminism and the Mastery of Nature*. New York: Routledge.

Polanyi, Karl. 2001 [1944]. *The Great Transformation*. Boston: Beacon.

Pulkingham, Jane, Sylvia Fuller, and Paul Kershaw. 2010. "Lone Motherhood, Welfare Reform and Active Citizen Subjectivity." *Critical Social Policy* 30 (2): 267–91.

Putnam, Robert D. 1993. *Making Democracy Work: Civic Traditions in Modern Italy*. Princeton: Princeton University Press.

Raghuram, Parvati, Clare Madge, and Pat Noxolo. 2009. "Rethinking Responsibility and Care for a Postcolonial World." *Geoforum* 40 (1): 5–13.

Razavi, Shahra. 2007. "The Political and Social Economy of Care in a Development Context: Conceptual Issues, Research Questions and Policy Options." In *Gender and Development Programme*. Geneva: United Nations Research Institute for Social Development.

Reader, Soran. 2007. *Needs and Moral Necessity*. London: Routledge.

Richards, David A. J. 2010. *Fundamentalism in American Religion and Law*. New York: Cambridge University Press.

Roberts, Dorothy. 1997. "Spiritual and Menial Housework." *Yale Journal of Law and Feminism* 9 (1): 51–80.

Roberts, Sam. 2010. "New York State Ranks Last for Voter Turnout." *New York Times*, November 17.

Robin, Corey. 2011. "Why the Left Gets Neoliberalism Wrong: It's the Feudalism, Stupid!" Brooklyn, NY: Wordpress.

Robinson, Fiona. 1999. *Globalizing Care: Ethics, Feminist Theory, and International Relations*. Boulder, CO: Westview.

———. 2008. "The Importance of Care in the Theory and Practice of International Security."*Journal of International Political Theory* 4 (2): 167–88.

Robinson, Mary. 2007. "The Value of a Human Rights Perspective in Health and Foreign Policy." *Bulletin of the World Health Organization* 85 (3): 241–42.

Romero, Mary. 1992. *Maid in the USA*. New York: Routledge.

———. 2001. "Unraveling Privilege: Workers' Children and the Hidden Costs of Paid Childcare." *Chicago-Kent Law Review* 76: 1651–72.

———. 2002. *Maid in the USA*. 2nd ed. New York: Routledge.

Rose, Richard, and William Mishler. 1996. "Testing the Churchill Hypothesis: Popular Support for Democracy and Its Alternatives." *Journal of Public Policy* 16 (1): 29–58.

Ross-Sheriff, Fariyal, and Mary E. Swigonski. 2006. "Women, War, and Peace Building." *Affilia: Journal of Women and Social Work* 21 (2): 129–32.

Rowe, William L. 1991. "Responsibility, Agent-Causation, and Freedom: An Eighteenth-Century View." *Ethics* 101 (2): 237–57.

Rubenstein, Caren. 1993. "Consumer's World: Finding a Nanny Legally." *New York Times*, January 28, C1.

Ruddick, Sara. 1989. *Maternal Thinking:Toward a Politics of Peace*. Boston: Beacon.

Sander-Staudt, Maureen. 2006. "The Unhappy Marriage of Care Ethics and Virtue Ethics." *Hypatia* 21 (4): 21–39.

Sarti, Raffaela. 2005. "Conclusion: Domestic Service and European Identity." In *Proceedings of the Servant Project*, ed. S. Pasleau and I. Schopp. Liege: Editions de l'universite de Liege.

———. 2006. "Domestic Service: Past and Present in Southern and Northern Europe." *Gender and History* 18 (2): 222–45.

Sarvasy, Wendy. 1992. "Beyond the Difference versus Equality Debate: Postsuffrage Feminism, Citizenship, and the Quest for a Feminist Welfare State." *Signs* 17 (2): 329–62.

———. 2003. "Transnational Social Democracy: Post–World War I Feminist Practice and Theory." Conference Paper read at the Annual Meeting of the American Political Science Association.

Sarvasy, Wendy, and Patrizia Longo. 2004. "Kant's World Citizenship and Filipina Migrant Domestic Workers." *International Feminist Journal of Politics* 6 (3): 392–415.

Sassen, Saskia. 2001. *The Global City: New York, London, Tokyo.* Princeton: Princeton University Press.

Schor, Juliet B. 1998. *The Overspent American.* New York: HarperCollins.

———, ed. 2000. *Do Americans Shop Too Much?* Boston: Beacon.

———. 2004. *Born to Buy.* New York: Scribner's.

Schwartz, Joseph M. 2009. *The Future of Democratic Equality: Rebuilding Social Solidarity in a Fragmented America.* New York: Routledge.

Schwarzenbach, Sibyl A. 1996. "On Civic Friendship." *Ethics* 107 (1): 97–128.

Scully, Jackie Leach. 2008. *Disability Bioethics: Moral Bodies, Moral Difference.* Lanham, MD: Rowman and Littlefield.

Seccombe, Karen. 1999. *"So You Think I Drive a Cadillac?" Welfare Recipients' Perspectives on the System and Its Reform.* Boston: Allyn and Bacon.

Sen, Amartya. 1992. "Missing Women." *British Medical Journal* 304 (6827): 587–88.

———. 2009. *The Idea of Justice.* Cambridge: Harvard University Press.

Sevenhuijsen, Selma. 1998. *Citizenship and the Ethics of Care: Feminist Considerations on Justice, Morality, and Politics.* London: Routledge.

———. 2000. "Caring in the Third Way: The Relation between Obligation, Responsibility and Care in Third Way Discourse." *Critical Social Policy* 20 (1): 5.

———. 2003. "The Place of Care." *Feminist Theory* 4 (2): 179.

Sexton, J. B., E. J. Thomas, and R. L. Helmreich. 2000. "Error, Stress and Teamwork in Medicine and Aviation: Cross Sectional Surveys." *British Medical Journal* 320 (7237): 745–49.

Shapiro, Ian. 2001. *Democratic Justice.* New Haven: Yale University Press.

———. 2002. "Why the Poor Don't Soak the Rich." *Daedalus* 131 (1): 118–29.

Shi, Leiyu, James Macinko, Robert Politzer, and Jiahong Xu. 2005. "Primary Care, Race, and Mortality in US States." *Social Science and Medicine* 61 (1): 65–76.

Shonkoff, J. P., and D. A. Phillips, eds. 2000. *From Neurons to Neighborhoods: The Science of Early Childhood Development.* Washington, DC: National Academies Press.

Siddle Walker, Vanessa, and John R. Snarey, eds. 2004. *Race-ing Moral Formation: African American Perspectives on Care and Justice.* New York: Teachers College Press.

Siddle Walker, Vanessa, and Renarta H. Tompkins. 2004. "Caring in the Past: The Case of a Southern Segregated African American School." In *Race-ing Moral Formation: African American Perspectives on Care and Justice,* ed. V. Siddle Walker and J. R. Snarey. New York: Teachers College.

Silvers, Anita. 1995. "Reconciling Equality to Difference: Caring (f)or Justice for People with Disabilities." *Hypatia* 10 (1): 30–55.

Sim, Joe. 2009. *Punishment and Prisons: Power and the Carceral State.* Thousand Oaks, CA: Sage.

Simien, Evelyn M. 2007. "Doing Intersectionality Research: From Conceptual Issues to Practical Examples." *Politics and Gender* 9 (2): 264–71.

Simmons, William. 1999. "The Third: Levinas' Theoretical Move from An-archical Ethics to the Realm of Justice and Politics." *Philosophy and Social Criticism* 25 (6): 83–104.

Simonstein, Frida. 2006. "Artificial Reproduction Technologies (RTs): All the Way to the Artificial Womb?" *Medicine, Health Care and Philosophy* 9 (3): 359–65.

Skocpol, Theda. 1992. *Protecting Soldiers and Mothers: The Political Origin of Social Policy in the United States.* Cambridge: Harvard University Press.

Slater, Don, and Fran Tonkiss. 2001. *Market Society: Markets and Modern Social Theory.* Cambridge, UK: Polity.

Slote, Michael A. 2008. *The Ethics of Care and Empathy.* New York: Routledge.

Smiley, Marion. 1992. *Moral Responsibility and the Boundaries of Community: Power and Accountability from a Pragmatic Point of View.* Chicago: University of Chicago Press.

Smith, Adam. 1976 [1776]. *An Inquiry into the Nature and Causes of the Wealth of Nations.* Edited by R. H. Campbell and A. S. Skinner. 2 vols. Indianapolis: Liberty.

———. 1981. *The Theory of Moral Sentiments.* Indianapolis: Liberty.

Smith, Anna Marie. 2007. *Welfare Reform and Sexual Regulation.* New York: Cambridge University Press.

Stacey, Clare L. 2011. *The Caring Self: The Work Experiences of Home Care Aides.* Ithaca: Cornell University Press.

Stacey, Judith. 1990. *Brave New Families: Stories of Domestic Upheaval in Late-Twentieth-Century America.* Berkeley: University of California Press.

Stanford, John, and Robin Simons. 1999. *Victory in Our Schools: We Can Give Our Children Excellent Public Education.* New York: Random House.

Stiehm, Judith Hicks. 1982a. "The Protected, the Protector, the Defender." *Women Studies International Forum* 5 (3–4): 367–76.

———. 1982b. "Women, Men, and Military Service: Is Protection Necessarily a Racket?" In *Women, Power and Policy*, ed. E. Boneparth. Oxford: Oxford University Press.

———. 1984. "Our Aristotelian Hangover." In *Discovering Reality*, ed. M. Hintikka and S. Harding. Amsterdam: Elsevier.

Stillman, Sarah. 2011. "The Invisible Army: For Foreign Workers on U.S. Bases in Iraq and Afghanistan, War Can Be Hell." *New Yorker*, June 6.

Stone, Deborah. 2000. "Why We Need a Care Movement." *The Nation*, March 13.

———. 2008. *The Samaritan's Dilemma: Should Government Help Your Neighbor?* New York: Basic Books.

Straus, Murray A., Richard J. Gelles, and Suzanne K. Steinmetz. 1980. *Behind Closed Doors: Violence in the American Family.* New York: Anchor.

Strawson, P. F. 1962. "Freedom and Resentment." *Proceedings of the British Academy* 48: 1–25.

Strobl, Staci. 2009. "Policing Housemaids: The Criminalization of Domestic Workers in Bahrain." *British Journal of Criminology* 49 (2): 165–83.

Tännsjö, Torbjörn. 2002. *Understanding Ethics: An Introduction to Moral Theory.* Edinburgh: Edinburgh University Press.

Tessman, Lisa. 2000. "Moral Luck in the Politics of Personal Transformation." *Social Theory and Practice* 26 (3): 375–95.

———. 2005. *Burdened Virtues: Virtue Ethics for Liberatory Struggles.* New York: Oxford University Press.

———. 2009. "Expecting Bad Luck." *Hypatia* 24 (1): 9–28.

Thatcher, Margaret. 1987. "Interview for *Woman's Own.*" Margaret Thatcher Foundation, http://www.margaretthatcher.org/document/105577.

Thomson, Judith Jarvis. 1986. *Rights, Restitution, and Risk.* Cambridge: Harvard University Press.

Tilly, Charles. 1998. *Durable Inequality.* Berkeley: University of California Press.

———. 2003. "Changing Forms of Inequality." *Sociological Theory* 21 (1): 31–36.

Tinto, Vincent. 2000. "Linking Learning and Leaving: Exploring the Role of the College Classroom in Student Departure." In *Reworking the Departure Puzzle,* ed. J. M. Braxton. Nashville: Vanderbilt University Press.

Tönnies, Ferdinand. 2001. *Community and Civil Society.* Translated by J. Harris and M. Hollis. Cambridge: Cambridge University Press.

Tronto, Joan C. 1987. "Beyond Gender Difference to a Theory of Care." *Signs* 12 (4): 644–63.

———. 1993. *Moral Boundaries: A Political Argument for an Ethic of Care.* New York: Routledge.

———. 1995. "Caring as the Basis for Radical Political Judgments." *Hypatia* 10 (2): 141–49.

———. 2001. "Does Managing Professionals Affect Professional Ethics? Competence, Autonomy, and Care." In *Feminists Do Ethics,* ed. P. DesAutels and J. Waugh. Lanham, MD: Rowman and Littlefield.

———. 2002. "The 'Nanny Question' in Feminism." *Hypatia* 17 (2): 34–51.

———. 2003. "Time's Place." *Feminist Theory* 4 (2): 119–38.

———. 2006. "Vicious Circles of Unequal Care." In *Socializing Care,* ed. M. Hamington. Lanham, MD: Rowman and Littlefield.

———. 2010. "'The Servant Problem' and Justice in Households." *Iris: European Journal of Philosophy and Public Debate* 2 (2): 67–86.

Tucker, Robert, ed. 1977. *The Marx Engels Reader.* New York: Norton.

Turner, Brian S. 1997. "Citizenship Studies: A General Theory." *Citizenship Studies* 1 (1): 5–18.

Ubel, Peter A. 2009. *Free Market Madness: Why Human Nature Is at Odds with Economics—and Why It Matters.* Boston: Harvard Business School Publishing.

Ungerson, Clare. 1997. "Social Politics and the Commodification of Care." *Social Politics* 4 (3): 362–81.

Uttal, Lynn. 1999. "Using Kin for Child Care: Embedment in the Socioeconomic Networks of Extended Families." *Journal of Marriage and the Family* 61 (4): 845–57.

———. 2006. "Organizational Cultural Competency: Shifting Programs for Latino Immigrants from a Client-Centered to a Community-Based Orientation." *American Journal of Community Psychology* 38 (3–4): 251–62.

Van Parijs, Philippe. 1995. *Real Freedom for All: What (If Anything) Can Justify Capitalism?* Oxford, UK: Clarendon.

Vazquez-Arroyo, Antonio Y. 2008. "Liberal Democracy and Neoliberalism: A Critical Juxtaposition." *New Political Science* 30: 127–59.

Verkerk, Marian. 1999. "A Care Perspective on Coercion and Autonomy." *Bioethics* 13 (July): 358–68.

Verkerk, Marian, Hilde Lindemann, Els Maeckelberhe, Enne Feenstra, Rudolph Hartough, and Menno De Bree. 2004. "Enhancing Reflection: An Interpersonal Exercise in Ethics Education." *Hastings Center Report* 34 (6): 8.

Vico, Giambattista. 1990 [1709]. *On the Study Methods of Our Time*. Translated by E. Gianturco. Ithaca: Cornell University Press.

Vives, A. 2008. "Corporate Social Responsibility: The Role of Law and Markets and the Case of Developing Countries." *Chicago-Kent Law Review* 83: 199.

Vogel, Ursula. 1994. "Marriage and the Boundaries of Citizenship." In *The Condition of Citizenship*, ed. B. van Steenbergen. London: Sage.

Wadsworth, Martha E., Tali Raviv, Christine Reinhard, Brian Wolff, Catherine DeCarlo Santiago, and Lindsey Einhorn. 2008. "An Indirect Effects Model of the Association between Poverty and Child Functioning: The Role of Children's Poverty-Related Stress." *Journal of Loss and Trauma* 13 (2–3): 156–85.

Waerness, Kari. 1984a. "Caring as Women's Work in the Welfare State." In *Patriarchy in a Welfare Society*, ed. H. Holter. Oslo: Universitetsforlaget.

———. 1984b. "The Rationality of Caring." *Economic and Industrial Democracy* 5: 185–211.

———. 1990. "Informal and Formal Care in Old Age: What Is Wrong with the New Ideology in Scandinavia Today?" In *Gender and Caring: Work and Welfare in Britain and Scandinavia*, ed. C. Ungerson. London: Harvester, Wheatsheaf.

Wagstaff, Adam. 2002. "Poverty and Health Sector Inequalities." *Bulletin of the World Health Organization* 80 (2): 97–105.

Walker, Margaret Urban. 1998. *Moral Understandings: A Feminist Study of Ethics*. New York: Routledge.

———. 1999. "Getting Out of Line: Alternatives to Life as a Career." In *Mother Time: Women, Aging and Ethics*, ed. M. U. Walker. Lanham, MD: Rowman and Littlefield.

———. 2006. *Moral Repair: Reconstructing Moral Relations after Wrongdoing*. New York: Cambridge University Press.

———. 2007. *Moral Understandings: A Feminist Study of Ethics.* 2d ed. New York: Oxford University Press.

Walzer, Michael. 1983. *Spheres of Justice: A Defense of Pluralism and Equality.* New York: Basic Books.

Waring, Marilyn. 1988. *If Women Counted: A New Feminist Economics.* New York: HarperCollins.

Warner, Judith. 2009. "Dude, You've Got Problems." *New York Times,* April 17, 2009.

Weaver, R. Kent. 2000. *Ending Welfare as We Know It.* Washington, DC: Brookings Institution Press.

Weber, Max. 2003 [1905]. *The Protestant Ethic and the Spirit of Capitalism.* Translated by T. Parsons. Mineola, NY: Dover.

Weir, Allison. 2005. "The Global Universal Caregiver: Imagining Women's Liberation in the New Millennium." *Constellations: An International Journal of Critical and Democratic Theory* 12 (3): 308–30.

Weldon, S. Laurel. 2006. "The Structure of Intersectionality: A Comparative Politics of Gender." *Politics and Gender* 2 (2): 235–48.

White, Julie A. 2000. *Democracy, Justice and the Welfare State: Reconstructing Public Care.* University Park: Penn State University Press.

———. 2007. "The Hollow and the Ghetto: Space, Race, and the Politics of Poverty." *Politics and Gender* 9 (2): 271–80.

Williams, Bernard. 1985. *Ethics and the Limits of Philosophy.* Waukegan, IL: Fontana.

———. 1994. *Shame and Necessity.* Berkeley: University of California Press.

Williams, Fiona. 1999. "Good-Enough Principles for Welfare." *Journal of Social Policy* 28 (4): 667–88.

———. 2001. "In and beyond New Labour: Towards a New Political Ethics of Care." *Critical Social Policy* 21 (4): 467.

———. 2004. *Rethinking Families.* London, Calouste Gulbenkian Foundation.

Williams, Joan. 2000. *Unbending Gender: Why Family and Work Conflict and What to Do about It.* New York: Oxford University Press.

Williams, Patricia J. 1991. *The Alchemy of Race and Rights.* Cambridge: Harvard University Press.

Windsong, Elena Ariel. 2010. "There Is No Place Like Home: Complexities in Exploring Home and Place Attachment." *Social Science Journal* 47 (1): 205–14.

Winters, Jeffrey A. 2010. *Oligarchy.* New York: Cambridge University Press.

Wolin, Sheldon S. 1960. *Politics and Vision: Continuity and Innovation in Western Political Thought.* Boston: Little, Brown.

———. 2008. *Democracy Inc.: Managed Democracy and the Specter of Inverted Totalitarianism.* Princeton: Princeton University Press.

Wong, Sau-ling C. 1994. "Diverted Mothering: Representations of Caregivers of Color in the Age of 'Multiculturalism.'" In *Mothering: Ideology, Experience, Agency,* ed. E. N. Glenn, G. Chang, and L. R. Forcey. New York: Routledge.

Workpermit.com. 2006. *UN report—Economic Role of Immigrant Women Over-looked*, October 24, http://www.workpermit.com/news/2006_10_24/global/immigrant_women_remittances.htm.

Xenos, Nicholas. 1989. *Scarcity and Modernity*. London: Routledge, Chapman and Hall.

Yak, Bernard. 1993. *The Problems of a Political Animal*. Berkeley: University of California Press.

Yeates, Nicola. 2004. "A Dialogue with 'Global Care Chain' Analysis: Nurse Migration in the Irish Context." *Feminist Review* (77): 79–95.

Young, Iris Marion. 1990. *Justice and the Politics of Difference*. Princeton: Princeton University Press.

———. 2000. *Inclusion and Democracy*. New York: Oxford University Press.

———. 2003. "The Logic of Masculinist Protection: Reflections on the Current Security State." *Signs: Journal of Women in Culture and Society* 29 (1): 1–24.

———. 2006. "Responsiblity and Global Justice: A Social Connection Model." *Social Philosophy and Policy* 23 (1): 102–30.

Yuval-Davis, Nira. 1997. "Women, Citizenship and Difference." *Feminist Review* 57: 4–27.

ABOUT THE AUTHOR

Joan C. Tronto is Professor of Political Science at the University of Minnesota and author of *Moral Boundaries: A Political Argument for an Ethic of Care.*

www.ingramcontent.com/pod-product-compliance
Lightning Source LLC
Chambersburg PA
CBHW032129020426
42334CB00016B/1098